THE PHILOSOPHICAL THEOLOGY
OF JONATHAN EDWARDS

The Philosophical Theology of Jonathan Edwards

Expanded Edition

Sang Hyun Lee

PRINCETON UNIVERSITY PRESS

PRINCETON, NEW JERSEY

This book has been composed in Linotron Sabon

Third printing, and first paperback printing, 2000

Library of Congress Cataloging-in-Publication Data

Lee, Sang Hyun, 1938–
The philosophical theology of Jonathan Edwards / Sang Hyun Lee — [Rev.]
expanded ed.
p.   cm.
Includes bibliographical references and index.
ISBN 0-691-07325-2 (cl : alk. paper)
ISBN 0-691-04942-4 (pbk. : alk. paper)
1. Edwards, Jonathan, 1703–1758 — Contributions in philosophical
theology.   2. Philosophical theology — History — 18th century.   I. Title.
BT40. L44 2000
230'.58'092 — dc21   99–046065

The paper used in this publication meets the
minimum requirements of ANSI/NISO Z39.48-1992
(R1997) (*Permanence of Paper*)

http://pup.princeton.edu

Printed in the United States of America

10 9 8 7 6 5 4 3

TO

Inn Sook,
Cy Suh Hyong,
and the memory of Mi Hyong,

AND TO

Richard R. Niebuhr

Contents

CONTENTS

Preface to the Expanded Edition

THIS EXPANDED EDITION contains a revision of ten pages (pp. 186–96) of the original edition published in 1988. This rewriting was necessary in order to state clearly that the coincidence of actuality and disposition, according to Edwards, is true for the divine being *as the Trinity* — thus, for each of the three Persons. The remainder of the text is exactly the same.

I am grateful for the helpful conversations I had with Daniel L. Migliore and E. David Willis of Princeton Theological Seminary, and Robert W. Jenson of the Center of Theological Inquiry. I also benefited from Amy Plantinga Pauw's doctoral dissertation, "The Supreme Harmony of All: Jonathan Edwards and the Trinity." However, I am solely responsible for the interpretation of Edwards' doctrine of the Trinity that is presented in this book.

This edition also includes, as an appendix, an essay on Edwards' view of the physical universe and its ecological implications. This material was previously published in S. H. Lee, W. Proudfoot, and A. Blackwell's book, *Faithful Imagining: Essays in Honor of Richard R. Niebuhr*. I am grateful to Scholars Press for permission to reprint that essay here.

In the original edition of this book, I used the volumes of the Yale edition of *The Works of Jonathan Edwards* that were available at the time. Since then several additional volumes have been published. Unfortunately, due to time constraints and other considerations, these later volumes could not be incorporated into the current edition.

I am delighted that Princeton University Press decided to re-issue this book. I am especially grateful to Ms. Deborah Tegarden for her gracious and expert guidance through the entire process of preparing this edition. It is also this author's good fortune to be a beneficiary of the meticulous and elegant work done by Ms. Tegarden's colleagues and staff, especially Ms. Donna Kronemeyer.

Acknowledgments

It is my pleasure to acknowledge the generous assistance I have received from many individuals and institutions in completing this project. I am deeply grateful to my mentor and friend, Professor Richard R. Niebuhr of Harvard University, who first introduced me to the writings of Edwards during my Divinity School years, guided me through my doctoral dissertation on Edwards' concept of habit, and then, during the many years of the writing of this present volume, has sustained me with his unfailing support and enthusiasm. His enduring conviction that I should develop further my particular reading of Edwards' thought has been the crucially important source of encouragement in all stages of this project. My appreciation for what I owe him intellectually and in other ways continues to grow. I am also deeply indebted to Professor Alan Heimert of Harvard for his strong support of this project and helpful guidance over the years.

My thanks go to Professor John E. Smith of Yale University, the General Editor of the Yale edition of Edwards' works, who has generously given me the benefit of his counsel and encouragement on a number of occasions. As most other students of Edwards' thought, I am also indebted to Professor Thomas A. Schafer of McCormick Theological Seminary for allowing me to use his transcriptions of Edwards' "Miscellanies" at the Beinecke Library of Yale University as well as for sharing with me his wide-ranging knowledge of Edwards scholarship in general. Discussions with a number of other scholars have also helped me become clearer about my own interpretation—especially, the late Professor Wallace E. Anderson of Ohio State University, Professor Roland Delattre of the University of Minnesota, Professor Paul Ramsey of the Center of Theological Inquiry in Princeton, and Professor Wilson H. Kimnach of the University of Bridgeport.

ACKNOWLEDGMENTS

My very special thanks go to President Thomas W. Gillespie of Princeton Theological Seminary for his keen interest in and warm support of faculty research in general and this project on Edwards in particular. I am also indebted to Dr. James I. McCord, the former president of Princeton Seminary, for his encouragement over the years. Professor E. David Willis, my colleague at Princeton Seminary, read a portion of the manuscript and offered me helpful comments. Professor Daniel L. Migliore, also of Princeton Seminary, graciously allowed me to try out some ideas with him while I was working on the final chapters of the book. To my other colleagues in theology and other departments at Princeton Seminary, as well as to Professor John F. Wilson of Princeton University, I am also grateful for all the conversations about Edwards and theology and philosophy in general. This book is certainly better than it might have been because of what I have learned from them. I would like to express my special thanks to my former student, Professor Gregory Boyd of Bethel College, who read with great care the entire first draft and offered me many helpful suggestions about both style and content. His assistance has been indispensable in the preparation of the final draft. The friendship and encouragement of numerous other individuals in the Princeton Seminary community has been important in completing this project.

Parts of the first draft were written during a sabbatical year (1975–1976) made possible by a fellowship from the American Council of Learned Societies. I am grateful to Princeton Theological Seminary for a research leave during the spring term of 1983, and to Hope College, Holland, Michigan, for a number of faculty research grants while I taught there between 1970 and 1980. I recall with much gratitude the encouragement that my former colleagues at Hope College gave me.

In getting this volume ready for publication, I have been fortunate to have the assistance of the superb staff of Princeton University Press, particularly the editorial work of Ms. Diane Grobman and Ms. Janet Stern. I owe a special debt to its Editor-in-Chief, Mr. Sanford G. Thatcher, who encouraged me over the years with his interest in the project and has helped

xii

me in the final preparation of the manuscript with his high standards as well as with his continuing support.

I am grateful for the courtesies I received from the staff of Andover-Harvard and Widener Libraries of Harvard University, Speer Library of Princeton Seminary, and Firestone Library of Princeton University. I am especially indebted for the kind assistance I received from the staff of the Beinecke Rare Book and Manuscript Library of Yale during my many visits there over the years, and for their kind permission to publish a number of items from the unpublished manuscripts of Edwards as specified in the footnotes. My thanks also go to Ms. Lynn H. Kosanovich for her expert typing and for many stylistic suggestions, and to Ms. Byong-Jean Choy for typing the index.

The writing of this book has been very much a family project. The depth of my indebtedness and gratitude to my wife and children cannot really be expressed in words. But something must be said. My wife, Inn Sook, has sustained me during the many years of working on this volume with her steadfast confidence in me as well as in the project. Without her loving companionship and support, this volume certainly could not have been completed. My son, Cy Suh Hyong, and my daughter, Mi Hyong, during her brief but excellent life in this world, somehow believed that this project was important and encouraged me with their frequent and supportive greeting, "Are you working on Edwards?" My parents, the late Reverend Won Woo Lee and Mrs. Young Ok Cha Lee, who sent their seventeen-year-old boy away from home to America for education have been an enduring source of inspiration during the entire process of my work on this volume.

Abbreviations

FAJ   *Jonathan Edwards: Representative Selections*, ed. Clarence H. Faust and Thomas H. Johnson (New York: Hill and Wang, 1962)

HGT   *The Philosophy of Jonathan Edwards from His Private Notebooks*, ed. Harvey G. Townsend (Eugene: University of Oregon Press, 1955)

PH   *Treatise on Grace and Other Posthumous Writings Including Observations on the Trinity*, by Jonathan Edwards, ed. Paul Helm (Greenwood, S.C.: Attic Press, 1971)

THA   *Exercises Commemorating the Two-Hundredth Anniversary of the Birth of Jonathan Edwards* (Andover, Mass.: Andover Press, 1904)

WC   *The Works of President Edwards*, 4 vols. (New York: Robert Carter and Brothers, 1868)

WEA   *Scientific and Philosophical Writings*, ed. Wallace E. Anderson, vol. 6 of *The Works of Jonathan Edwards*, ed. John E. Smith (New Haven: Yale University Press, 1980)

WG   *The Works of President Edwards*, 4 vols. (New York: G. and C. and H. Carvill, 1830)

WL   *The Works of President Edwards*, 4 vols. (New York: Leavitt and Allen, 1852)

WS   *The Works of President Edwards*, 10 vols. (New York: S. Converse, 1829–1830)

YALE MSS   Yale Collection of Edwards' Manuscripts, Beinecke Rare Book and Manuscript Library, Yale University

THE PHILOSOPHICAL THEOLOGY
OF JONATHAN EDWARDS

CHAPTER I

Introduction: The Idea of Habit and Edwards' Dynamic Vision of Reality

PERRY MILLER, who is largely responsible for the recent revival of interest in Jonathan Edwards, has claimed that the Puritan philosopher-theologian was "intellectually the most modern man of his age" and that in some of Edwards' insights he was "so much ahead of his time that our own can hardly be said to have caught up with him."[1] Miller based this judgment on Edwards' creative appropriation of various philosophical developments of the late seventeenth and early eighteenth centuries, especially Lockean empiricism and Newtonian science, in his restatement of the Augustinian-Calvinistic theological tradition for his own time.

My contention in the present volume is that Edwards was actually more radically creative than Miller himself might have realized.[2] What Edwards accomplished in the course of his search for a philosophical understanding of the Christian faith was a thoroughgoing metaphysical reconstruction, a reconception of the nature of reality itself. There is in Edwards' thought a shift of categories in terms of which the very nature

[1] Perry Miller, *Jonathan Edwards* (Cleveland: World, 1959), pp. vi, 305.

[2] Miller's claim for Edwards' "modernity" gave rise to many other studies of Edwards but certainly did not go unchallenged. For the opposing point of view, see, for example, Vincent Tomas, "The Modernity of Jonathan Edwards," *New England Quarterly* 25 (1952): 60–84; Peter Gay, *A Loss of Mastery: Puritan Historians in Colonial America* (Berkeley and Los Angeles: University of California Press, 1966), pp. 88–117; Robert C. Whittemore, "Jonathan Edwards and the Theology of the Sixth Way," *Church History* 35 (March 1966): 60–75. For a post-modern reading of Edwards, see Stephen H. Daniel, *The Philosophy of Jonathan Edwards* (Bloomington: Indiana University Press, 1994).

of things is explicated. Edwards departed from the traditional Western metaphysics of substance and form and replaced it with a strikingly modern conception of reality as a dynamic network of dispositional forces and habits. Dispositions and habits, conceived as active and ontologically abiding principles, now play the roles substance and form used to fulfill. It is this dispositional ontology that provides the key to the particular character of Edwards' modernity as well as the interpretive clue for the underlying logic, the original vision, in terms of which Edwards' thought can be seen as a unity.

The most innovative element in Edwards' dynamic perspective on reality is that it is a dispositional conception. Dispositions and habits, as shall be seen in detail below, can mediate between being and becoming, permanence and process. The mediating capacity of Edwards' ontology functions in his philosophical theology, enabling him to reaffirm in the strongest possible terms his theological tradition within a thoroughly modern philosophical framework. It is precisely at this point that Edwards is not only historically important but also an enduring source of insight even for the philosophical and theological tasks of the twentieth century.

A prime example of the way Edwards' thought contributes to the discussions of contemporary philosophical theology is his dispositional reconception of the nature of the divine being. The traditional Western doctrine of God, the so-called classical theism, understood God's perfect actuality and self-sufficiency as implying God's absolute changelessness—that is, as God's inability to be affected in any way whatsoever by his relation to the world. This view has been seriously challenged in modern theology. Critics have asked, How can a totally changeless God, without any element of potentiality in him, be capable of any creative and purposive activity? If God's own life is unaffected by God's relation to the world, how can God's involvement in time and history have any genuine meaning? This demand to see the divine being as more dynamic than the classical theism sees it has been prompted by the increasing stress upon the dynamic nature of being in modern thought in general as well as by the considerations arising from Christian theology's inherent and continuing task of reexamining itself in light of the Biblical affirmations about the divine being.[3]

The most extreme alternative to the classical theism has come from process theology, a theology largely inspired by the philosophy of Alfred North Whitehead. Process theology attempts to portray God's being as at once complete or eternal and also engaged in becoming by positing a dipolar, or two-sided, nature of the divine being. God's primordial or conceptual side, according to the process perspective, is changelessly complete, while God's consequent or concrete nature is an ongoing process of becoming. God's concrete actuality, which is the temporal actualization of God's eternal nature, in other words, is growing or becoming ever more complete through the creative advance of the world. Process theology has adopted process philosophy's conception of reality as inherently processive, and has defined God's own concrete actuality as a part of the general process of the becoming of reality. If the classical theism went too far in emphasizing God's unchangeability and self-sufficiency, process theology has overstated God's involvement with the changing world thereby compromising God's prior actuality and transcendence. God, in process theology, is an instance of the process of becoming rather than the perfect actuality upon which all being and creative process are ultimately dependent.[4]

[3] For recent discussions of the issue of being and becoming in God by theologians and philosophers other than process thinkers, see, for example, Eberhard Jüngel, *The Doctrine of the Trinity: God's Being Is in Becoming* (Grand Rapids, Mich.: Eerdmans, 1976); Keith Ward, *Rational Theology and the Creativity of God* (Oxford: Blackwell, 1982); Colin E. Gunton, *Becoming and Being: The Doctrine of God in Charles Hartshorne and Karl Barth* (Oxford: Oxford University Press, 1978); Robert C. Neville, *Creativity and God: A Challenge to Process Theology* (New York: Seabury Press, 1980); Royce G. Gruenler, *The Inexhaustible God: Biblical Faith and the Challenge of Process Theism* (Grand Rapids, Mich.: Baker Book House, 1983).

[4] It should be noted that there are important differences among various process thinkers in their conceptions of God. What I have offered here is a description of the general tendency among those conceptions. Two of the classic texts in process thought are Alfred North Whitehead, *Process and Reality:*

Writing over two hundred years ago, Jonathan Edwards had already confronted this modern question of the being and becoming of God and had worked out a highly innovative solution that introduces dynamism into the very being of God without compromising God's prior actuality. For Edwards, God is essentially a perfect actuality as well as a disposition to repeat that actuality through further exercises.[5] This divine disposition, according to Edwards, is completely exercised through the inner-Trinitarian relationships. In other words, the Second and the Third Persons of the Trinity perfectly repeat the primordial actuality of the First Person. God, for Edwards, therefore, is and always has been completely actual as God. But the divine essence remains a disposition, and now exercises itself externally in time and space by creating the world. The world, in other words, is meant to be the spatio-temporal repetition of the prior actuality of the divine being, an everlasting process of God's self-enlargement of what he already is. At this point, Edwards has made a basic modification of the traditional conception of the deity and has introduced an element of dynamic movement into the heart of the divine being. But at the same time, Edwards avoids the failure of contemporary process theology to see God as primordially and fully self-actualized. And the key to the balancing of being and becoming in Edwards' doctrine of God is the notion of the divine disposition as ontologically productive—that is, as capable of repeating what is already actual through further exercises. Thus, God can be seen as fully actual and at the same time engaged in a process of self-extension. In this way Edwards offers a compelling alternative to process theology— an alternative that deals creatively with the drawback of much

---

An Essay in Cosmology (New York: Macmillan, 1929); and Charles Hartshorne, *The Divine Relativity: A Social Conception of God* (New Haven: Yale University Press, 1948). For the different ways in which various philosophical theologians have appropriated process philosophy, see *Process Philosophy and Christian Thought*, ed. Delwin Brown, Ralph E. James, and Gene Reeves (Indianapolis: Bobbs-Merrill, 1971).

[5] See Chap. 7.

of traditional theology but without compromising the central tenets of the historic Christian belief about the divine being.

Edwards' dispositional ontology, which underlies his reconception of the divine being, is the clue to the originality and unity of Edwards' philosophical theology as a whole. The aim of this volume is to explicate the dynamic character of the central aspects of Edwards' thought with his category of disposition as the interpretive key. Here in the introductory chapter I shall offer a brief sketch of what will be argued in detail in the chapters that follow.

The crux of the matter is Edwards' realistic (as opposed to nominalistic) and relational definition of "habit," which the Scholastics called *habitus* and is now better known as "disposition" or "tendency."[6] Habit or disposition, for Edwards, is not mere custom or regularity of events. Habit is an active and ontologically abiding power that possesses a mode of realness even when it is not in exercise. Habit, for Edwards, is also a relational principle—that is, a general law that governs the manner or character of actual actions and events.

If the essence of being is habit or disposition, then an entity is an abiding reality as a habit or disposition and attains full actuality through the exercise of that habit or disposition. Actions, events, and relations, then, are not mere accidents or qualities of the being of an entity, but are, rather, internally related to it. Through actions and relations the actuality of an entity is moved from its dispositional or virtual real-ness to its full actuality.[7] Further, since the essence of an entity does not cease to be a disposition, the being of an entity is capable of being increased in and through further exercises of the dispositional essence. Being, in short, is inherently dynamic and relational.

When habit is the disposition of a perceiving mind, moreover, it functions as the principle of knowing—that is, as the propensive power of the imagination's synthesizing activity through which the mind's apprehension of the relational

6 See Chap. 2.
7 See Chap. 4.

structure of reality becomes possible. Habit, therefore, is not the thoughtless way in which a sort of activity is mechanically carried out. The habit of mind, for Edwards, functions as the very possibility of rationality and moral action. Habit, therefore, is at once the principle of being and becoming and the principle of knowing. Through habit, knowing is connected with being and becoming.[8]

What results from Edwards' recasting of Christian thought in the frame of his dispositional reconception of being and knowledge is a novel and dynamic perspective on God, the world, and history. It is axiomatic in Edwards that God is the absolutely sovereign and eternally perfect ground of all existence and creativity. But the essence of the divine being, as I have already noted, is now conceived of as a disposition as well as a full actuality. God, therefore, is inherently inclined to enlarge or repeat his primordial actuality through further exercises of his dispositional essence. And it is Edwards' dispositional ontology of the divine self-enlargement (and not, as is sometimes suggested, Neoplatonic philosophy) that explains the logic of the ongoing purposive and creative activity of an already truly actual and sovereign God.[9]

The created world is a network of divinely established habits and dispositions (or the so-called laws of nature) whose ultimate telos is to know and to love God so as to repeat in time and space God's own being. The world as a system of dispositional powers possesses a relative and yet abiding reality of its own.[10] The true exercise of those dispositions, or the created world's attainment of its true actuality, however, requires the direct involvement of the exercises of God's own disposition to repeat his own prior actuality in time and space. History and nature, in other words, are inherently dynamic and purposive, but their dynamic life becomes actual only as they actively participate in, and actively function as the medium of, God's own life in time and space.

The focal point in the creation through which God's own

---

[8] See Chaps. 5 and 6.
[9] See Chap. 7.
[10] See Chap. 3.

temporal self-enlargement and also the life of history and nature come together and reach their goal is the imaginative activity of the divinely transformed human mind and heart. The shaping and expansive power of the imagination enables the mind to know and love what it experiences as meaningful wholes in their ultimate relational context. In this way the finite mind is enabled to know and love the world as the temporal repetition of the divine glory. And since the activity of the imagination is the exercise of the perceiving human self, it is through the imagination in the knowledge process that the human self's own dispositional essence is actualized. Further, such an activity of the human imagination is made possible by the immediate involvement of God's own disposition in and through the human disposition. Thus, through the activity of the sanctified imagination, the perceiving self and the perceived world attain their actuality. And such an attainment of their actuality is none other than their participation in God's sovereign work of repeating his internal being in time and space. Through the imagination, then, history and nature come alive and also achieve their union with God.[11]

The created existence, therefore, is at once a repetition of the eternal and also a teleological movement toward a goal. History repeats God who is already actually God but also moves toward the goal of God's self-repetition in time. The ultimate goal of history (the Kingdom of God) is at once immanent in history and also beyond it. God's own being is directly involved in history (in the sense of self-repetition), and every moment in history can, therefore, be understood as a repetition of his own eternal glory. But the *absolutely complete* repetition in history of the infinite glory of God cannot be accomplished within history. It is an unending process. Such an interpretation helps one to understand how Edwards can stress the possibility of a historically immanent millennium while not losing sight of the transcendent character of the complete fulfillment of the Kingdom of God.[12]

As many interpreters have pointed out, Edwards worked

[11] See Chaps. 5 and 6.
[12] See Chap. 8.

out his philosophical theology with a keen awareness of the philosophical and scientific developments of his day.[13] My explication of Edwards' dynamic and relational vision of reality with the idea of habit as the interpretive key opens up, I believe, the way to achieve a deeper insight into the creativity and historical importance of the resolutions that Edwards offered for the most fundamental problems of seventeenth- and eighteenth-century Western thought.

The basic problem that seventeenth-century thought bequeathed to Jonathan Edwards' generation was that of revising the Aristotelian-Scholastic world view so as to come up with a perspective that could accommodate the new methods and categories of thought presented by mechanicoexperimental science.[14] The issue can be broadly divided into two areas: the ontological (cosmological) and the epistemological. The ontological problem stemmed from the inadequacy of the old metaphysics of substances and substantial forms to function as the intellectual framework in an age that was increasingly thinking of reality in terms of motion, power, and relational laws. The notions of substance and substantial forms were also branded as occult qualities by mechanical science as it pursued its empirical and experimental methodology.

This ontological problem remained unresolved in Newton, for example, and caused extreme tension within his cosmology.[15] On the one hand, the static and nonrelational view of

[13] Among studies of Edwards' intellectual background, some of the most important are Miller, *Jonathan Edwards*; Norman Fiering, *Jonathan Edwards' Moral Thought and Its British Context* (Chapel Hill: University of North Carolina Press, 1981); William S. Morris, "The Genius of Jonathan Edwards," in *Reinterpretation in American Church History*, ed. Jerald C. Brauer (Chicago: University of Chicago Press, 1968), pp. 29–65; Thomas H. Johnson, "Jonathan Edwards' Background of Reading," *Publications of the Colonial Society of Massachusetts* 28 (1931): 193–222.

[14] For similar interpretations of Edwards' understanding of his own philosophical task, see Herbert W. Richardson, "The Glory of God in the Theology of Jonathan Edwards: A Study in the Doctrine of the Trinity" (Ph.D. diss., Harvard University, 1962), chap. 3; Anderson, "Editor's Introduction," in WEA, pp. 37–52.

[15] See Chap. 4.

being remained in his conception of the material world as consisting of particulate, inert particles, while on the other hand, he could not ignore the existence of what might be called the relational forces, such as attraction and repulsion. According to the particulate view, causation is always by impact, and relations are external to bodies. But the forces of attraction and repulsion seemed to Newton to be forces that act at a distance, thus calling for a view of matter as essentially active and relational. Edwards' resolution of this problem was his dynamic view of being that is based upon his idea of the laws or habits of forces as ontologically real. The permanence of being is no longer defined in terms of substance or inert matter but rather in terms of the abiding reality of laws themselves. Entities are essentially active and relational, and causality is at a distance and not by impact. And the empirical banishment of the occult qualities is honored since the laws that make up the essence of being are the very patterns of motion that can be discerned through observation.

The dynamic view of being was suggested by Newton himself as well as by other thinkers who influenced Edwards, particularly Locke. Newton's universe was much more significantly populated by forces and "active principles" than by inert particles. And Locke's discussion of the dispositional power of the primary qualities as the causes of the secondary qualities was also pointing toward the primacy of forces and powers.[16] The central difference between these thinkers and Edwards was that neither Newton nor Locke departed completely from the static and particulate view of entities while their young disciple in New England did.

Many contemporaries of Edwards in the eighteenth century also began to speak of entities as essentially power rather than as substance. Also, such Neoplatonic thinkers at Cambridge as Cudworth, whom Edwards read as a youth, maintained that the teleological forces called "plastic natures" functioned within the very fabric of the world.[17] The distinc-

[16] See Chap. 2.
[17] See Chap. 4.

tiveness of Edwards' view is that he very clearly invests the patterns of phenomena themselves with an ontological significance without either speaking vaguely about forces and powers as essential to matter or introducing new occult qualities not directly deducible from phenomena themselves as his contemporaries did. In this way, Edwards tries to bring together into a coherent conception the traditional concern with permanence, mechanical and empirical science's insistence upon the primacy of the laws of motion and of observable phenomena, and the Cambridge Platonists' stress upon teleology. And in working out such a perspective, Edwards makes a firm move toward a truly modern conception of the universe.

The epistemological problem that Edwards inherited from his predecessors had to do with the issue of power and activity. The question was, What is the exact role of the mind's own activity in the cognitive process? A redefinition of the nature of mental activity emerged as an urgent question in the eighteenth century because the new atomistic conception of the materials of knowledge brought with it a serious problem—namely, the question of the possibility of experiencing order and structure in the world.[18] Locke, for example, believed that the primacy of sense experience in the knowledge process required that the simple, unmixed ideas of sensation and reflection be regarded as the sole foundation of our knowledge of the world.[19] Since the materials of knowledge are not the forms of composite entities, as they were in Scholastic epistemology, but the unmixed atoms of sensation, the traditional conception of the mental activity of abstraction could no longer be maintained. At this point, Locke simply asserts that it is the mind's own activity of putting together simple ideas that makes an experience of order in reality possible. Locke's pointing to the mind's own activity as the source of human experience of order in reality precipitated the rise of many theories of the imagination in modern thought.[20] But

[18] See Chap. 5.
[19] See Chap. 5.
[20] See Ernest Lee Tuveson, *The Imagination as a Means of Grace: Locke*

Locke himself left the psychology of the mind's creative activity largely unanalyzed and unexplained. So the task was defined for the young Jonathan Edwards: How could one develop a theory of the mind's imaginative or ordering activity in such a way that the empirical emphasis upon the direct sense contact with the world as the foundation for all legitimate knowledge is preserved? The Cambridge Platonists, especially Cudworth and Shaftesbury, undoubtedly inspired Edwards with their insistence upon the important contribution that the mind itself makes to the knowledge process. But their epistemologies had not paid enough attention to the Lockean empiricism to suit Edwards.

Edwards' grappling with the Lockean problem resulted in his theories of the imagination and of aesthetic perception—what Edwards called the "sense of the heart"—and here again the idea of habit is the key. The habit of mind as an active force enabled Edwards to formulate a dispositional theory of the mind's activity of ordering sense ideas into meaningful relationships. Habit as a relational and conditional law is, according to Edwards, triggered into action only upon appropriate occasions—that is, upon the mind's passive reception of sense ideas from the external world. In this way, Edwards was able to give both the mind and the sense ideas necessary roles to play in the knowledge process. Moreover, the idea of habit of mind as the character or the direction of the total human personality was the basis of Edwards' notion that the mind's reception of sense ideas, the mind's imaginative activity, and the mind's affectional response, all together constitute an event of direct apprehension or sensation of the way things are.[21] David Hume also developed a kind of dispositional theory of the association of ideas, but due to his positivistic conception of habits and dispositions and his nonrelational view of being, the associative activity of the mind's habits could not be conceived as possessing any veritable epistemic connection

***

and the Aesthetics of Romanticism (Berkeley and Los Angeles: University of California Press, 1960), pp. 5–41.

[21] See Chap. 6, n. 16, below.

with the structure of reality.[22] At any rate, the Shaftesburian insistence upon the active role of the mind in the knowledge process and the Lockean emphasis upon the simple ideas of sensation as the sole material of knowledge merge into a creative synthesis in Edwards' theories of the imagination and aesthetic perception—theories that anticipated the Coleridgian aesthetics of nineteenth-century romanticism.

In Edwards' philosophical theology, the reality and activity of God have an absolute priority. The existence and meaning of the created world depend completely and continually upon God. Edwards' dynamic conception of knowing and being is grounded in his reconception of the divine being as inherently dynamic. In my exposition here, however, I will, so to speak, work my way up to the doctrine of God. I will in the following chapter begin by establishing a firm grasp of my interpretive principle—that is, Edwards' reconception of the idea of habit. I will then move, in Chapters 3 through 6, to ontology and epistemology. I will attempt to explicate Edwards' dispositional reconception of being as at once permanent and dynamic, and then move to his dispositional theory of the role of the imagination in the knowledge process. The activity of the imagination will be shown to be the point in the created existence in and through which the dynamic life of God, as well as the becoming of the world, attain their ends. In chapter 7, I will focus upon Edwards' crucial reconception of the being of God as at once actual and also becoming. The inherently dynamic nature of the divine being will be shown to be the foundation for the being and becoming of the world. The final chapter will make explicit some of the most basic implications of Edwards' reconception of God and God's creative activity for his understanding of temporality and human history.

[22] See Robert P. Wolff, "Hume's Theory of Mental Activity," in *Hume: A Collection of Critical Essays*, ed. V. C. Chappell (Garden City, N.Y.: Doubleday, 1966), pp. 99–128.

CHAPTER II

The Idea of Habit

EDWARDS USES many terms to refer to the basic idea of an
active and real tendency. The most important and fre-
quently used words are "habit," "disposition," "tendency,"
"propensity," "principle," "temper," and "frame of mind."[1]
These words are all used whether Edwards has in mind an
acquired tendency or an innate disposition. But "habit" is
the most representative term because, for one thing, Edwards
refers to it when he gives his carefully worded definition of an
active tendency in "Miscellanies," No. 241.[2] "Habit" is also
the term that connects Edwards' conception with the history
of that idea which goes as far back as Aristotle, and, in using
this term, Edwards undoubtedly had this fact in mind. Aristotle was probably the first to give "habit," or *hexis* as he
called it, a philosophical usage. In the Middle Ages, Saint
Thomas Aquinas continued the Aristotelian usage but also
gave it a greater elaboration as well as an enlarged metaphys-

---

[1] See *Religious Affections*, vol. 2 of *The Works of Jonathan Edwards*, ed.
John E. Smith (New Haven: Yale University Press, 1959), pp. 206–207, 282–
283; Jonathan Edwards, *The Nature of True Virtue*, ed. William K. Frankena
(Ann Arbor: University of Michigan Press, 1960), pp. 5, 8, 99; "The Mind,"
No. 69, WEA, pp. 384–385. An analysis of the significance of habit in all as-
pects of Edwards' thought was initially presented in my doctoral dissertation,
"The Concept of Habit in the Thought of Jonathan Edwards" (Ph.D. diss.,
Harvard University, 1972). Norman Fiering has also discussed Edwards' idea
of habit but limits its importance to ethics and psychology. See Fiering, *Moral
Thought*, pp. 308–313, and his earlier essay, "Benjamin Franklin and the
Way to Virtue," *American Quarterly* 30 (1978): 199–223. Wallace E. Anderson has acknowledged the importance of dispositions in Edwards' theory of
the mind. See his "Editor's Introduction," in WEA, pp. 124–129.

[2] Edwards' definition reads, "All habits [are] a law that God has fixed, that
such actions upon such occasions *should* be exerted" ("Miscellanies," No.
241, Yale MSS). A number of passages from the previously unpublished portions of Edwards' manuscripts are published in this study with the kind permission of the Beinecke Rare Book and Manuscript Library, Yale University.

ical significance. The idea appears in the writings of important thinkers of Edwards' own time, and it plays a critically important role in such key American philosophers as Charles Sanders Peirce and William James.[3] So, in spite of the fact that many modern discussions of what Edwards meant by "habit" are carried on in terms of disposition or dispositional properties, I use the term "habit" both because it is Edwards' own technical term, and also because it will help place Edwards' conception of it within the context of its development in European and American philosophical thought.[4]

As many other things in the seventeenth and eighteenth centuries, the idea of habit was in a state of flux and even confusion when Edwards was doing his thinking. The Aristotelian conception of habit as an active and ontologically significant

[3] See Murray G. Murphey, *The Development of Peirce's Philosophy* (Cambridge: Harvard University Press, 1961), pp. 157–163; Ralph J. Bastian, "The 'Scholastic' Realism of C. S. Peirce," *Philosophy and Phenomenological Research* 14 (1953): 246–249; John Boler, *Charles Peirce and Scholastic Realism* (Seattle: University of Washington Press, 1963); William James, *Habit* (New York: Henry Holt, 1914). The similarity between Edwards' and Peirce's definitions of habit is intriguing. How much of Edwards Peirce actually might have read is an interesting historical question. It is most likely that both thinkers arrived at a realist conception of habit as the result of their grappling with the same problem—namely, how to overcome the positivistic and nominalistic implications of the writings of John Locke and David Hume.

[4] For a brief history of the idea of habit, see Paul A. Janet and Gabriel Scailles, *A History of the Problems of Philosophy*, trans. A. Monahan (New York: Macmillan, 1902), pp. 352–353; the article on "Habit," in *The Great Ideas*, vol. 2 of *Great Books of the Western World*, 54 vols., ed. Robert Hutchins (Chicago: Encyclopaedia Britannica, 1952). In recent years, there has been a significant and lively discussion in philosophy on the nature of dispositional properties, real possibilities, and counterfactuals. This recent resurgence of an interest in the ontological status of dispositions and the category of possibility makes my dispositional interpretation of Edwards' thought very timely, although I cannot in this present study of Edwards take an account of the contemporary discussions. See, for example, David Weissman, *Dispositional Properties* (Carbondale: Southern Illinois University Press, 1965); *The Possible and the Actual: Readings in the Metaphysics of Modality*, ed. Michael J. Loux (Ithaca: Cornell University Press, 1979); Andrew P. Ushenko, *Powers and Events* (Princeton: Princeton University Press, 1946), esp. pp. 80–154.

16

principle was still preserved in the writings of some thinkers, but many of the scientifically and empirically oriented philosophers were beginning to regard habit in a wholly nominalistic and positivistic manner—that is, as merely custom or the regularity of some aspects of observable phenomena. In regarding habits as active and real tendencies, Edwards in a sense goes back to Aristotle and Saint Thomas. And yet Edwards' "habit" is Aristotle's *hexis* and Saint Thomas's *habitus* in radically new dress. Edwards wanted to restore the old idea of habit without jettisoning the spirit of empiricism and of the Newtonian science. The result is Edwards' redefinition of Aristotle's *hexis* in terms of general laws that are real and yet are deducible on the basis of the observation of phenomena. With this new idea of habit as law, Edwards in effect turns upside down some of the central aspects of the Aristotelian and Scholastic world view. To place Edwards' idea of habit in its proper context, one must then begin with a brief, bird's-eye view of the tradition.

THE ARISTOTELIAN-THOMISTIC TRADITION
Aristotle

His term for habit is *hexis* (ἕξις), which is derived from the verb "to have." The root meaning of *hexis*, therefore, allows a wide-ranging use of the term, even in the very general sense in which a person is said "to have a coat or tunic."[5] Aristotle, however, gave the term a set of specific and philosophically significant meanings. First of all, *hexis* is an active tendency to behavior of a specific kind. Aristotle wrote, "Habit means a disposition according to which that which is disposed is well or ill disposed."[6] Habit as *hexis* then is not mere custom but a propensity toward a certain sort of behavior.

Second, habit also "a kind of existent thing."[7] Aristotle

---

[5] Aristotle, *Metaphysics*, trans. Hippocrates G. Apostle (Bloomington: Indiana University Press, 1966), p. 95; "Habit," *Great Ideas*, p. 665.

[6] Aristotle, *Metaphysics*, p. 94.

[7] See W.F.R. Hardie, *Aristotle's Ethical Theory* (Oxford: Clarendon Press, 1968), p. 108.

seems to have believed that habits have an abiding reality apart from the actual behavior that is their manifestation. Habits are more permanent than disposition and are called a "second nature." So Aristotle criticized the megarian view that habits have no existence except when they are being exercised. He objected that on this view a builder, for example, would not have the capacity to build when he or she was not actually building something.[8]

Another important meaning that Aristotle gives to *hexis* is that it enhances a human being's intellectual and moral life. Knowledge, when it has attained the form of a habit, for example, is a virtue and represents the enhancement of what was there before. By giving a person's capacities a desirable direction and form, habits facilitate, not hinder, the natural functioning of those capacities. Habit is an automatic force. But this automatic efficacy of habit does not function to inhibit the full functioning of the normal powers of human beings; rather it facilitates such functioning. Used in this sense, "habit" means something quite different from the modern usage according to which the term is used mainly in reference to those kinds of habituations (e.g., the habit of smoking) which induce thoughtless and even involuntary behavior. "Habit" as *hexis*, as W.F.R. Hardie points out, can also be translated as a "state of character," a phrase that is helpful because it shows that for Aristotle habits do not violate the integrity of the rational capacities of a person but rather function as his or her "character" or the overall direction of the self—that is, in and under, so to speak, all the natural powers of the self.[9]

Habit, in Aristotelian philosophy, is primarily a principle of operation and not a principle of being. So Aristotle deals with habits mainly as the intellectual and moral virtues—the developed states of the capacities to know and to act. There are places in his writings, however, where habits are treated as if they could also be principles of being. For example, Aristotle

---

[8] Ibid.
[9] Ibid., p. 103.

refers to the bodily state of health, and such a state describes the general way a being is.[10]

One must also place habits in Aristotle's metaphysics of substance and accident. Here his teaching is clear. Habits are accidental qualities that inhere in substances.[11] Habits, in other words, do not constitute the existence of an entity; they rather determine the nature of the operation of an already existing entity. In the Aristotelian-Scholastic metaphysics in general, substances are seen as either fully actual or purely potential, thus not allowing any middle point between potentiality and actuality. So a substance or the existence of an entity cannot be in the state of a habit. Although the place of habits in the potentiality/actuality metaphysics is fully developed only in Saint Thomas, it is clear already in Aristotle that habits play a role only on the level of the accident and not the substance.

Finally, habit, for Aristotle, is primarily an acquired propensity toward a determinate type of behavior. That is to say, "habit" refers to a tendency that has received a specific direction and facility through the repetition of a certain type of action. However, certain passages can be found in Aristotle's writings wherein he uses the term *hexis* to refer to innate tendencies—innate, in the sense that a particular type of propensity is common to all members of a class. In the *History of Animals*, for example, he differentiates various species according to the differences in their habits.[12] In this way, Aristotle sets a precedent for giving "habit" a double meaning—the specific meaning of an experientially acquired propensity and the more general meaning of all kinds of tendencies, whether acquired or innate.

[10] Aristotle, *Metaphysics*, p. 94.
[11] *The Basic Works of Aristotle*, ed. Richard McKeon (New York: Random House, 1941), pp. 771–772, 952–955. See also Jacques Maritain, *An Introduction to Philosophy* (New York: Sheed and Ward, 1962), pp. 182–183; Vernon J. Bourke, "The Role of Habitus in the Thomistic Metaphysics of Potency and Act," in *Essays in Thomism*, ed. Robert Brennen (New York: Sheed and Ward, 1942), p. 107.
[12] "Habit," *Great Ideas*, p. 665.

Further Development of Aristotle's Hexis in Saint Thomas's Habitus

Saint Thomas accepted all the salient aspects of Aristotle's concept of *hexis*, but he also gave some of them a greater systematization and introduced some further developments as well. The most important way in which Saint Thomas gives a further systematization to Aristotle's idea of habit is in regard to the latter's view that habits give enhancement to human beings' natural capacities. I am referring to Saint Thomas's discussion of the role of *habitus* in his metaphysics of potentiality and actuality.[13] According to Saint Thomas, there are three kinds of operational potencies. The first kind are wholly in act (such as the divine potency and the agent intellect). The second kind (such as the powers of sensation) are wholly passive and can be in act only while actuated by some active potency. Neither of these two kinds of potencies allows a metaphysical development. The third kind also has to be actuated by its corresponding active potency, but the actuation produces not merely a passion (as in the case of the second kind of potency) but also a quality that remains after the event of actuation has ceased and gives the potency an added facility and a specificity of direction. Human beings' rational power is an example of this kind of operational potency. In this view, this rational power of human beings can be developed and brought to a new state—namely, to the condition of virtue or *habitus*. Habits then give the original powers a perfection; they are now the propensities to act well and with a greater strength.

The unique metaphysical status of *habitus* is that it is a mean between full actuality and pure potentiality. Thus, habits can bring a potency to a degree of actuality without giving it a full actuality. Saint Thomas's notion of the intermediary role of *habitus* is clearly described by Vernon J. Bourke:

13 I am indebted to Vernon J. Bourke's studies of St. Thomas's idea of habitus. In addition to Bourke's essay mentioned in n. 11 above, see also Bourke, "Habitus as a Perfectant of Potency in the Philosophy of St. Thomas Aquinas" (Ph.D. diss., University of Toronto, 1938).

If the original state of an operative be that of pure potency, then habitus is a new state of that potency in which it is somewhat in act without being wholly in act. As a principle of operation, it is in potency in regard to the act which is operation; as a quality, it is already in act. This introduces the need of a terminological distinction of acts. The act which is in operation is called second act, or second perfection; that which brings the potency to the state in which it can perform its specific operation perfectly is called first act, first perfection, *virtus*, or habitus. Thus we have the development of a term, intentionally complex in meaning, denoting a condition in which its subject is at once in act and in potency. This is neither ambiguous, nor paradoxical, for that to which it is in potency (i.e., perfect operation) is quite different from that to which it is in act (i.e., pure, indeterminate potency).[14]

So habits, according to Saint Thomas, occupy the unique ontological status of being neither fully actual nor purely potential. By participating both in potentiality and in actuality, habits help explain how potency can be moved to actuality. Habits, for Saint Thomas, thus give an enhancement to the life of a human being.

Saint Thomas also amplified Aristotle's conception of habit by designating the sanctifying grace as an entitative habit, that is, a habit that functions on the level of being. For the Aristotelian-Scholastic tradition, the substance of a human being is a *forma completiva*; the substance either actually exists or does not. There cannot be any room for habit on the level of substance. However, Saint Thomas allows an exception in the case of a supernatural enhancement of one's being through the infusion of supernatural habits of being.[15] The being of a human being that is naturally complete can be subject to a supernatural growth. Saint Thomas of course puts a qualification

---

[14] Bourke, "The Role of Habitus," p. 107. See Thomas Aquinas, *The Summa Theologica*, vol. 20 of *Great Books of the Western World*, p. 4.

[15] Aquinas, *Summa Theologica*, pp. 7–8; Bourke, "The Role of Habitus," pp. 107–108.

on the role of habit on the entitative level by stating that such a role is possible only in an analogical sense.[16] The function of a supernatural habit on the level of being is analogical because habit, in the usual sense, refers to a natural principle and also because habit, in the usual sense, is an accidental quality that functions only on the level of quality (such as operation of a substance) and not on the level of being. Nevertheless, Saint Thomas's designation of the supernatural grace as an entitative habit, though in an analogical sense, is a significant amplification of Aristotle's conception of *hexis*.

IDEAS OF HABIT IN EDWARDS' BACKGROUND

As the young Jonathan Edwards delved into the philosophical and theological literature of his day, he faced a confusing state of affairs in the uses of the idea of habit as well as some exciting new possibilities for that idea. Neoplatonic philosophers at Cambridge contrasted the habitual against the eternal or permanent and spoke disparagingly of the former, while empiricistic thinkers tended to water down habits to customs. But some of these philosophers also brought up the idea of habit in connection with some of the new ontological and epistemological issues of their period, thereby laying a groundwork, at least implicitly, for new ways of conceiving the philosophical importance of habit. At the same time, there were also those who were faithfully reiterating the traditional Aristotelian conception. The young metaphysician studying at the newly founded Yale College did not lack in materials for creative thinking.[17]

The Aristotelian Idea of Habit in Burgersdicius, Chambers, and Reformed Theologians

Franciscus Burgersdicius was a Dutch Calvinist logician whose *Monitic Logica* was a set textbook at Harvard and Yale

[16] Bourke, "The Role of Habitus," p. 108.

[17] For a discussion of Edwards' early intellectual background and of the dating of Edwards' acquaintance with the writings of various authors, including Locke, see Anderson, "Editor's Introduction," in WEA, pp. 1–37.

at least up to 1923.[18] Working within the framework of the Aristotelian doctrine of substance and accident, Burgersdicius defines habit as "an adventitious quality of operating or doing anything with ease." Distinguishing habit from the natural powers of human beings, he writes:

> The same [i.e., natural powers] differ from Habit, both because it is from Nature, Habit elsewhere, and because it only renders the Subject fit to do or suffer. Whereas Habit also renders a Subject propense, and that to do expeditiously, and with facility.[19]

So, like Aristotle's *hexis*, habit for Burgersdicius is an active propensity with agency and a specificity of direction. He then gives the examples of such bodily habits as industry, and such mental habits as intelligence, wisdom, and prudence.[20]

Like Aristotle's *hexis*, Burgersdicius' habit is primarily an acquired disposition—an "adventitious quality," "not flowing from the essence of the subject." But again like Aristotle, Burgersdicius admits a broader use of the term to include any accidental form: "natural power, habit strictly so called, patible quality, form, operation, habit in the tenth category [i.e., in the sense of 'having' as opposed to 'privation'], etc."[21] The strict meaning of "habit," then, is an acquired and active propensity that perfects and enhances the operational powers of humanity. Broadly speaking, however, "habit" refers to all qualities and abilities, acquired or innate.

Ephraim Chambers' *Cyclopedia; or An Universal Dictionary of Arts and Sciences* was another source that provided Edwards with the Aristotelian concept of habit. In language closely resembling that of Burgersdicius, Chambers defined "habit" as "a quality adventitious to a thing, fitting, and disposing it either to act or suffer" and again as "an aptitude, or disposition either of the mind or body, acquired by a frequent

---

[18] W. S. Morris, "The Genius of Jonathan Edwards," p. 30.
[19] Franciscus Burgersdicius, *Monitic Logica* (London: R. Cumberland, 1697), pp. 14–16.
[20] Ibid., p. 15.
[21] Ibid., pp. 14, 91.

repetition of the same act." Strict and broad meanings of
"habit" are also found in Chambers. After defining "habit" as
"acquired by a frequent repetition of the same act," Chambers
goes on to add that "all natural habits, whether of body or
mind, are no other than the body and mind themselves."[22]

Various Reformed and Puritan divines, whose writings Edwards was familiar with, used the idea of habit basically in the
Aristotelian-Thomistic sense, primarily in their discussions of
regeneration, grace, and virtue. Their interest was not primarily in the Aristotelian metaphysical significance of habit, but
the meaning of the term "habit" as used in their doctrinal formulations includes most of the main features of the Aristotelian-Thomistic conception. The habit of grace, infused into a
person by God, for example, is said to be an active propensity—"a disposition active and inclining," and not just a "remote power," according to John Owen, an English Puritan divine.[23] William Ames, in his *Marrow of Theology*, pointed out
that a "virtuous habit moves the faculty, which otherwise
would not be so moved, toward good."[24] Habits are "active
and living powers," taught John Flavel, which are "to a course
of action as fountains or springs to the streams and rivers that
flow from them."[25]

The habit of grace is also a "state of character" that enhances and perfects the life of the whole person. Ames speaks
of habit as "a state of mind of various perfection." Habits of
grace give the regenerate person a newly acquired ability and
propensity "to do well." The habit of grace as a "state of character," furthermore, is an abiding, real principle. It constitutes
a "new life of the soul," a "second nature."[26] Thomas Shepard

[22] Ephraim Chambers, *Cyclopaedia; or, An Universal Dictionary of Arts
and Sciences*, 7th ed. (London: printed for W. Innys, J. P. Knapton [and
others], 1751), s.v. "habit."

[23] John Owen, *The Works of John Owen*, 17 vols. (Philadelphia: Leighton
Publications, 1865), 3: 289, 295, 468–485.

[24] William Ames, *The Marrow of Theology*, trans. John D. Eusden (Boston:
Pilgrim Press, 1968), p. 228.

[25] John Flavel, *The Method of Grace* (New York: American Tract Society,
1820), p. 102.

[26] Ames, *The Marrow of Theology*, p. 224; see also Thomas Shepard, *The*

specifically noted the fundamental, abiding nature of the change that God brings about in regeneration. He wrote, "And hence the act of grace ceaseth sometimes, because 'tis opposed by corruption, yet the being of it remains in full power, though not in exercise thereof."[27]

In short, explicitly or implicitly, these philosophical and theological predecessors and contemporaries of Edwards taught or made use of the basically Aristotelian-Thomistic idea of habit as an active and abiding tendency. The logicians were preserving intact the whole Aristotelian metaphysics, while the theologians were simply making use of that idea in their doctrinal formulations.

Changing World Views and New Possible Functions of Habit

Thus, Edwards had before him the Aristotelian *hexis* as a resource. But the seventeenth and eighteenth centuries were a time when the entire Aristotelian-Scholastic metaphysics of substance and quality was undergoing fundamental revisions under the pressure of Newtonian science and the associated tenets of empiricism. Motion, laws of motion, and power were now the key categories of thought, and the empirical or observational method the key method of inquiry. Before I analyze Edwards' definition of habit, I must briefly make note of how the old idea of habit reemerges in those philosophers who were hard at work in formulating new conceptions of the nature of things. In such thinkers as Locke, Hume, Newton, and the Cambridge Platonists, the idea of habit appears often in oblique ways. But their discussions contain suggestions for new possible philosophic functions of the idea of habit, and these suggestions provided Edwards with fertile ground for a reconception of the old idea of habit as well as for a formulation of a new perspective on reality.

Parable of the Ten Virgins Opened and Applied, Being the Substance of Divine Sermons on Matt. 25:1–13 (London: J. Rothwell, 1660), p. 173; Peter van Mastricht, *A Treatise on Regeneration* (New Haven: T. and S. Green, 1769), p. 27.

[27] Shepard, *The Parable of the Virgins*, p. 238.

The first area in which the idea of habit reappears is epistemology, or, to be more specific, the issue of the mind's apprehension of the order and relationships among ideas. Using as
his model the atomistic cosmology of Newtonian science,
Locke held that the fundamental materials of knowledge were
simple, unmixed ideas of sensation and reflection.[28] One of the
resultant problems of this view was that the traditional notion
of abstraction as the process of apprehending the order among
ideas became no longer serviceable. The mind could abstract
common elements or connecting links from the parcels of experience only if those parcels were conceived of as composite
particulars as the Scholastic had taught. Now, however, the
sense ideas are thought of as simples, and there is nothing to
abstract from them. At this point, Locke basically slurs over
the problem by declaring that "it is the office and excellency
of our reason to trace" the connections among ideas.[29] Locke
never really analyzes the nature of the process of such an activity of the reason, and this part of Locke's teaching remains
as a remnant of the rationalistic side of his thought.

But something new happens in a chapter in his *Essay* called
"Of the Association of Ideas." As he discusses the accidental,
"unnatural," or erroneous relationships among ideas in the
mind, Locke does not designate the "reason" as the source of
error but appeals to a wholly different principle—custom or
habit. By a customary association of ideas, "ideas, that in
themselves are not at all of kind, come to be so united in some
men's minds that it is very hard to separate them." Noting the
automatic or inevitable character of the influence of custom,
Locke writes that "the one no sooner at any time comes into
the understanding but its associate appears with it." Such a
phenomenon, Locke writes, is "wholly owing to chance or
custom" and to "habits of thinking" that have been settled by

---

[28] John Locke, *An Essay concerning Human Understanding*, ed. John W.
Yolton (London: J. M. Dent and Sons, 1961), bk. 2, chap. 1, nos. 1–5; chap.
2, nos. 1–3. See also Basil Willey, *The English Moralists* (Garden City, N.Y.:
Doubleday, 1967), p. 193.
[29] Locke, *Essay*, bk. 2, chap. 33, no. 5. See also C. R. Morris, *Locke-
Berkeley-Hume* (London: Oxford University Press, 1963), p. 50.

custom.[30] In Locke's discussion, the scope of the epistemic function of habit is limited as he applies it only to the aberrational connections among ideas. Nevertheless, something of fundamental significance is suggested here for the epistemic role of habit. In traditional epistemologies, habit primarily provided the element of facility, specific direction, or added strength to the functioning of the rational capacity of the mind. But now, in the context of the Lockean atomistic conception of sense data, the principle of habit emerges as what is directly responsible for the very presence of relations and order among ideas in the mind. In other words, the mind's own habitual activity of relating simple ideas of sensation could effectively replace the theory of abstraction. Habit, now, emerges as the rational capacity of the mind rather than a mere ancillary principle to the rational capacity—to use the term "rational" in a broad sense to mean the mind's ability to apprehend the structure of reality. As is well known, David Hume extended the Lockean principle of the association of ideas to all, including the natural and normal, connections among ideas, and thus took a further step in making explicit the suggestion of the new possible roles of habit in epistemology.[31]

But in both Hume and Locke, such an epistemic role of habit remained essentially a suggestion. Both thinkers vacillated between the ideas of habit as an active, purposive power on the one hand, and a mere custom or the regularity of actual events on the other. Concerning this latter tendency, it may be noted that both Locke and Hume liked to compare the association of ideas to the mutual attraction of atoms in physics. The pressure was on both men to follow one of the cardinal principles of seventeenth-century mechanical philosophy—the idea that all motion in the cosmos is due to causation by contact and efficient causation among the particles themselves.[32] Any teleological explanation was to be avoided so far as was

[30] Locke, *Essay*, bk. 2, chap. 33, nos. 5–6.
[31] David Hume, *A Treatise of Human Nature*, ed. L. A. Selby-Bigge (Oxford: Clarendon Press, 1960), bk. 1, pt. 1, sect. 4.
[32] C. R. Morris, *Locke-Berkeley-Hume*, pp. 123, 141.

possible. Thus, both Locke and Hume were eager to describe the phenomenon of the association of ideas as something that happens mechanically among the ideas themselves and not something that is brought about by an intentional activity of a purposive power. Neither Hume nor Locke could, however, avoid noting the involvement of a dispositional and inclinational power of the mind in the total phenomenon of the association of ideas. Locke spoke of the "settled habits of thinking," and Hume referred to the "propensity" of the mind as influencing the way sense ideas are related in the mind.[33]

Another dimension of this same ambiguity in the treatment of habit in both thinkers has to do with the ontological status of that principle. The "constant conjunction" among certain ideas that is brought about by custom is viewed by Hume as incapable of referring to the "necessary connection" that obtains in the real nature of things in the world. Neither did Hume think that the disposition of the experiencing subject could in any way enjoy a correspondence with the way things are in themselves.[34] The principles of habitual connections are thus considered as not necessarily referring to reality either from the objective, or from the subjective, pole. For Locke, as I noted above, the habitual associations of ideas represent only the "unnatural" connections among them and thus cannot refer to their "necessary" connections—those connections

[33] Locke, *Essay*, bk. 2, chap. 33, no. 6; Hume, *Treatise*, bk. 1, pt. 4, sect. 2. Two scholars of Hume's philosophy have argued that Hume found a mechanical interpretation of the association of ideas inadequate and had to supplement that interpretation with a theory of the mind's "propensities," which play an active role in the mind's experience of relations. Such an interpretation would bring Hume's theory of the mind closer to that of Edwards. See John Passmore, *Hume's Intentions* (London: Cambridge University Press, 1952); Robert P. Wolff, "Hume's Theory of Mental Activity," pp. 99–128. Edwards seems to have read Hume only late in his life, perhaps as late as 1755, and thus Hume would not have been an important influence in Edwards' early formulations of his theory of the mind. A comparison and contrast between Edwards and Hume would make an interesting study, however. See "Editor's Introduction," in *Freedom of the Will*, ed. Paul Ramsey, vol. 1 of *The Works of Jonathan Edwards* (New Haven: Yale University Press, 1957), p. 14, n. 11.

[34] C. R. Morris, *Locke-Berkeley-Hume*, pp. 138–145.

which have to do with the objective structure of reality. Habit is not yet seen as an ontological category.[35] A positivistic or nominalistic conception of habit prevails, and the possible epistemic role of habit remained unrecognized in Locke and only implicit in Hume.

The other area in which the old idea of habit appears with hints for a new possible philosophic role is that of ontology itself. The suggestions here are more explicit in Hume than in Locke. On Hume's empiricistic presuppositions, no basis could be found for continuing to speak about such traditional categories of being as substance and causality. The world that is experienced by the mind can only be described as "constant conjunctions" or "customary associations." And the experiencing self could only be described as "nothing but a heap or collection of different perceptions,"[36] that is, as habits of thought. In Basil Willey's words, "Reality ('Nature')," for Hume, "is the mental habits of all men—except perhaps lunatics, lovers, and poets."[37] Again, the old idea of habit emerges with hints for possibilities of a new philosophic function. In the context of the empiricistic criticism of the substance metaphysics of the Scholastics, habit now seems to be the only aspect of the motion-filled world, mental or material, that possesses at least a relative degree of permanence and stability. In the traditional substance metaphysics, habit was only an accidental quality and thus played a role only on the level of operation. But now habit could perhaps emerge as an ontological principle. Perhaps the real nature of things in the world is the habitual pattern of relations among ideas. Perhaps the real essence of the human self is its habits of thought and behavior. Such a metaphysical reconstruction was not forthcoming from the pen of David Hume, however, because of his positivistic presuppositions about habits. The experimental spirit weighed heavily upon him, and he was not pre-

[35] Ibid., p. 47.
[36] Hume, *Treatise*, bk. 1, pt. 4, sect. 2.
[37] Basil Willey, *The Eighteenth Century Background* (Boston: Beacon Press, 1961), p. 118.

pared to think of the regular patterns of behavior as the abiding structure of the world.

Such a new ontological function of habit was in an implicit and oblique way present also in Locke in his discussion of primary and secondary qualities. Our ideas of primary qualities, according to Locke, really refer to certain qualities in the objects themselves. But our ideas of the secondary qualities refer to nothing in the objects except to certain powers that the objects have to produce various sensations in us. These powers, Locke asserts, are not ontologically substantive qualities, rather "nothing but bare powers . . . depending on its primary qualities, whereby it is filled to produce different operations on different parts of our bodies."[38] They are, still, dispositional powers that do have observable and regular effects. A question arises however: If these dispositional powers can be regarded as possessing reality as abiding dispositions (as they seem to be by Locke) could they not then function as the permanent and substantive essences of things? Taking such an alternative could have saved Locke from his reluctant admission of the existence of something called "substance" ("a supposed I know not what") that lies behind all qualities, powers, and behavior but is not itself observable.[39] What is more, such a

---

[38] Locke, *Essay*, bk. 2, chap. 23, no. 8.

[39] Ibid., bk. 2, chap. 23, no. 15. Locke tended to think of the secondary qualities or powers as relational or dispositional properties that have real effect on the perceiving mind. "So the paper I write on having the power in the light . . . to produce in me the sensation which I call white, it cannot but be the effect of such a power in something without the mind." The secondary qualities or dispositional powers, however, according to Locke, are not the constitutive principles of the essence of things. The being of an object is defined in terms of its substance and the original or primary qualities, both of which are hidden to human experience. Thus, the metaphysics of substance prevails, and Locke is not prepared to think of the essence of things as powers or dispositions. So, he writes, "since the powers or qualities that are observable by us are not the real essence of that substance but depend on it and flow from it, any collection whatsoever of these qualities cannot be the real essence of that thing" (ibid., bk. 2, chap. 31, nos. 12–13). Scholars have argued, however, that Locke's discussion of powers, together with Newton's speculations about the "active principles," gave an impetus to many eighteenth-century thinkers to dispense with the problematic notion of substance and to think of

replacement of substances with dispositional powers could have laid the foundation for a dynamical view of reality that would bring philosophy closer to the findings of natural science. But Locke's uneasiness about the ontological status of powers and dispositions foreclosed such a turn of thought. He keeps insisting that powers are "barely" powers and "nothing but" powers—in other words, not ontologically real qualities. As was the case with Hume, here again the positivistic conception of habits and dispositions prevails and makes a metaphysical reconstruction impossible. The remnants of the old substance metaphysics and the borrowings from the new world of natural science remain in Locke in an unresolved conflict.

I have tried to indicate how the possibilities for new ontological and epistemological functions of habit and disposition were present in the writings of Locke and Hume, and also how some aspects of the mechanistic, scientific ways of thinking, as they were understood and applied by them, made such new functions of habit and disposition impossible. A nonpositivistic and nonmechanistic definition of disposition was needed. Such a reconception of habits and dispositions, as I will argue, is precisely what Jonathan Edwards attempted. What is ironical is the fact that the scientists of his day (for example, Isaac Newton himself) were not themselves purely positivistic or mechanistic in their thought, and indeed some of the inspirations for Edwards' own metaphysical conception of habit can be found in their writings.[40] Thus, for example, while Newton did indeed espouse the mechanical philosophy of Descartes and Gassendi, he also found that there were many phenomena, such as magnetism, chemical reactions, and gravity itself,

---

the essence of the being of things as none other than powers. Edwards was one of those thinkers who took the bold step toward a dynamic ontology. See P. M. Heimann and J. E. McGuire, "Newtonian Forces and Lockean Powers: Concepts of Matter in Eighteenth-Century Thought," *Historical Studies in the Physical Sciences* 3 (1971): 233–306.

[40] Wallace E. Anderson dates Edwards' acquaintance with Newton's works as Edwards' two graduate years at Yale (1720–1722). See Anderson, "Editor's Introduction," in WEA, pp. 21–23.

that did not seem to be best explained by the causation-by-impact principle.[41] He was, therefore, led to speak about those forces which seem to defy the principles of mechanical philosophy. His umbrella term for all such forces or causes of forces was "active principles," and he associated them closely with the activity of such an immaterial and teleological power as God's providential will.[42] Reading Newton, Edwards must have been inspired by the scientist's broadening of mechanical philosophy's narrow conception of motion and causation, which inspiration may have encouraged Edwards in seeing the dispositional principle of habit as playing the key role in both epistemology and ontology.

But how would Newton defend the reality of "active principles" on the basis of his methodological principle that a scientist's task is not to speculate about "occult qualities" but rather "to subject the phenomena of nature to the laws of mathematics"?[43] Locke was unsure, and Hume explicitly skeptical, about the ontological status of powers and dispositions that are not directly observable. But the scientist Newton did not espouse the positivistic outlook. He seems to have held that the "active principles," such as gravity, in spite of the fact that they were in a sense unobservable, were not "occult qualities" (such as substances and forms) but rather "general laws of nature, by which the things themselves are form'd: their truth appearing to us from phenomena."[44] Here Newton is arguing that the general law of gravity, though in itself not directly observable, is the pattern of the observable and regularly occurring instances of gravitational pull and thus not an occult quality—such as the substantial form that is ontologi-

[41] Ibid., p. 23. See also J. E. McGuire, "Force, Active Principles, and Newton's Invisible Realm," *Ambix* 15 (1968): 186. Heimann and McGuire have observed that "action at a distance is a doctrine which never seriously troubled Newton" ("Newtonian Forces and Lockean Powers," p. 242).

[42] Heimann and McGuire, "Newtonian Forces and Lockean Powers," p. 236.

[43] Quoted in E. A. Burtt, *The Metaphysical Foundations of Modern Science* (Garden City, N.Y.: Doubleday, 1954), p. 214.

[44] Ibid., p. 222.

cally and temporally prior to the actual observable effects of it. In other words, Newton is suggesting that, if certain conditions are met, the reality of certain unseen principles can be argued on the basis of their observable effects. This kind of argument must have been an inspiration to Newton's young disciple in the Colonies.[45] As shall be seen, Jonathan Edwards rejects the positivistic conceptions of dispositions and habits on the *basis* of the observable phenomena.

The insistence upon a concept of power broader than the one offered by seventeenth-century mechanical philosophy had already been voiced by philosophers even before Newton—particularly by the Cambridge Platonists. And there is good reason to believe that these Neoplatonic thinkers had an important influence upon Newton and Edwards. Reacting to the mechanistic cosmology of Hobbes, such thinkers as Cudworth and More held that the principle at work in the nature of things was an incorporeal, organic, and teleological force, which they called "plastic nature" or "spirit." Plastic natures, as seen by them, were unconscious and yet purposive, self-active, and life-giving powers. The laws of nature talked about by Hobbes and other mechanistic and materialistic thinkers, Cudworth argued, were "really nothing but a plastic nature" that works within or upon material and immaterial entities in the cosmos, regulating their movements in a harmonious manner. They are the instruments of God's creative and providential activity of giving life and order to the world.[46] Such a con-

[45] See Heimann and McGuire, "Newtonian Forces and Lockean Powers," pp. 251–252; Miller, *Jonathan Edwards*, pp. 71–99.

[46] Ralph Cudworth, "On Plastic Nature," in *The Cambridge Platonists*, ed. Gerald R. Cragg (New York: Oxford University Press, 1968), p. 240. The influence of the Cambridge Platonists on Edwards' early development is now widely recognized. Anderson documents the impact of Henry More's writings upon Edwards in the very early stages of the latter's intellectual formation. Scholars do not completely agree on how early in his life Edwards read Ralph Cudworth, but the idea of "plastic nature" or the "spirit of nature" appears in the writings of both More and Cudworth, and it is safe to assume that Edwards was aware of this notion by the time he was doing graduate work at Yale. See Anderson, "Editor's Introduction," in WEA, pp. 23–24, 59–61, 111–112; Fiering, *Moral Thought*, pp. 24, 46; Emily Watts, "Jonathan Edwards

ception of a teleological force may have been an inspiration to Newton, who found evidence in the observable phenomena themselves for the existence of powers that seem to work in a way different from the efficient causes of mechanical philosophy. Newton and Edwards, however, did not completely adopt this notion of plastic natures as spelled out by those Cambridge men for a number of reasons. They were, first of all, pictured too much on the model of Platonic forms and ideas and not sufficiently in line with the new scientific ideas of relational laws. Neither were they sufficiently based upon the observable phenomena as the Newtonian laws of nature were. What is more, there was the additional theological concern that such intermediaries seemed to weaken the direct involvement of God within the ongoing life of the cosmos.[47] Nevertheless, there is no doubt that those ideas gave encouragement to Edwards, as well as to Newton, in his attempt to revise the narrow mechanistic view of powers and motion.[48]

EDWARDS' IDEA OF HABIT

The idea of habit has a long history that goes back to Aristotle. In his metaphysics, and then in the Scholastic thought, the idea of habit played an important philosophic role, essentially as a dynamic principle that perfects the operations of human beings. In Edwards' own times, one deals with a chaotic and also creative period in which the Aristotelian-Scholastic metaphysics is being torn apart by the demand of natural science to see the world in terms of power and motion rather than in the language of substance and form. The idea of habit, as I have shown, reappears in this context with oblique but intriguing promises for possible new roles in the emerging new world view. But, as I have tried to indicate, be-

---

and the Cambridge Platonists" (Ph.D. diss., University of Illinois, 1963); Burtt, *Metaphysical Foundations*, pp. 135–150.

[47] For a discussion on Newton's reservations about, as well as enthusiasm for, the Cambridge Platonists' concept of "plastic nature," see McGuire, "Force, Active Principles, and Newton's Invisible Realm," pp. 184–185.

[48] For further discussion, see below, Chap. 4.

fore habit could play new philosophic roles, it needed a redefinition and a reconception in light of the new ways of thought that were fast becoming part and parcel of modern life. Such a work required a restoration of the Aristotelian conception as well as a modification of it. This Edwards attempted to carry out. One must, then, now proceed to examine Edwards' redefinition of habit.

Habit as an Active Tendency

Edwards has not left a systematic and detailed treatment of his idea of habit. So my work has to be one of piecing together various statements of Edwards scattered throughout his writings. As previously noted, habit is, according to Edwards, much more than mere custom or the usual way something is done or the regular way something happens. It is, rather, an active tendency that governs and brings about certain types of events and actions. It is a causal and purposive power. "All habits," wrote Edwards, "[are] a law that God has fixed, that such actions upon such occasions *should* be exerted."[49] Therefore, habit is an active law that prescribes that if certain conditions are given, a certain type of action would certainly result.

I can specify two senses in which habit is an *active* tendency in Edwards' conception. Habit is active, first of all, in that it certainly issues forth in certain types of actions or events if certain conditions are fulfilled. Writing about grace as a habit or principle of action, Edwards asserts:

> True grace is not an unactive thing; there is nothing in heaven or on earth of a more active nature. . . . Godliness in the heart has as direct a relation to practice . . . as a habit or principle of action has to action.[50]

That to which an active tendency tends, then, is not just a "bare possibility" but what might be called a "real possibil-

---

[49] "Miscellanies," No. 241, Yale MSS.
[50] *Religious Affections*, p. 398.

ity."[51] Edwards made this distinction in a note in the "Miscellanies." He was concerned about the claim that the "light of nature" without special revelation could lead humankind to salvation.

> When it is asserted that the light of nature, or the means and the advantages which all mankind have by pure nature to know the way of their duty & happiness, are absolutely sufficient, without any additional means & advantages; one of these two things must be meant by it, if it is has any meaning: wither that they are sufficient in order to a meer possibility [sic] of obtaining all needful & useful knowledge in these important concerns; or that these natural means have a sufficient tendency actually to reach the effect, either universally, or at least generally, or at least in a prevailing degree, as the state of mankind is.

Edwards then continues:

> If the former of these be meant: viz. that the means of knowledge & understanding of these things, which all mankind have by meer nature is sufficient in order to a bare possibility of obtaining this knowledge; that, if it should be allowed, will not at all prove, that further light is not extremely needed by mankind. A bare possibility as here distinguished from all tendency to the actual attaining the effect or end may be, & yet there be no tendency or probability, that ever the effect (however necessary, and however dreadful the consequence will be of its failure) will be reached, in one single instance in the whole ☉ [world] of mankind, from the beginning of the ☉ to the end of it, tho' it should stand millions of ages.
>
> But if by the sufficiency of these natural means be meant, a sufficiency of tendency actually to reach the effect, either universally or in a prevailing degree, considering all things belonging to the state & circumstances of mankind: I say, if

---

[51] In my interpretation of Edwards' idea of "real possibility," I have found instructive a similar idea in Charles Sanders Peirce. See Boler, *Peirce and Realism*, pp. 99–107.

this be means, asserting the light of nature to be sufficient to obtain the effect; it is the very same thing as to say, that it actually does obtain the effect. for if the tendency, all things considered, be sufficient actually to obtain the effect, doubtless it does actually obtain the effect. for what should hinder a cause from actually obtaining the effect, that it has a sufficient tendency to obtain all things consider'd?[52]

A tendency to the "meer possibility" of a certain event, if the term "tendency" could be used in this way, may or may not bring about such an event. But an active tendency to a kind of event will actually bring about such an event whenever a certain set of conditions are met. Is Edwards here saying that habit as an active tendency operates with a kind of conditional necessity? That is to say, assuming that certain conditions are fulfilled, habit as an active tendency would necessarily bring about a kind of event? This is in fact precisely what Edwards asserts in his book on the freedom of the will. After defining "necessity" as "a full, fixed, and certain connection," Edwards distinguishes "moral necessity" from "natural necessity."

By "moral necessity" is meant the necessity of connection and consequence, which arises from such *moral causes*, as the strength of the inclination, or motives, and the connection which there is in many cases between these, and such volitions and actions. . . . By "natural necessity," as applied to men, I mean such necessity as men are under through the force of natural causes; as distinguished from what are called moral causes, such as habits and dispositions of the heart, and moral motives and inducements.[53]

Habit, then, functions with a kind of necessity in bringing about a type of event or operation under a type of circum-

---

[52] "Miscellanies," No. 1337, Yale MSS. Edwards used this sign for the word "world." See Townsend, "Editor's Introduction," in HGT, p. xxi.

[53] *Freedom of the Will*, p. 156. For a discussion of Edwards' distinction between "moral and natural necessity," see Paul Ramsey, "Editor's Introduction," in *Freedom of the Will*, pp. 34–37.

stances. Habit is an active, causal power, and Edwards explicitly refers to habits as causes, as in the above quotation.

Habit, in Edwards' view, is an active principle in another way—in the sense that it governs the *type* of events or actions and the *type* of occasions upon which those events or actions would become actual. Habit is a law that "*such* actions upon *such* occasions should be exerted" (emphasis added). Again, habit is more than custom or the regular way something happens or is done. It is more than a summation of the character of some actual events. Habit actively brings about events of a particular sort. So habit is a purposive power that works with a design. Edwards is here maintaining that a teleological activity does not have to be associated with consciousness; habit as an automatic principle can still seek an end. Habit then functions like a formal and final cause.

Edwards' conception of habit is something like Plato's conception of form in that habit regulates and constitutes the pattern or character of events and behavior. But habit in Edwards is certainly more than Plato's form; it is in fact more like the Aristotelian notion of form, because it is in itself a nisus, or a push, toward the existence of the events or behavior of a type. Habit is, in other words, an active and causal power as well as a form or a pattern. In short, it is clear that Edwards is restoring a version of the Aristotelian concept of *hexis* as an active tendency, thereby rejecting the nominalistic and positivistic notion of habit as mere custom or regularity.

Habit as Law

It is true that Edwards retrieved from the Aristotelian-Scholastic tradition the notion of habit as an active, causal power. But Edwards did not simply repeat that notion with the associated metaphysics of substance and form, as Burgersdicius and Chambers did, at a time when all the developments in the intellectual world were calling the adequacy of that metaphysics into question. Edwards redefined "habit," as I have already quoted, as a relational law "that such actions upon such occasions should be exerted." A quite early entry in "The Mind" contains Edwards' equally relational definition of powers in general. After defining a cause "to be that after, or upon the existence of which, or its existence in such a manner, the existence of another thing follows," Edwards goes on to say that "the connection between these two existences or between the cause one effects is what we call power."[54] This is not just an accidental or occasional sort of connection but one that always obtains given two events of a particular type. By power, then, Edwards means an active tendency, a habit. I shall return to this point later. What I must note here is that habit or an active power is, for Edwards, a lawlike relation between events or actions and not an accidental quality that inheres in a substance. At this point, Edwards has effectively left the old world of the substance/form metaphysics.

Edwards was in all this really only honoring the fundamental methodological concerns of Newtonian science. Newton considered his task to be "to subject phenomena of nature to the laws of mathematics." He further explained that "these principles [mass, gravity, cohesion, etc.] I consider not as occult qualities, supposed to result from the specific forms of things, but as general laws of nature, by which the things themselves are formed."[55] By "phenomena," Newton primarily meant motion. And motion was to be studied in terms of the mathematical rules it follows. It was natural, therefore, for Edwards to want to think of habits and powers in terms of the lawlike relations that obtain among events and actions. Newton was also eager to get away from static and self-contained forms of traditional metaphysics and to focus upon the patterns of motions themselves. This seventeenth-century tendency to reject a sharp division between being and function or activity is also at work in Edwards' move away from a definition of habit as a quality or form to a conception of it as something that is embedded in, and can be read out of, motion or activity itself.[56] This naturally leads to Newton's epistemolog-

[54] "The Mind," Nos. 26, 29, WEA, pp. 350, 352. For a similar conception of habit as a relational law in Peirce, see Boler, *Peirce and Realism*, pp. 102–103; Murphey, *The Development of Peirce's Philosophy*, pp. 154–158.
[55] Quoted in Burtt, *Metaphysical Foundations*, p. 222.
[56] Ibid., pp. 220–225.

ical concern not to talk about anything that cannot be in some fashion based upon observable phenomena. He wants to deal with the laws of nature themselves and not with some occult qualities that are far removed from nature as it is plainly observed. Edwards, no less an empiricist, wanted also to speak of the laws of phenomena rather than the forms and properties "behind" the phenomena.

Eager as Edwards was to follow certain methodological principles of Newtonian science, however, he did not accept all of its conclusions. For Edwards, a law as habit is an active and causal power. The important question of whether all the laws of nature are regarded by Edwards as active tendencies will be extensively dealt with at a later point. What is now evident, however, is that at least some laws of motion, according to Edwards, are habits. Newton was inclined to regard all laws of phenomena as mere uniformities, and to insist on looking elsewhere for their causes. For Edwards, however, a law, when it is a habit, is a general law that functions prescriptively or purposively and is, therefore, more than a descriptive summation of actual events. This is so because habit, as Edwards says, is a law that a type of event or action "should" occur upon occasions of a particular sort. Habit then governs the future actions and events as well as the past and present ones. Habit is a general law that governs *all* events of a particular class and is, therefore, more than the uniformity that obtains in the actually observed events of the past and the present.

On what grounds does Edwards argue for the ontological reality of habit over and above the phenomenal reality of nature's uniformities and regularities? I will deal with this crucial question in the following section. What needs to noted presently is that in defining "habit" as a general law, Edwards is holding that a law of motion can be regarded as a causal power; in doing so, he is carving out an alternative to Newton's (as well as Locke's and Hume's) tendency to regard all laws of phenomena as mere descriptions of uniformities. Here, as in many other aspects of his thought, Edwards the theologian plunges into the very depth of the scientific and philosophical thought of his day and tries to reshape it.

To define "habit" as a law also means a break with the causality-by-impact perspective—a perspective that lingered on in Newton, thus causing a tension with his discovery of those forces which did not seem to function by impact.[57] To say that habit as an active power is a lawlike relationship among events or activities is to maintain that things happen or are done because the relationship calls for them. Things happen because it is fitting or appropriate that they do so according to a kind of relationship that already exists in the mode of a general law or habit. Edwards has moved away from impact causality to an aesthetic or relational causality. This implies further that one thing does not cause another thing all by itself. Relational causality implies a confluence of all entities in the system of being into a nexus of relationships in which all are involved in causing one another. So Edwards declares that "there is no such a thing as mechanism if that word is taken to be that whereby bodies act each upon other purely and properly by themselves."[58]

Still another implication of Edwards' relational definition of habit is that the meaning and content of a habit is constituted by the character of its effects. "Propensities are no propensities," writes Edwards, "any otherwise, than as taken with their objects" (i.e., effects).[59] Writing about the necessity of holy practice for the regenerate, Edwards also asserts that "certainly the proper nature and tendency of every principle, must appear best and most fully, in its most perfect exercises."[60] Habit is not like the forms of the Scholastic meta-

---

[57] Cf. Heimann and McGuire, "Newtonian Forces and Lockean Powers," p. 242.

[58] "Of Atoms," WEA, p. 216. Herbert Richardson discusses Edwards' conception of "aesthetic causality"; see "The Glory of God," chap. 4. See also Roland Delattre, *Beauty and Sensibility in the Thought of Jonathan Edwards* (New Haven: Yale University Press, 1968), pp. 184–206.

[59] *Original Sin*, ed. Clyde Holbrook, vol. 3 of *The Works of Jonathan Edwards* (New Haven: Yale University Press, 1970), p. 126.

[60] *Religious Affections*, p. 436.

physics that have a self-contained nature and meaning within themselves. Habit is a relationship or pattern among actions and events themselves, or between occasions and events or actions. One cannot, therefore, talk about the content of a habit without talking about the actions and events in which it is exercised. The Scholastics also spoke of the actions as clues to the nature of a being: *operari sequitur esse* (operation follows being).[61] But Edwards is contending that the essence from which actions flow is not to be thought of as a self-contained form but rather as the lawlike relation of actions themselves.

Habit as Possessing a Mode of Reality

Although habit has content and meaning only in reference to the actual actions and events of which it is a law, it is in an ontological sense more than actual events. As was shown in the previous section, habit for Edwards is a general law and not just the phenomenal uniformity of actual events. Habit as a general law is an active, prescriptive law that governs all the events of a particular type. Does habit, then, have a mode of reality apart from the actual events of which it is a general law? Edwards answered this question affirmatively in "The Mind":

> In memory, in mental principles, habits, and inclinations, *there is something really abiding in the mind when there are no acts or exercises of them,* much in the same manner as there is a chair, in this room when none perceives it, *we mean that the minds would perceive chairs here according to the law of nature in such circumstances.* So when we say, a person has these and those things laid up in his memory, we mean they would actually be repeated in his mind upon certain occasions, according to the law of nature—though we cannot describe, particularly, the law of nature about these mental acts so well as we can about other things. (Emphasis added)[62]

[61] See Boler, *Peirce and Realism*, p. 102.
[62] "The Mind," No. 69, WEA, p. 385.

According to Edwards, laws and habits are something real. And the meaning of this assertion is that certain laws and habits *would* certainly manifest themselves in actual events if certain circumstances exist. But the laws and habits are ontologically present, whether manifested or not. Edwards argued that the laws of nature are not merely in the order of knowing but also in the order of being. But did not Newton caution that all reliable knowledge has to be based upon phenomena and that the occult qualities have no such experimental bases? If Edwards maintains that habits and laws are real, is he not setting up occult qualities that have no bases in phenomena?

It seems that Edwards meant to justify the reality of habits and laws precisely on Newton's own ground—namely, on the ground of the phenomena. Edwards seems to argue that the very phenomenon itself points to the reality of laws and habits. Consider the following statements made by Edwards:

> I shall here consider . . . whether such an universal, constant, infallible event [i.e., the event of human sinfulness] is truly a proof of the *being* of any tendency or propensity to that event. . . .
>
> . . . To determine whether the unfailing constancy of the above-named event be an evidence of tendency, let it be considered, what can be meant by tendency, but a prevailing liableness or exposedness to such or such an event? Wherein consists the notion of any such thing, but some stated prevalence or preponderation in the nature or state of causes or occasions, that is followed by, and so proved to be effectual to, a stated prevalence or commonness of any particular kind of effect? Or, something in the permanent state of things, concerned in bringing a certain sort of event to pass, which is a foundation for the constancy, or strongly prevailing probability, of such an event? If we mean this by tendency (as I know not what else can be meant by it, but this, or something like this) then it is manifest, that *where we see a stated prevalence of any kind of effect or event, there is a tendency to that effect in the nature and state of its causes.* A common and steady effect shews, that there is

somewhere a preponderance, a prevailing exposedness or liableness in the state of things, to what comes so steadily to pass. (Emphasis added)[63]

Edwards' basic thesis seems to be that the actual phenomenon of "a stated prevalence of any kind of effect or event" leads one to belief in the "being" of an active tendency. Laws and habits, in other words, have a mode of being apart from the actual events because there is something in the actual exercise of those laws and habits which points to such a mode of reality.

This argument must be analyzed in further detail. What is the phenomenon of prevalence of certain types of events? Edwards was referring to the fact that certain events actually occur so regularly under certain circumstances that the law that is involved is not just a descriptive law of uniformity but a prescriptive general law. That is to say, what is called for by such a phenomenon of prevalence is a general law that governs not only the actual events of the past, or the actual events of the present, but the possible events of the future as well. In such a general law, there is something extra that goes beyond the actual events. This something extra is what needs to be noticed.

What is more, according to Edwards, a prescriptive general law or an active tendency operates with a kind of necessity. Laws and habits are not tendencies that *may* be realized but that would *certainly* be realized if certain conditions are met. On the basis of such a tendency, one *predicts* that a certain event would occur if certain conditions are met. In other words, that a certain event would occur if certain conditions are met is now a real fact. It is a present knowledge and a real fact that such and such event would occur if such and such circumstances obtain. How should one account for this odd fact that one can have a present knowledge of a present real fact about those possible events of the future? Peirce drew from this fact the conclusion that only actual events exist but the real is not exhausted by the actual events.[64] In other

---

[63] *Original Sin*, pp. 120–121.
[64] See Boler, *Peirce and Realism*, pp. 26, 106–107.

words, the active tendency that is involved here is a *real* tendency. The reality of certain future events to which there is an active tendency can be explained only by the reality of the active tendency. An active tendency or an active law as a general law, then, is not exhausted by the actual events that it governs. To use Peirce's example, the hardness of a diamond is a real tendency or a "would-be," because a diamond would, and not just may, resist pressure. Therefore, a diamond's hardness is a real fact even when it is not manifesting itself in actual events of resisting pressure.[65] Edwards said as much when he wrote that habits were "something really abiding in the mind when there are no acts or exercises of them."[66] When Newton discovered the law of gravity, he discovered, in Edwards' view, not only a law that merely describes certain uniformities in actual events; he discovered real tendencies that in a sense cause, and therefore explain, the observed events. It was noted in the previous section that habit as a relational law has a content only in reference to its observable effects. If this is all that Edwards maintained, he would be, as Peirce would have later called it, a nominalistic pragmatist. Like Peirce, however, Edwards is a realistic pragmatist because he, too, held that habit, though it is the very pattern of the observable events themselves, is more than those events: it is an abiding principle with its own sort of reality.

If it is true that Edwards restored Aristotle's *hexis*, it is equally true that he reshaped *hexis* into a modern conception. Like Aristotle's *hexis* and Saint Thomas's *habitus*, habit for Edwards is an active, teleological, and causal power that is also an ontologically real, abiding principle. Habit is to be distinguished both from pure potentiality and also from mere pattern or uniformity of events and actions. Habit is a virtual principle that stands at a midpoint between mere potentiality and full actuality. It is a virtual principle, a real potential. It is a pattern that governs and brings about events and actions. And this virtual power and prescriptive pattern belongs not only to the order of knowing but also to the order of being.

[65] Ibid., pp. 99–101.
[66] "The Mind," No. 69, WEA, p. 385.

This essentially Aristotelian concept is then reconceived by Edwards in the language of relations. Habit is not the self-contained form of Aristotelian-Scholastic metaphysics, but rather a general law among events and actions. Edwards agreed with the Cambridge Platonists' replacement of Hobbes' mechanical and efficient causality with the teleological principle of "plastic nature." But the latter concept was not relational enough for Edwards. By defining the causal power of habit as a relational law, Edwards introduced the concept of relational or aesthetic causality. Habit is a power that functions conditionally—that is, in a manner appropriate or fitting to all the interrelated terms.

It is said that the movement from the Aristotelian-Scholastic thought to the modern perspective consists in the movement from being to function. In Edwards' time, the notions of substance and form were being given up as inadequate. Newton, Locke, and Hume all exemplify, in various degrees, this new stress upon activity and the pattern or law of that activity. The paramount question was the ontological status of that pattern or law. A dynamic ontology based on motion and not on substance was destined to come. But on what abiding structural principle could such a new ontology be built? Should one throw up one's hands and give up as Hume seems to have done? By defining the pattern or law of motion as an ontologically real and abiding principle (i.e., as a habit), Edwards was prepared to get on with that task of a metaphysical reconstruction.

There are many aspects of what Edwards has to say about habit that have not yet been explicitly analyzed—such questions as, What is its origin? And does it apply equally to the material as well as to the mental realm? These and other issues, however, would best be discussed as they emerge in Edwards' actual application of his notion of habit to various philosophical and theological questions. I shall now move directly to an analysis of Edwards' reconception of ontology, which I referred to above.

CHAPTER III

Being as Habit

AS ALREADY INDICATED in the preceding chapter, many explicit as well as implicit moves toward an ontology that takes adequate account of the scientific and empiricistic developments were present in the writings of many of Edwards' philosophical predecessors, including Newton and Locke. Newton's preoccupation with "forces" and "active principles," and Locke's allusions to the "powers" behind the observable qualities in things are cases in point. The Cambridge Platonists, with whose writings Edwards was also acquainted early in his youth, were also speaking about the dynamic principles of "plastic natures" as immanent in the very nature of things.[1]

Edwards learned from all of the above ideas, but he had a different strategy. Newton, Locke, the Cambridge Platonists, and other predecessors of Edwards still thought of the world as essentially consisting of individual substances and forms. Edwards, however, makes a clean break with this Aristotelian-Scholastic conception and sets out to give the substances and forms themselves a new meaning. It is my contention that one does not even begin to understand Edwards' world view without noticing that he introduced an essentially new understanding of the very nature of reality, replacing substance metaphysics with a dynamic and relational conception. And it is my thesis that Edwards' conception of habit is an important clue to his reconstruction of ontology.

Edwards' concern, however, was not only a philosophical reconstruction in light of the developments in experimental science and empiricistic epistemology. Supremely important for him was the principle of God's absolute sovereignty in all

[1] For a discussion of Edwards' acquaintance with the writings of the Cambridge Platonists, see Anderson, "Editor's Introduction," in WEA, pp. 20–26.

aspects of reality, both the material and the spiritual. From the day when Edwards attained an experiential conviction of the truth of God's sovereignty, this doctrine remained for him a fundamental principle of all that he thought and wrote.[2] The refutation of deistic and materialistic world views was very high on Edwards' intellectual agenda. I hope to indicate in the present chapter the various ways in which Edwards' notion of habits and laws played a key role in his attempt to restate a strong doctrine of God's sovereignty without completely compromising the ontological integrity of the created world.

EDWARDS' DISPOSITIONAL ONTOLOGY

I shall begin by offering an initial sketch of the main features of Edwards' new ontology. Summing up the various speculations and observations in his early notes, "The Mind," Edwards jotted down the following as two of the "Subjects to Be Handled in the Treatise on the Mind":

> The manifest analogy between the nature of the human soul and the nature of other things; how laws of nature take place alike; how *it is laws that constitute all permanent being in created things, both corporeal and spiritual.*
>
> In how many respects *the very being of created things depend on laws*, or stated methods fixed by God, of events following one another. (Emphasis added)[3]

Referring specifically to spiritual or perceiving beings, Edwards wrote in "Miscellanies," No. 241: "[Soul's] essence consists in powers and habits."[4] Habits and laws, Edwards is saying, are the abiding principles of being. They do not merely *belong to* entities but rather are constitutive of their being.

---

[2] Ibid., pp. 26–27. Anderson here dates Edwards' conversion experience as having occurred during the first year of his graduate study. See also Edwards, "Personal Narrative," FAJ, pp. 58–59.

[3] "Subjects to Be Handled in the Treatise on the Mind," Nos. 36, 50, WEA, pp. 391–392.

[4] "Miscellanies," No. 241, Yale MSS.

Things, in other words, do not have habits but *are* habits and laws, which are the essence of things.

There are other principles besides habits and laws that are basic to Edwards' ontology. God's immediate and continual exertion of his power is or results in the resistance or actuality of entities. Further, being is also beauty or proportion. I shall discuss below the relationship among God's activity, beauty, and habits or laws, all of which are the constitutive principles of being. My immediate focus here, however, is on the meaning of Edwards' assertion that being is essentially habits and laws.

The revolutionary character of Edwards' conception can be initially sketched if one compares and contrasts it with the basic categories of the Aristotelian-Scholastic ontology, which was the prevailing view in the late seventeenth and the early eighteenth centuries. In that tradition, the idea of substance explained the self-subsisting and abiding aspect of the existence of an entity, and the categories of substantial form and essence referred to the character and structure of being. It should be acknowledged that Edwards occasionally uses the word "substance," but what he means by it is radically new.[5]

According to Edwards, habits and laws make up the relative yet real permanence of created things. The actual existence of a thing is the result of the continuing and immediate exercise of God's own power. But God exercises his power "according to certain fixed and exact established methods and laws."[6] These laws are "constant and regular,"[7] and, as I have shown, are ontologically real apart from the actual events (i.e., they constitute and govern God's particular exercises of his power). And it is in the constancy of these laws that the permanence of created things lies. Of course, this permanence is itself ontologically contingent since these laws themselves are established and upheld by God and are dependent upon God's immediate exercise of his power for their application or exer-

---

[5] See, for example, "Of Atoms," WEA, p. 215.

[6] "The Mind," No. 13, WEA, p. 344.

[7] "The Mind," No. 27, WEA, p. 351.

cise. Creatures exist *per se* (by themselves or in themselves), while only God exists *a se* (not only in himself but also from himself). The point to be noted here is that Edwards uses his notion of habits and laws to give the created existence an integrity of its own, thus avoiding absolute monism. Further, Edwards understands the substantial or abiding character of the created things as dispositional and not as static. Things are abiding because they are essentially lawlike habits and not because they are substances or substantial forms.

Edwards' conception of being as essentially lawlike habits also means that being is essentially relational. Habits and laws, as shown above, are relations of relations—that is, the patterns according to which existences (resistances) are caused by God. And these patterns are the habits and laws that make up the abiding aspect of entities as well as the very ways in which one thing is related to other things. Relations, in other words, are internal to being. A thing *is* only as it is related to other things. In this way, Edwards has left behind him the traditional conception of the world as consisting of particulate and individual entities or substances, each of which exists by itself independent of its relations to others.

Finally, Edwards' conception of being in terms of habits and laws results in a dynamic view of reality. To say that the abiding nature of entities consists of habits and laws is to maintain that entities are abidingly active tendencies. Things are essentially dispositional and thus inherently and unceasingly tending to actual existences through the exercise of habits and laws and through the immediate exercise of God's own power. The traditional notion of substance receives a radical revision here. Potentiality and activity are being brought into the very inner nature of being. The substances of things used to be thought of as *forma completeva*; things either exist or do not exist. But habits and laws that for Edwards now function on the most basic level of being are active tendencies. Reality is not something that is achieved once and for all but something that is achieved again and again. Reality is a permanent process of the multiplications of actualities (relations). Further, if what the Scholastics used to call substances are habits and laws, then the operations or exercise of entities now attain an ontological significance. The operations of an entity are the exercise of its potency for existence and not only of its potency for activity.

The burden of this chapter is to trace the development of Edwards' new ontology in his early philosophical and scientific writings with a special focus on his conception of the permanence of being as essentially dispositional. Chapter 4 will deal with the other important aspects of Edwards' dispositional ontology: habits and laws as the structural and dynamic principles of being.

HABITS AND LAWS AS THE PERMANENCE OF THE CREATED WORLD

The Development of a Dispositional Ontology in Edwards' Early Philosophical and Scientific Writings

The fundamental principles of Edwards' view of reality were worked out in the pages of his early philosophical and scientific writings, which fall roughly between the year he graduated from Yale College (1720) and the early years of his pastorate in Northampton (late 1720s and early 1730s). Among the most important concerns in these writings, as Wallace Anderson has pointed out, are the refutation of materialism and the formulation of a "phenomenalistic idealism."[8] And it is out of Edwards' discussion of these concerns that a dispositional definition of the permanence of the created world emerges.

In his refutation of metaphysical materialism, Edwards was joining many of his predecessors, especially the Cambridge Platonists, who saw that the philosophy of Thomas Hobbes was a serious threat to morality and religion. Since Edwards was acquainted with the writings of these Cambridge men very early in his youth, it is not surprising that he picks up this issue in his earliest philosophical and scientific writings.[9] He

---

[8] Anderson, "Editor's Introduction," in WEA, pp. 52–111. See also nn. 43 and 44 below.

[9] See above, n. 1.

begins his essay entitled "Of Atoms" with the definition of "atom" as a body "that cannot be made less, or whose parts cannot by any finite power whatsoever, be separated from one another." An atom is a solid body or an indivisible continuum of parts. Such a body is "absolutely full" and "has every part of space included within its surface solid and impenetrable."[10] To the question of whether a small part of such a solid body could be broken off without endangering the existence of that body, Edwards answers that if an atom could be divided, it could then be divided into every part and thus annihilated.

Edwards then infers that if solidity means impenetrability or indivisibility, solidity is nothing other than the activity of resisting annihilation. "Solidity, indivisibility, and resisting to be annihilated are the same thing." And, since "being and persevering to be are the same thing," solidity or "resistance" is the very being of an atom. "The solidity of bodies and the being of bodies is the same."[11] An atom is a solid body; solidity is nothing other than the act of resisting, which is the same thing as existing. Thus, solidity is not just a quality of an atom but the very being of an atom. At this point, Edwards has already done away with the notion that a material entity is a hidden substance or subject to which solidity or the activity of resisting belongs. A body is not a substance but rather solidity, and solidity is an activity.

The analysis does not stop here. Edwards further notes that an atom resists annihilation to any other finite force. An atom's solidity must then be an infinite power of resistance to any division or separation of its parts. How can we account for such a power? Edwards answers that it can only be the infinite power of God. Resistance or the existence of a body must, then, be the very activity of God himself. So Edwards concludes that "solidity results from the immediate exercise of God's power," and that "all body is nothing but what immediately results from the exercise of divine power in such a particular manner."[12]

[10] "Of Atoms," WEA, p. 212.
[11] Ibid., p. 211.
[12] Ibid., p. 215.

Now Edwards is ready to clinch his case against metaphysical materialism by drawing the logical conclusion from his analysis that a material body is not a substance that exists by itself.

> The certain unknown substance, which philosophers used to think subsisted by itself, and stood underneath and kept up solidity and all other properties, which they used to say it was impossible for a man to have an idea of, is nothing at all distinct from solidity itself; or, if they must needs apply that word to something else that does really and properly subsist by itself and supports all properties, they must apply it to the divine Being or power itself.[13]

So "the substance of bodies at last becomes either nothing, or nothing but the Deity acting in that particular manner in those parts of space where he thinks fit."[14] In this way, Edwards sees no need to speak of the material body as an independent and hidden substance in order to account for its existence. The divine power, the solidity or resistance that results from the exercise of that power at a point in space, and the manner of the exercise of the divine power are all that are required to explain the being of matter. Against the materialist principle that all entities are to be explained as material substances, Edwards has argued that matter does not even exist as independent substance. "No matter is, in the most proper sense, matter."[15] Bodies are God's actions, which are executed according to the divinely established rules.

In this way, Edwards' earliest discussions of the nature of material bodies are much more than an antimaterialist argument. Emerging here is a view of things radically divergent from the traditional substance cosmology. Hobbes, the materialist, and also his opponents (Cartesians, Cambridge Platonists, and Newtonians) still worked with the traditional notion of substance. Unlike them, Edwards is proposing that the nature of things be explained without resorting to that notion.

[13] Ibid.
[14] Ibid.
[15] "Things to Be Considered and Written Fully About," No. 26, WEA, p. 235.

If the term "substance" is to be used at all, its meaning is now changed. Substance in the sense of the essence of an entity is now seen as the dynamic activity of resisting, and not some hidden principle to which activities belong. As Wallace Anderson has put it, Edwards' "predecessors thought of substance as the owner of properties; while Edwards thought of substance as the doer of deeds."[16] Substance in the sense of the subject of properties and activities is not needed or is collapsed into the activity of resistance itself. Or, if one were to speak of the ultimate source of the existence of an entity, the substance of bodies is nothing other than God's power.[17]

So far Edwards has accomplished at least two things. He has argued that a new ontology that adopts as its basic principles the scientific categories of motion and the laws of motion need not end up, as Hobbes had maintained, in metaphysical materialism. And, in this argument, Edwards is beginning to outline an ontology sharply divergent from the traditional metaphysics of substance. Further, Edwards has shown that the created world can be understood in terms of the new scientific categories without undermining the absolute sovereignty of God. Edwards sees God's activity as constituting the very being of the scientifically conceived cosmos of atoms and their motions. Atoms as resistances are none other than God's own activity, and the laws of the motions of those atoms are none other than "the stated methods of God's acting with respect to bodies."[18]

But a most crucial question arises at this point. If bodies are nothing but God's activity in time and space, do they possess any sort of permanence distinguished from God's actions? The generalized form of this question would be, If the created world is nothing but the result of God's continuous activity of causing resistance, does it have an abiding reality or an integrity of something that can be distinguished from God? In "Of Atoms" and a series of notes called "Natural Philosophy,"

[16] Anderson, "Editor's Introduction," in WEA, p. 67.
[17] "Of Atoms," WEA, p. 215.
[18] Ibid., p. 216.

which are the very earliest serious philosophical and scientific writings of Edwards, he does not explicitly raise the question of the permanence of the created world. And one does not yet find here a dispositional conception of the relative permanence of the created world in terms of habits and laws. There are, however, seeds of such a conception even at this early date. In one of the entries in "Natural Philosophy," Edwards reminds himself to write further about "how all *nature* consists in things being precisely according to strict rules of justice and harmony."[19] Further, whenever Edwards speaks about God's continuous activity of causing resistance, it is emphatically stated that such divine activities are according to the fixed and constant methods or laws.[20] But Edwards does not yet raise a new conception of laws and habits as ontologically real principles and define the permanence of the world in terms of such a concept.

In fact, Edwards' explicit statements at this point only highlight God's all-pervasive involvement in the created world. Since bodies are the result of God's immediate activity, "there is neither real substance nor property belonging to bodies; but all that is real, it is immediately in the first being," says Edwards. Edwards then goes so far as to say that "the universe is created out of nothing every moment."[21] Does this mean, one might ask, that Edwards' rebuttal of metaphysical materialism is turning into a pantheistic and monistic perspective in which the external world, and, by implication, the created world as a whole, possess no integrity of their own? Is Edwards willing to settle for an extreme sort of occasionalism? That such was not his intention becomes clear if one carefully analyzes Edwards' writings that immediately follow "Of Atoms" and the early portions of "Natural Philosophy." And it is in the context of Edwards' discussions of some problems arising out of his idealistic speculations that he explicitly raises

[19] "Things to Be Considered and Written Fully About," No. 16, WEA, p. 231.
[20] Ibid., "Unnumbered Series," No. 6, WEA, p. 265.
[21] Ibid., Nos. 44, 47, WEA, pp. 238, 241.

the issue of the ontological integrity of the created world in general and of material existence in particular.

Edwards' Solution to the Problem of the Reality of Unperceived Objects, and the Dispositional Conception of the Permanence of the World. A few years after Edwards worked on his rebuttal of materialism in "Of Atoms," he began developing another important theme—his so-called idealistic doctrine that nothing can be without being known. In a "Miscellanies" entry numbered "pp," written early in 1723, Edwards states, "For how doth one's mind refuse to believe, that there should be being from all eternity, without its being conscious to itself that it was; that there should be being from all eternity and yet nothing know, all that while, that anything is."[22] A few months later, in "Of Being," he gave a much fuller elaboration of the same point. And then many of the issues that arise from this assertion are discussed in "The Mind," which Edwards began writing at about the same time.[23]

Initially, Edwards maintains that his idealist doctrine is self-evident. "One's mind refuses to believe" that anything could be without being perceived or known, and it "is really a contradiction" to suppose such a possibility.[24] Later, in "The Mind," however, Edwards offers some arguments in support of his contention. Most important, in No. 27 of "The Mind," Edwards asserts that material bodies (which are really nothing but resistances) could not be conceived as resisting (and thus existing) independent of a perceiving mind. Resistances can be resistances only by resisting other bodies, but all bodies are none other than activities of resisting. How, asks Edwards, can an activity of resisting be thought of as resisting other activities of resisting? As a matter of fact, however, ideas in the mind can be observed as resisting and relating to other ideas. Therefore, Edwards concludes, resistances (bodies) can exist only as ideas in the perception of a mind. Edwards' conclusion

---

[22] "Miscellanies," No. "pp," HGT, p. 74. See also Anderson, "Editor's Introduction," in WEA, p. 75.

[23] Anderson, "Editor's Introduction," in WEA, pp. 76, 326.

[24] Ibid., p. 75.

is that "the world is therefore an ideal one; and the law of creating, and the succession of these ideas, is constant and regular."[25]

The basis of Edwards' idealist doctrine, however, is not the main concern here. My interest is in the way Edwards' earlier view of the material world is now recast in terms of his new doctrine, and in the question of the integrity and permanence of the material world that Edwards now explicitly raises. In "Of Atoms," bodies were shown to be resistances that were caused by God's activity. Now Edwards maintains that bodies (resistances) actually exist only as ideas that are communicated by God according to some fixed rules. The ultimate ontological ground of the being of material bodies remains God himself, but their actual existence is now considered as inseparably connected with the actual ideas that are "communicated to us, and to other minds, according to certain fixed and exact established methods and laws."[26]

At this point, the question of the permanence of the created world arises again. In the context of Edwards' rebuttal of materialism, the question was, If bodies are nothing but the resistances that are immediately caused by God, does the created world possess any degree of independence and permanence? Now, in light of Edwards' idealist doctrine, the question is, If nothing can be without being perceived or known, do things cease to exist when they are not actually perceived? This question, however, really involves two questions: First, if the actual existence of things is to be understood as the actual ideas that are communicated to human minds by God himself, does the created world possess any degree of independence or permanence distinguishable from God's activity of communicating those ideas? In other words, does the created world pos-

---

[25] "The Mind," No. 27, HGT, p. 351.

[26] For further discussion of Edwards' "idealism," see, for example, Egbert Smyth, "Jonathan Edwards' Idealism," *American Journal of Theology* 1 (1897): 950–964; H. N. Gardiner, "The Early Idealism of Jonathan Edwards," *Philosophical Review* 9 (1900): 573–596; George Rupp, "The 'Idealism' of Jonathan Edwards," *Harvard Theological Review* 62 (1969): 209–226; Miller, *Jonathan Edwards*, pp. 60–63.

sess any degree of being when God is not actually communicating those ideas to human minds? Second, if things do not exist unless they are being perceived, do they have any sort of exteriority and independence from the perceiving minds?

Within the context of Edwards' discussions, these two questions are of course closely related. They both have to do with the broader question of the permanence of the created world—either its permanence distinct from God or its permanence apart from human minds. It is important to distinguish these two questions, however, because Edwards' explicit discussion is more on the second question than on the first, although his treatment of the second question, has ramifications for the first.

Edwards' initial answer to the question of the existence of unperceived objects (and thus of their exteriority to the human minds) is that they exist in God's consciousness. In "Miscellanies," No. "pp," Edwards writes:

> Supposing a room in which none is, none sees in that room, no created intelligence; the things in the room have no being any other way than only as God is conscious [of them], for there is no color, nor any sound, nor any shape, etc.[27]

In "Of Being," Edwards also writes that "a room close shut up, that nobody sees, can have nothing in it; there is nothing other way [sic] than in God's knowledge."[28] But this answer contains serious difficulties. For one thing, there is, within Edwards' own scheme, a contradiction in saying that God knows certain created entities when he is not communicating ideas of them to human minds. The existence of things is, for Edwards, nothing other than ideas communicated to human minds. Thus, if they are not actually being communicated (as would be the case for unperceived things), there is nothing existent for God to know. Furthermore, there is the problem of confusing the divine and human modes of knowledge. If God and

[27] "Miscellanies," No. "pp," HGT, p. 74.
[28] "Of Being," WEA, p. 204.

the creatures are to be distinguished, the eternal and infinite mind of God presumably does not know in the same way that the finite human minds know. God cannot, then, be said to know the finitely conditioned, actually existing things that are temporarily not being perceived by any human mind. Even if one says that God is in some eternal way perceiving those things which are not being perceived by human minds, one is talking about two radically different sorts of knowing. And God's eternal knowledge of things would not establish their temporal existence. On the other hand, if Edwards argued that human minds have the very same ideas that God in his eternal mind has, Edwards then would end up holding the view of Nicholas Malebranche that we see things in God. This latter view, of course, has the problem of collapsing human knowing into the divine, thus resulting in pantheism.[29]

Bishop Berkeley had his own strategy in his own treatment of the problem of the reality of unperceived objects. Like the early Edwards, he also affirms that they exist in God's consciousness. In order to avoid the problem of collapsing the human mode of knowing into the divine, he then makes the distinction between the "archetypal and eternal existence" of things in God's mind on the one hand, and the "ectypal or natural existence" of things in a human mind on the other.[30] Things that are not being perceived by a human mind, in other words, have an archetypal existence in God's mind. And when God communicates the ideas to a human mind, their ectypal existence in time and space begins. This solution does avoid the collapse of the human knowing into the divine, a problem

[29] Norman Fiering considers it very possible that Edwards read the French philosopher-monk Malebranche, possibly before 1726. Malebranche's *Treatise concerning the Search after Truth* was available at Yale Library during Edwards' student years there. See Fiering, *Moral Thought*, pp. 40–45; Anderson, "Editor's Introduction," in WEA, pp. 20–21.

[30] *The Works of George Berkeley, Bishop of Cloyne*, ed. A. A. Luce and T. E. Jessop, 9 vols. (London, 1948), 2: 254, quoted in Frederick Copleston, *Modern Philosophy* (pt. 2), vol. 5 of *A History of Philosophy*, 9 vols. (Garden City, N.Y.: Doubleday, 1964), p. 50. For a recent discussion of Edwards' relation to Berkeley's thought, see Anderson, "Editor's Introduction," in WEA, pp. 26, 123–124.

in Malebranche of which Berkeley was aware, but makes it impossible to speak of the same ideas of things in the human mind as existing in God's mind when one is not perceiving them. One could not speak in such a way when the ideas one perceives are categorically different from the ideas in God's mind. Furthermore, Berkeley has left unanswered the question of the reality of those things which actually exist in time and space when they are not being perceived by any human mind. Those things would, in Berkeley's view, possess an archetypal existence in God's mind but would not be real in time and space. In this way, Berkeley's discussion illustrates the difficulties in preserving the exteriority or independence of the material world when its abiding existence is made dependent upon God's knowledge of it.

Edwards did not stay very long with his initial contention that the unperceived objects are real by existing in God's consciousness. In the early pages of "The Mind," Edwards shows a serious concern for the objectivity and continuity of the external world that common sense believes is there and that natural science investigates. It is at this point that Edwards makes an explicit move toward a dispositional theory of the permanence of the created world. He does this by raising the fixed and regular laws according to which God causes the actual ideas of resistances and by conceiving of those laws as constituting the abiding character of the created world. The abiding being of the created world, in other words, is defined neither as consisting in God's consciousness of it (a view that tends to do away with any distinction between eternal and finite modes of being and knowing) nor as consisting in the perception of it by finite minds (a view that results in a subjectivistic idealism). The permanent nature of the created world is rather to be seen as consisting in the abiding character of the laws according to which the actual existences (ideas) are caused by God and known by human minds.

In No. 34 of "The Mind," Edwards expresses his concern about the objectivity of the material world by insisting that "things are where they seem to be" and that his idealist assertions do not "make void natural philosophy, or the science of the causes or reasons of corporeal changes." In the same entry, Edwards offers the following revision of his earlier contention that unperceived things exist in God's consciousness:

> Though we suppose that the existence of the whole material universe is absolutely dependent on idea, yet we may speak in the old way, and as properly and truly as ever: God in the beginning created such a certain number of atoms, of such a determinate bulk and figure, which they yet maintain and always will; and gave them such a motion of such a direction, and of such a degree of velocity in a continued series. Yet perhaps all this does not exist anywhere perfectly but in the divine mind. But then, if it be inquired what exists in the divine mind, and how these things exist there, I answer: there is his determination, his care and his design that ideas shall be united forever, just so and in such a manner as is agreeable to such a series.[31]

Edwards is here speaking about the pre-Adamic world. And he is obviously considering it as having a being although no human mind is perceiving it. How does it have a being? Edwards' answer is, "in the divine mind," but now with an extremely important qualification. Edwards clearly does not say that the unperceived pre-Adamic world can be said to have existed only because God perceived it. Edwards now states that the reality of unperceived things lies in "God's determination" that "ideas shall be united forever, just so and in such a manner"—in other words, in the abiding nature of the *divinely determined laws* that govern God's activity of causing resistances. Edwards makes essentially the same point in entry No. 36:

> Things as to God exist from all eternity alike. That is, the idea is always the same, and after the same mode. The existence of things, therefore, that are not actually in created minds, consists only in power, or in the determination of

[31] "The Mind," No. 34, WEA, pp. 353–354.

God that such and such ideas shall be raised in created
minds upon such conditions.[32]

Here again Edwards makes a clear distinction between the
"eternal existence" of things in God and their temporal existence via human minds. And Edwards, in contrast to Berkeley,
does not explain the reality of unperceived finite things in
terms of their "eternal existence" in God's mind. Edwards is
clearly set on making a meaningful distinction between God
and the world and thus on giving the created world an integrity of its own *in actual time and space*. The dispositional conception of the permanence of the created world is becoming
clearer in this entry. "That such and such ideas shall be raised
in created minds upon such conditions," it will be recalled, is
the definition of a habit or a general law—that is, an active
and ontologically real disposition.[33]

Edwards expands on this notion toward the end of "The
Mind":

> In memory, in mental principles, habits and inclinations,
> there is something really abiding in the mind when there are
> no acts or exercises of them, much in the same manner as
> there is a chair in this room when no mortal perceives it. For
> when we say there are chairs in this room when none per-
> ceives it, we mean that minds would perceive chairs here
> according to the law of nature in such circumstances.[34]

Here, God's determination of the laws of nature is not even
mentioned. That God establishes them is simply assumed.
What is highlighted is the abiding nature of the law of nature
in terms of which the abiding reality of all things, including
the unperceived objects, is defined. The next logical step from
this point is stated in an entry in the "Subjects to Be Handled
in the Treatise on the Mind"—namely, his generalized conclusion that "laws . . . constitute all permanent being in created

[32] "The Mind," No. 36, WEA, p. 355.
[33] Compare this quotation with Edwards' statement that "all habits [are] a
law that God has fixed, that such actions upon such occasions should be exerted" ("Miscellanies," No. 241, Yale MSS).
[34] "The Mind," No. 69, WEA, p. 385.

things, both corporeal and spiritual."[35] Edwards' discussion of the permanent being of material things is now generalized to cover the created world as a whole, and his definition of the permanence of the world in terms of laws is unequivocally stated.

Here is a dispositional conception of the world. The created world abides as a system of the permanently fixed general laws or tendencies that God has established and according to which he causes actual existences (actual ideas) in time and space. The world, therefore, exists abidingly in the mode of *virtuality* or *real possibility* that is a midpoint between pure potentiality and full actuality. That there is a general law means that God has determined that he would cause an actual existence of such and such a nature at a certain time and at a certain point in space. The virtual being of the world, in other words, has a mode of reality because general laws, as was shown, are ontologically real principles even apart from their manifestations in actual applications. And, as God causes the actual existences (actual ideas) according to these general laws, the world is constantly being moved from the mode of virtuality to full actuality.

It will be recalled that Edwards asserted in an early note in "Natural Philosophy" that "the universe is created out of nothing every moment." This still obtains in the sense that it is God who constantly preserves the established general laws *and* causes actual existences according to those laws. But it is not a continual *creatio ex nihilo* in a simple sense. The divinely established general laws are given a permanence, and are in a sense not created ex nihilo every moment. Edwards' view is an occasionalism only in the sense that God moves the world from virtuality to full actuality every moment through an immediate exercise of his power. Edwards' view is not an unqualified occasionalist position, however, since the world has an abiding reality in a virtual mode.[36]

It is in the light of what I have called "virtual existence" that

---

[35] "Subjects to Be Handled in the Treatise on the Mind," No. 36, WEA, p. 391.

[36] For an example of the interpretation of Edwards as an "occasionalist," see Fiering, *Moral Thought*, pp. 279–280, 307–308.

one can best understand Edwards' notion of the "supposed existence" of unperceived things. I have already referred to the entry No. 34 of "The Mind" where Edwards qualifies his earlier view that unperceived objects exist in the divine consciousness. Their existence is now affirmed as consisting in God's determination to abide by the general laws that he himself has established. Edwards then goes on to ask exactly what sort of being an unperceived object has in the scheme of the divinely established general laws.

> All the ideas that ever were or ever shall be to all eternity, in any created mind, are answerable to the existence of such a peculiar atom in the beginning of the creation. . . . God supposes its existence; that is, he causes all changes to arise as if all these things had actually existed in such a series in some created mind, and as if created minds had comprehended all things perfectly.[37]

The being of a pre-Adamic atom that neither God nor a human mind actually perceives, in other words, is a "supposed" being. And the reality of an unperceived but supposed being has a mode of reality because the supposition is based on the general laws that unite all things and are ontologically real principles. Edwards actually says that an unperceived atom exists "in a sense in created idea, for that exists in created idea which necessarily supposes it."[38]

The connection between the supposed existence of unperceived things and the world as a system of general laws is expanded further in No. 40 of "The Mind":

> Yea, there must be an universal attraction in the whole system of things from the beginning of the world to the end; and to speak more strictly and metaphysically we must say, in the whole system and series of ideas in all created minds, so that these things must necessarily be put in to make complete the system of the ideal world. That is, they must be supposed if the train of ideas be in the order and course

[37] "The Mind," No. 34, WEA, p. 354.
[38] Ibid.

settled by the supreme mind. So that we may answer in short, that the existence of these things is in God's supposing of them, in order to the rendering complete the series of things—to speak more strictly, the series of ideas—according to his own settled order and that harmony of things which he has appointed.[39]

In communicating to human minds the ideas of actually existing things, God must "suppose" other things that are not perceived because they are all together in a single system of mutually connected systems of things—that is, in an integrated network of general laws that governs their existence. And this network of general laws is ontologically real. Thus, to suppose something as being part of that network is to consider it real—real in the mode of virtuality. This is why Edwards can say that the existence of the unperceived things is in God's "supposing" of them.

James Tufts observed that running through Edwards' writings there are two lines of thought that are at variance with each other—the first, a realist perspective with its description of the world of Newtonian science as an objectively existing world, and the other, an idealist point of view in which an independently existing world is denied.[40] My interpretation, however, would indicate that these two perspectives are not at variance in Edwards' thought but rather are brought together in his dispositional conception of the permanence of the world. Edwards does remain an idealist to the extent that he could not conceive of being as being apart from the knowing mind. But there is a realist element in Edwards in that the external world is accorded an abiding reality in the mode of virtuality distinct from either the divine or human knowledge. In this sense, Edwards is an objective idealist. He is a precursor

[39] "The Mind," No. 40, WEA, p. 357. Wallace Anderson has remarked: "Nothing is more apparent in [Edwards'] theory of supposed existence than that Edwards conceives general laws of nature to be ontologically prior to the objects and events of the world" ("Editor's Introduction," in WEA, p. 109).

[40] James H. Tufts, "Edwards and Newton," *Philosophical Review* 49 (1940): 609–622.

of Charles Sanders Peirce, who also avoided the Humean skepticism by affirming the continuity of the world through a realist definition of laws and habits.[41]

One might question my reading of Edwards by arguing that the laws of nature are really none other than the order according to which God himself causes finite existences and, therefore, cannot constitute the permanence of a world that is to be distinguished from the divine reality. In other words, one could ask, Where else are the laws of nature except "in God" to the extent that they are the manner of God's own actions? It is true that the laws of nature are none other than "the proportion of God's acting."[42] But, it is important to note, they are for Edwards the patterns of God's operation ad extra in time and space. The laws of nature thus are clearly distinguished from the Logos or the inner wisdom of God. The laws of nature, unlike the divine wisdom ad intra, have a temporal reference, and are as such the objective structure of the universe that scientists can investigate through observable phenomena. The laws of nature, therefore, occupy a peculiar metaphysical position in Edwards' thought; they are like the borderline that is shared by two adjoining countries—in this case, between the divine being and the created world. Edwards' intention is clear. The laws of nature are to be distinguished from God's inner being and as such constitute the relative but real permanence of the created world.

In this and the preceding sections, I have traced in Edwards' earliest philosophical notes the emergence of a dispositional

---

[41] For a discussion of Charles Sanders Peirce's critical response to Hume, see Murphey, *The Development of Peirce's Philosophy*, pp. 116–118. For a characterization of Edwards' thought as "objective idealism," see William H. Becker, "The Distinguishing Marks of the Christian Man in the Thought of Jonathan Edwards" (Ph.D. diss., Harvard University, 1964).

[42] "The Mind," No. 34, WEA, p. 353. Egbert Smyth made the following suggestive observation, which, I believe, moves in the direction of my own interpretation: "The external world [according to Edwards], ultimately, exists only mentally in God's idea, yet it is not a mere act or state of the divine consciousness; it is God operating *ad extra*, expressing himself in finite modes, forms, creations, according to a stable purpose and by an established constitution" (Smyth, "Jonathan Edwards' Idealism," p. 959).

conception of the permanent being of the created world. Already in Nos. 34 and 36 of "The Mind," which were probably written during Edwards' tutorship at Yale (1724–1726), he clearly identifies the laws and habits, as well as God's direct action, as the constitutive elements of the being of created entities. In No. 241 of the "Miscellanies," probably written early in 1727, is found a firmly settled statement of a dispositional conception of the soul as well as a definition of habit itself. Therefore, certainly by the early months of 1727, and perhaps as early as sometime in the 1724–1726 period, a dispositional reconception of reality, at least in its basic form, was firmly crystallized in Edwards' own mind. It is true that in "Of Atoms" and "Of Being," written between 1720 (when Edwards graduated from Yale) and 1723, he already saw the laws of nature as the fixed methods according to which God acts to cause the existence (solidity) of created beings.[43] But, as my discussion has shown, it took just a little further thought and perhaps a couple of years for Edwards to become clear about the ontological status of the fixed methods of God's acting (i.e., habits and laws) and thus to reach a dispositional conception of the essence of things. Once established, this new ontology became the cornerstone of Edwards' reconstruction in philosophical theology, and also provides, as this present volume attempts to demonstrate, the lens through which Edwards' writings as a whole can be seen in a systematic unity.[44]

[43] For the dating of these early writings of Edwards, I am indebted to Thomas A. Schafer. See also, Anderson, "Editor's Introduction," in WEA, pp. 29–36. I am solely responsible for the estimation of the time of Edwards' formulation of a dispositional reconception of reality.

[44] Most of Edwards' lifetime work that I discuss in this volume followed the 1724–1726 period—that is, it came after the time of his formulation of a dispositional ontology. I will, however, freely refer to some of the very earliest philosophical notes that predate the 1724–1726 period—e.g., "Of Atoms," "Of Being," and the entries at the very beginning of "The Mind" and "Miscellanies," all of which were written between 1720 and 1723. I do so because, as previously noted, the primary task of the present volume is to demonstrate the way in which Edwards' dispositional ontology enables one to see the coherence of his thought taken as a whole. The manner in which Edwards' dispositional ontology harmoniously incorporates the relational perspective on

God's Providential Activity and the Integrity of the Finite Order

Before I move on to discuss laws and habits as the structural and dynamic principles of being, I must briefly note the way Edwards holds together God's immediate and continual activity in the world *and* a relative and yet abiding permanence of the created order. Edwards' conception of God's providential activity as at once immediate and also in accordance with the established laws will confirm and illustrate Edwards' dispositional definition of the permanence of the world.

Edwards articulates the nature of God's activity vis-à-vis the world by means of a distinction between what he calls "arbitrary operation" and "natural operation."[45] In medieval theology, this distinction was made in terms of God's *potentia absoluta* and *potentia ordinata*: his absolute and ordained power. The so-called voluntarist tradition in theology, which originated in the late medieval period, viewed the reality of the created order as dependent upon the completely free and sovereign activity of the divine will rather than upon the archetypes or "divine ideas" of God's intellect. The radical contingency of the finite order is thereby highlighted, and the laws of nature are now seen as imposed and established by God rather than as immanent in or even intrinsic to the cosmos. The impetus that this voluntarist tradition gave to the development of natural science in the West has become quite well known.[46] The distinction between God's absolute and ordained power is this voluntarist tradition's way of stressing the radical dependence of the world upon God's sovereign will without completely denying the obvious fact that he usually operates by following the regular patterns of phenomena. With his ordained power, God works by concurring with the

---

reality, developed in entry No. 1 on "Excellency" (written in 1723), is a case in point. For the dating cited here, see Anderson, "Editor's Introduction," in WEA, pp. 8–9, 28–29.

[45] "Miscellanies," No. 1263, HGT, pp. 184–193.

[46] See Eugene M. Klaaren, *Religious Origins of Modern Science: Belief in Creation in Seventeenth-Century Thought* (Grand Rapids, Mich.: Eerdmans, 1977), pp. 29–52.

order that he himself has fixed. But God always retains his absolute power by which he can at any time change, abolish, or temporarily suspend the established order. In Edwards' time, this distinction was widely utilized by English and Puritan theologians as well as by natural philosophers, implicitly even Newton himself.[47] Edwards basically accepted this distinction but added to it some important new meanings. His treatment is quite systematic and is contained in "Miscellanies," No. 1263.

Edwards' distinguishes God's "arbitrary operation" from God's "natural operation." The latter is "confined to, limited by, those fixed establishments and laws commonly called the laws of nature." The "arbitrary operation" of God, however, is not limited by previously established laws. "Arbitrary operation," then, is God's immediate and direct operation. "Natural operation," on the other hand, is a "secondary" activity of God in which he is "directed" by certain existing laws. God's creation of the world ex nihilo, his act of establishing a new law, and his departure from an established law are examples of the divine operations that involve, at least partially, an arbitrary activity of God. On the other hand, natural operation is involved, for example, in God's act of causing the actual movement of a previously created atom. In such a case, "some use was made of laws of nature before established, such, at least, as the laws of resistance and attraction or adhesion and *vis inertiae*, that are essential to the very being of matter."[48]

Are there, then, divine acts that are purely arbitrary, or purely natural? Edwards holds that while there can be purely or absolutely arbitrary operations, there cannot be purely or absolutely natural operations. The original creation of the world ex nihilo, Edwards tells us, is the only divine operation that is absolutely arbitrary and not "mixed"; all other operations are mixed ones. Two of the examples I gave above for

[47] See McGuire, "Force, Active Principles, and Newton's Invisible Realm," pp. 187–194.
[48] "Miscellanies," No. 1263, HGT, p. 188.

arbitrary operations (God's act of establishing a new law and his act of departing from an established law) are not, then, purely arbitrary. Edwards' contention is that some already existing laws are used when God establishes a new law or when he departs from a particular law.[49]

Edwards' two main emphases are clear. On the one hand, he sees the efficacy of the fixed laws of nature as indeed universal. All of God's actions, except the original creation, involve some adherence to fixed laws. Laws, it is seen, are essentially permanent once created. This point of view flows out of Edwards' conception of the being of finite entities as consisting of those established laws. On the other hand, Edwards dissociates himself from the deists as far as is logically possible: there is no operation of God that does not involve, at least partially, the arbitrary, immediate, and direct causal activity of God. All created entities and events "must have their very being from His actions, and must be perfectly and most absolutely subject to and dependent on his action." The arbitrary operation, Edwards continues,

> is first and supreme, and to which the other is wholly subject and also wholly dependent, and without which there could be no divine operation at all, and no effect ever produced, and nothing besides God could ever exist. Arbitrary operation is that to which is owing the existence of the subject of natural operations—the manner, measure, and all the circumstances of their existence.[50]

An atom, it will be remembered, is defined by Edwards as God's immediate act of causing resistance according to certain fixed laws. So, God's arbitrary operation is continually necessary even for the very existence of entities. This, then, is the most important reason that there cannot be any purely natural operation: namely, the continual dependence of existence itself upon the arbitrary operation of God. In this way, without avoiding the abiding character of the established laws, Ed-

[49] Ibid., pp. 187–188.
[50] Ibid., p. 186.

wards makes God's direct involvement universal and constant.

The opposite poles in the seventeenth- and eighteenth-century views on God/world relations were the occasionalist doctrine that God, the only causal power, creates the world ex nihilo from moment to moment, on the one hand, and the deistic belief that God created the world machine in the beginning and now lets it exist and operate on its own according to the laws of nature, on the other. Most thinkers, however, fell somewhere between the extremes. Newton, for example, like many others, stressed God's continual involvement in the cosmos through the doctrines of the "divine concourse" with the laws of nature and of God's intermittent direct involvement. In other words, God continually preserves the mechanical laws themselves, operates in concurrence with them, and also occasionally modifies or changes them. Far from being a deist, Newton was very eager to affirm God's continual activity in the world. Newton even at times spoke about God being the direct cause of all motion. He would characteristically affirm that God is "able to act in all times & places for creating & governing the present universe."[51] As is well known, Newton persistently rejected the Cambridge Platonists' plastic natures lest any doctrine of self-active powers should undermine the world's radical dependence upon God. As is also well known, Newton further rejected the immanence of the force of gravity within the essence of bodies themselves, again to preserve the radical contingency of the created order. Nevertheless, Newton stopped short of taking the occasionalist position and strove for a more moderate view.[52]

The distinctiveness in Edwards' treatment of the *potentia absoluta* and *ordinata* dialectic, therefore, is the extention of God's *potentia absoluta* to all things and all events without voiding his *potentia ordinata*. God's arbitrary or immediate causal activity does not just preserve, modify, or suspend the

[51] Quoted in McGuire, "Force, Active Principles, and Newton's Invisible Realm," p. 201.
[52] Ibid., pp. 185, 202.

established laws. As conditional laws, the laws of nature cannot even function without God's immediate activity of causing (not just preserving) resistance (existence, events, etc.). The very existence of any thing and the operations of all things involve God's immediate activity—all this, without damaging the reality and efficacy of general laws. Unlike Newton, Edwards does in a sense see general laws as immanent within entities; to be more accurate, for Edwards, general laws are the essence of entities as their constitutive definitions. But this did not undermine God's direct causal activity, as Newton was afraid that the Cambridge Platonists' plastic natures might do. The effect was in fact exactly the opposite. Since Edwards' laws (which now make up the very permanence and essence of entities) are conditional laws requiring for their functioning God's immediate involvement, his making laws immanent in being now brings God's immediate activity (resistance) into the very being of finite entities. The plastic natures of the Cambridge Platonists were conceived as self-active principles that act on their own in God's behalf.[53] If such principles were made immanent in finite entities, therefore, these entities would indeed be self-active beings that were not radically dependent upon God's continual agency. In contrast to this, since Edwards' laws are abiding and yet conditional principles, his definition of being in terms of those laws had the effect of strongly reinforcing God's immediate involvement in the cosmos. In this way, Edwards' notion of habits and laws enabled him to maintain his loyalties to both the sovereignty of God and the objective reality of *rerum natura*.

Edwards' dual emphasis upon the all-inclusive nature of God's direct providential activity and the dependent and yet real integrity of the finite order is nowhere more clearly expressed than in his discussion of the various levels or scales in the system of created entities. As the divinely established laws and habits constitute the abiding identities of finite beings, the "scale or series of created existences" is organized "according to the degrees of excellency and perfection" of those laws.

[53] Ibid., pp. 184–185.

And one functional criterion of the perfection or excellency of laws is their singularity or particularity—that is, their independence from the more universally applicable laws such as the law of gravity. Edwards also believes that the more singular a law is, the more complex and "harder to be investigated and traced" it is. Thus, "the lowest rank of material things are almost wholly under the government of the general laws of matter and motion." And "if we ascend from them to plants . . . the laws of vegetation are doubtless, many of them, distinct from the general laws of matter and motion and therefore, by what was observed before, nearer akin to an arbitrary influence." As we move up from plants to animals, to human beings' natural and spiritual powers, to angels, even to the "man Christ Jesus," and ultimately to God himself, the laws are more and more singular and less tied down to the general laws of matter. At the very top, there is the law that governed God's act of the original creation of the world, and this law was absolutely arbitrary or "tied to no other rules and laws but the direction of His infinite understanding." The law of the being of Jesus Christ is the miracle of the Incarnation in which it is at once "united personally to the Godhead" and thus "infinitely above the laws of nature" and also a part of the finite existence. Human beings as intelligent creatures, according to Edwards, also occupy a unique position in this scale of beings in that their laws are singular enough, and their independence from the laws of matter great enough, so that they can be said to possess a "secondary and dependent arbitrariness."[54]

A closer look at the position of human beings is needed. What exactly is meant by the singularity of the laws that govern perceiving beings? Edwards attributes a "secondary and dependent arbitrariness" to them, saying that "they are not limited in their operation to the laws of matter and motion" and that "they can do what they please."[55] In "Miscellanies,"

[54] "Miscellanies," No. 1263, HGT, pp. 186, 189–190.
[55] Ibid., p. 186.

73

No. 383, Edwards explains the nature of human beings' special position further:

> 'Tis only the soul of man that does as that supreme principle [that is, God] does. This is a principle of action, has a power of motion in itself as that first principle has, and which no unperceiving being in this lower world has. Man's soul determines things in themselves indifferent, as motion and rest, the direction of motion, etc., as the supreme cause does. Man's soul has an end in what it does, pursues some good that is the issue of its action, as the first universal principle doth. Man's soul makes, forms, preserves, disposes, and governs things within its sphere as the first principle does the world. Man's soul influences the body, continues its nature and powers and constant regular motions and productions, and actuates it as the supreme principle does the universe.[56]

The essence of Edwards' point is that the distinctiveness of human beings vis-à-vis nature is their intelligence, purposiveness, and creativity. Edwards is viewing the position of human beings as both continuous with and also transcending nature. Intelligent beings as well as matter are all governed by similar principles—namely, laws. Edwards, in this sense, is considering humanity and nature very much as parts of one system. But humanity's uniqueness is equally stressed. There is an egalitarian note in Edwards' cosmology as well as due attention to the differences among created beings.

I shall return at a later point to this question of humanity's unique role in the cosmos. What I need to point out in the present context is how in Edwards' cosmology humanity's independence vis-à-vis material existence does not decrease human beings' contingency and dependence upon God but rather increases it. As God creates, sustains, and works through the laws that govern human beings, he is acting without making use of certain other laws (i.e., the laws of material existence). God's involvement in the existence and operation

---

[56] "Miscellanies," No. 383, HGT, p. 81.

of intelligent creatures, then, is more immediate and direct than his relationship with the material realm. Edwards affirms the reality and integrity of perceiving beings as strongly as to say that they possess a "secondary and dependent arbitrariness." But in the very core of that relative sovereignty lies a dependence upon God that is more radical than material existence's dependence upon him. To use Paul Tillich's terminology, autonomy is thoroughly grounded in theonomy.[57] And it has been my thesis throughout this chapter that Edwards' attempt to exalt the sovereignty of God without demolishing the integrity of *rerum natura* as a created reality is facilitated by his notion of habits and laws as ontologically real and abiding principles that require the fulfillment of certain conditions (most importantly God's own agency) in order to function.

[57] Paul Tillich, *Systematic Theology*, 3 vols. (Chicago: University of Chicago Press, 1967), 1: 147–150.

CHAPTER IV

Being as Relational and Dynamic

HABITS AND LAWS AS THE STRUCTURE OF BEING

I HAVE SHOWN how, for Edwards, the abiding nature of being consists in the divinely established habits and laws that are ontologically real and yet dependent upon God's immediate involvement for operation. A material entity, for example, is not a self-subsisting, hidden substance but rather an activity of resisting (persevering) brought about by God himself at a particular point in time and space "in a particular manner," that is, according to a stable law. Existing (resisting), then, occurs only in a particular manner: in the way a particular divinely established general law demands. Laws, therefore, not only constitute the abiding dimension of an entity but also determine *how* or *in what way* it should actually exist and does exist. Laws are the principles of the structure and order of reality. So it is that "the very being, and the manner of being, and the whole, of bodies depends immediately on the Divine Being," who causes resistance according to certain fixed laws.[1] The same principle applies to sentient beings as well. The soul's "essence consists in powers and habits," wrote Edwards.[2] In numerous places in Edwards' writings, one also finds his insistence that a person's habits and dispositions not only determine the direction and character of intellectual and moral actions but also constitute his or her nature.[3]

What does it mean to define the structure of reality in terms of laws and habits?

---

[1] "Things to Be Considered and Written Fully About," No. 23(a), WEA, p. 235.
[2] "Miscellanies," No. 241, Yale MSS.
[3] See *Religious Affections*, p. 206.

The Relational Nature of the Structure of Being

It will be remembered that for Edwards a habit or law of nature is a general law that describes and governs the relations among certain occasions and the actions or events that occur on those occasions. Habit is a law "that such actions upon such occasions should be exerted." Actions and occasions that are governed by a habit are not simply related; they are related in a particular manner. A habit specifies that such actions and such occasions should be related. That is, habit determines what type of actions or events would be and are related with what type of occasions. In short, a habit or law is a relation of relations.

Edwards is proposing a way of thinking about structure that is radically different from the way it used to be thought about. Aristotelian and Scholastic metaphysics thought of structure mainly in terms of forms, and forms, as conceived in that tradition, are essentially self-contained, particulate principles. Edwards' model of ontological structure is not form but a manner or relation of relations. This radical departure from the traditional metaphysics, as Edwards executes it, contains three important elements the implications of which are far-reaching.

First of all, for Edwards, *what an entity is, is inseparable from its relations.* In the Aristotelian ontology, being in the primary and most fundamental sense is substance. Substance lies underneath all other qualities; it is their subject. Substance is "that which is not asserted of a subject but of which everything else is asserted."[4] Other modes of being such as qualities and relations are secondary to substance. In contrast to substance, they are called accidents. Now, it is the substantial form that determines a substance to be what it is—a human being, an animal, a tree, and so forth. Accidental forms determine all the other things that an entity is and does. When Edwards defines the structure of an entity as a law or habit, he is

---

[4] W. D. Ross, *Aristotle* (London: Methuen, 1930), p. 166.

refusing to think of the what-ness of things in terms of individual, particulate forms. He is rather contending that the what-ness of entities can be conceived only in terms of their relations. *How* an entity is related with other entities is determinative of *what* that entity is.

Now, the permanence of being is constituted by laws and habits, according to Edwards. That is to say, laws and habits (or the relation of relations) function not only on the level of the Aristotelian accidents but also on the level of substance and substantial forms. Accidental forms and substantial forms, in a sense, are collapsed into one level in Edwards' ontology. Consequently, when Edwards defines the structure of an entity in terms of a relational law, he is letting relations function at the level of the very being of that entity. For Aristotle, an individual entity first exists and, in so existing, already is what it must be to be what it is—a human being, an animal, or a tree. Relations, in other words, are external to the being of entities. But in Edwards' ontology, relations are internal to being. Relations are elevated to the level of the substantial form. Being is being-in-relation. In short, habits and laws constitute *what* being is on its deepest level.

Edwards, however, did not wish to submerge all individuality into relations. Edwards defines an individual atom as an activity of resisting annihilation at a particular point in time and space. Nevertheless, individuality is never pure individuality. Since the law that governs the individual activities of resisting is a relation of relations, the acts of resisting can only be the acts of relating to other entities—that is, the acts of resisting in a particular sort of relationship with other entities. "In the existence of bodies," Edwards writes, "there has to be resistance or tendency to some place."[5] All resistances are thus resistances-in-relation. Individuality and relation are thus correlative categories.

This radically relational ontology is what lies behind Edwards' contention that being is essentially beauty. "For being, if we examine narrowly," writes Edwards, "is nothing else but

---

[5] "Miscellanies," No. 125, HGT, p. 76.

proportion."[6] Here Edwards is specifying the *content* of laws or relations of relationships that makes up the what-ness of being. Beauty is what the structure of being (i.e., laws and habits) looks like. I will return to a discussion of beauty at a later point. My point here is that Edwards' conception of habits and laws as functioning on the level of Aristotle's substantial forms indicates the depth of the relationality of the structure of being as he thinks of it. And this relational view of being in turn goes hand in hand with Edwards' thoroughly aesthetic vision of reality.[7]

The second aspect of Edwards' relational conception of the structure of being is that *relations determine the existence of an entity.* This point is implicit in what I said in the previous section, but it deserves to be made explicit. I have pointed out that since Edwards defines the structure of being as the manner or pattern of relationships, and since for him the distinction between substance and accident is collapsed into one category, relations are seen as making up not only some qualities of a secondary importance but the very quality or what-ness of the entity as a particular entity. Laws and habits are the very quality or what-ness of resistance (existence) itself. Now, if the act of resisting does not occur without following a particular law, then that law must be exercised if there is to be any resistance (existence). And, since the exercise of laws (the relations of relationships) can only mean a multiplication of relations of particular sorts, entities cannot actually exist without actual relations. So, not only the what-ness of an entity but also its that-ness is constituted by relations.

When God creates an entity, what he does is essentially to establish a nexus of laws according to which he would cause resistance in a particular spatiotemporal context. Even when he is not actually causing resistances, such would-be resistances have a mode of reality as real possibles (virtuals) via the nexus of general laws that govern and determine them. But it is only when the appropriate resistances are actually there,

---

[6] "The Mind," No. 1, WEA, p. 336.
[7] See Delattre, *Beauty and Sensibility*, pp. 15–57.

and thereby are establishing relations of a particular sort with other entities, that the entity whose essence is a nexus of laws is an actually existing being. The movement from virtuality to actuality, in other words, requires the actualization of relations. Edwards' dispositional conception of being, therefore, means that a being not only is *what it is* through its relations but also *exists* only through its relations.

To say that relations constitute both the structure and existence of finite entities, however, is not to forget God's continual and immediate involvement as the creator and governor of the world. The habits and laws according to which relations occur are originally created and constantly upheld by the divine being. Further, habits and laws are triggered into relational activities only as God's own power causes them in accordance to those very habits and laws. Ultimately, therefore, God's own activity constitutes that all things exist as well as what all things are. Nevertheless, God has given the real possibilities (virtuals) a mode of reality through the abiding habits and laws, and he causes actual relations (existences) in accordance with those habits and laws. Habits and laws as the general laws that govern the actual relations, therefore, exercise a dependent and yet real rule over finite existences, thereby participating in God's own activity. In this dependent and yet real sense, the relational activities governed by the habits and laws constitute the structure and existence of created beings.

The third element in Edwards' relational conception of the structure of being has to do with *the absolutely comprehensive extent of the mutual relations of all entities*. In Edwards' ontology an entity's structure is defined as a law or a nexus of laws, and, since laws are relations of relationships, the very existence as well as the essence (what-ness) of an entity are inseparable from its relations. In other words, resistances (existences) and a quality or manner of resistances cannot even be thought about without seeing them in their relations with other resistances and their respective qualities. Now it is time to attend to Edwards' view that entities are related not only with *some* other entities in the system of being but indeed with *all* other entities—that is, with the whole.

Each act of resisting (existing) occurs in a manner determined by the law that governs it, and each law has been established by God himself and thus is designed to function in a way fitting with the whole—that is, with the law of the entire universe or the external expression of the law of God's own being. There is the whole; the parts and their mutual relations are determined by the whole. An entity exists and stands in a relationship with other entities only as it stands in a fitting and harmonious relationship with the whole.

The most fundamental logical ground for such a perspective is Edwards' contention that the universe is the external expression and repetition of God's internal being.[8] As God is a unified being (with internal plurality), his existence ad extra can only be a unified system. The particularity of individual laws or nexuses of laws is recognized, but they must be conceived of as standing in just such a relationship with one another that the universe of all created laws as a whole constitutes an integrated quality—namely, the external expression of God's internal beauty. "The world was made to have all the parts of it nicely hanging together and sweetly harmonious and corresponding," writes Edwards.[9] And again, "This whole universe is no other than an immense multitude of particular regular systems all with a convenient mutual vicinity and proper relation and exact situation and commensuration."[10] In the context of his discussion of the universe as a hierarchy of divinely established laws, Edwards writes, "The nearer we come to God in the gradation or succession of created things, the nearer it comes to this, that there is no other law than only the law of the infinite wisdom of the omniscient first cause and supreme disposer of all things."[11]

There are three dimensions, Edwards is saying, in the relations of all things. There is the relationship an entity has to itself (in the sense of self-affirmation or self-preservation) and

---

[8] For an exposition of Edwards' conception of God's relation to the world, see below, Chaps. 7 and 8.

[9] "Miscellanies," No. "tt," HGT, p. 127.

[10] "Miscellanies," No. 880, HGT, p. 101.

[11] "Miscellanies," No. 1263, HGT, p. 192.

among its inner parts. Then there is the relationship with certain other entities. And finally, there is the relationship to the whole or the law of the whole. Edwards therefore typically speaks of the relationships of things in threefold ways. Contrasting the world of the spirit against the world of matter, for example, Edwards writes, "The glories of religion consist in the sweet harmony of the greater and more real world *within themselves, with one another*, and *with the infinite fountain and original of them*" (emphasis added).[12] Again, contrasting the ordinary human knowledge against the knowledge of the regenerate, Edwards writes, "Rationation, without this spiritual light, never will give one such an advantage to see things *in their true relations* and *respects to other things*, and *to things in general*" (emphasis added).[13] In other words, the law that is the essence of an entity governs the act of existing (resisting) considered in its particularity, governs the relationship of that existing with other existences, and does both of these in a manner appropriate and fitting to the nature of the whole of which it is a part.

This doctrine of the connections of all things with one another and with the whole can also be seen in Edwards' discussion of beauty. As noted previously, beauty or excellency is the content of the law according to which God creates and upholds the world, and thus the relational structure entailed in Edwards' doctrine of the laws and habits can only coincide with the relational logic of the concept of beauty.

"All beauty consists in similarness or identity of relation," writes Edwards.[14] This definition is quite in keeping with the traditional conception of beauty as harmony, uniformity, or symmetry. But the distinctive aspect of Edwards' conception is his view that there can be many kinds of similarness and that the true quality of a relation of similarity must be gauged or weighed against the kind of similarity or beauty that makes up the beauty of the whole. The created order as a whole is the

---

[12] "Miscellanies," No. 42, HGT, p. 238.
[13] "Miscellanies," No. 408, HGT, p. 249.
[14] "The Mind," No. 1, WEA, p. 334.

external repetition of God's internal being, and it is that being which is the true beauty or the ultimate form of similarity. God is the "foundation and fountain of all being and all beauty,"[15] and he is distinguished from all other beings, "chiefly by his divine beauty."[16] And "the beauty of the world is a communication of God's beauty."[17] God himself is the ultimate criterion of beauty.

Similarity, however, is not voided as a criterion of beauty by Edwards' placing the ultimate standard of beauty in God or in being as a whole. God's beauty is a beauty and thus a form of similarity. And even the lowest forms of similarity are beautiful since they are "images" or "shadows" of the ultimate form of similarity. Nevertheless, they are only what Edwards calls "confined beauty" and thus not the ultimate beauty.

> Excellence, to put it in other words, is that which is beautiful and lovely. That which is beautiful by itself separately and deformed considered as a part of something else more extended, or beautiful only with respect to itself and a few other things and not as a part of that which contains all things—the universe—is false beauty and a confined beauty. That which is beautiful with respect to the university of things has a generally extended excellence and a true beauty; and the more extended or limited its system is, the more confined or extended is its beauty.[18]

This priority of the whole over the parts gives rise to some important distinctions in Edwards' conception of beauty. The distinction between the "primary beauty" and the "secondary beauty" has to do with the difference between the spiritual (mental) and the natural (material) dimensions of reality. The kind of similarity or agreement that exists in primary beauty is the "consent" (love) between perceiving beings, and the agreement in secondary beauty is only an image of the spirit-

[15] *True Virtue*, p. 15.
[16] *Religious Affections*, p. 298.
[17] "Miscellanies," No. 293, HGT, p. 260.
[18] "The Mind," No. 14, WEA, p. 344.

ual consent. As the ultimate form of beauty is the consent or love that exists in God, consent is the form of beauty that is higher than mere agreement among nonsentient things.[19]

There is another distinction (and here the underlying principle is the priority of the whole), that between "simple beauty" and "complex beauty." The simple beauty consists of a simple equality. Edwards illustrates this distinction in "The Mind."[20] The equality between *AB* and *BC* in the following makes up a simple beauty:

```
|_____|_____|
A        B        C
```

A complex beauty involves a proportion among a complex nexus of relations, as in the following:

```
•    •    •  •
A    B    C  D
```

Here *BCD* is similar to *ABC*. Not only are more relations involved here than in the first figure, but also certain simple equalities are sacrificed or omitted so that a proportion of a more complex nature can be achieved. *BC* is not as *AB*, nor is *CD* as *BC*, but *BCD* is as *ABC*. It is necessary that there be certain partial irregularities so that the whole of a complex group of relations may be beautiful.

Complexity as such cannot be an absolute yardstick of beauty, however; a complex relationship can indeed be a greater deformity than a simple irregularity. What a complex nexus of relations is in its wholeness is the important question: it can be a high form of similarity or a high form of deformity.[21] At any rate, the important point here is that one's angle of vision must be that of the whole and not of parts if his or her estimate of the beauty of any nexus of relations is to be a valid one.

The upshot of this brief discussion of Edwards' concept of beauty is that a beautiful nexus of relations contains three ref-

[19] "The Mind," No. 1, WEA, pp. 336–338.
[20] Ibid., p. 334.
[21] "The Mind," Nos. 45, 64, WEA, pp. 393, 382.

erence points or dimensions. Edwards ends his longest discussion of beauty in "The Mind," No. 1, with the following cryptic and yet significant summary:

> Happiness strictly consists in the perception of these three things: of the consent of being to its own being; of its consent to being; and of being's consent to being.[22]

By "happiness" Edwards means the knowledge and love of beauty. In the light of all other things Edwards has to say about beauty and being, the above remark can be interpreted as referring to the three dimensions of a beautiful nexus of relations: (1) an entity's self-identity or the consent that exists within the parts of an entity ("the consent of being to its own being"); (2) an entity's relations with other entities ("its consent to being"); and (3) an entity's consent to the whole ("being's consent to being"). These three dimensions of a beautiful relation of course correlate with the three dimensions in the relatedness of every individual entity, as discussed in the previous section.

The Relational Essences of Created Beings and the Meaning of Their Actuality

The created world, according to Edwards, is a system of laws and habits that determine and govern the relations among events, actions, and their occasions, and these relations have reference to the laws or entities themselves, to other entities, and to the whole. Each entity, in other words, is a law of, and a tendency to, relations with those three dimensions. What does this three-dimensional structure of being mean for the nature of human beings and of matter, and what implications can be drawn in relation to the actualization of all entities in the created realm?

Human Being. The essential structure of a human being, first of all, is conceived by Edwards as a nexus of laws that is a tendency to three relationships: to one's self ("self-love"), to

[22] "The Mind," No. 1, WEA, p. 338.

85

others (to know and love others), and to the whole (to know and love God as manifested in Christ, and then to know and love all other things in relation to that first love and knowledge). The two primary functions of the human self are the understanding by which one "discerns and views and judges of things," and the inclination or "the heart" by which "the soul does not merely perceive and view things, but is in some way inclined with respect to the things it views or considers"—that is, by which one is "pleased or displeased." The direction and manner in which these two "faculties" function is determined by the underlying habits, dispositions, or the "principles of nature."[23] These principles are the basic orientations of the entire self and operate in, under, and through, so to speak, the intellectual and the inclinational activities. The principle of "self-love" is simply one's ability to value what he or she is inclined to value or, in Edwards' own words, "a man's love of his own good."[24] Self-love then is a human being's intellectual and inclinational relationship to one's self. Human beings are also determined to relate to other beings through their knowledge and love of them. In *The Nature of True Virtue*, Edwards writes that by "a law of nature which God has fixed" human beings are capable of knowing and loving the secondary beauty that makes up the inner structure of all created beings. But the relations of human beings do not end there; their ultimate destiny is to relate to the whole or God himself by knowing and loving his beauty. This divine beauty is the principle in harmony with which all finite beings are created. The reason that the secondary beauty is delightful to perceiving beings is really their congruence with that ultimate form of beauty.[25] So human beings truly know and love themselves and others only if they know them in their relationship with God's beauty. "A natural [man] may love others, but 'tis some way or other as appendages and appurtenances

[23] *Religious Affections*, pp. 96–98, 206.
[24] "Miscellanies," No. 530, HGT, p. 203.
[25] *True Virtue*, pp. 30–35.

86

to himself," writes Edwards, "but a spiritual man loves others as of God, or in God, or some way related to Him."[26]

There is, then, a three-dimensional structure in the essence of human being. And the first two relational dimensions are to be governed by the third dimension—the self's intellectual and inclinational relation to the whole. At numerous places, Edwards speaks about the end of creation itself as the external communication of God's own being through the knowledge and love of his beauty. In a typical passage, Edwards writes:

> Intelligent beings are the consciousness of the world. The end, therefore, of the creation must necessarily be that they may receive the goodness of God and that they may be happy. It appears also from the nature of happiness which is the perception of excellency. For intelligent beings are created to be the consciousness of the universe, that they may perceive what God is and does. This can be nothing else but to perceive the excellency of what He is and does.[27]

The Material World.   The relatedness of all things to the whole applies no less to nonperceiving beings. An atom is related to itself in the sense that it affirms itself through its resistance against annihilation. Material things are also related to one another. "The whole material universe is preserved by gravity or attraction, or the mutual tendency of all bodies to each other," writes Edwards.[28] Indeed, "the motion, rest, and direction of the least atom has an influence on the motion, rest, and direction of every body in the universe."[29]

Further, material things, just as perceiving beings, have that third or ultimate dimension in their relational essences. The laws that govern the being of physical bodies are inherently the tendencies to be in a fitting relation to the law of the

[26] "Miscellanies," No. 821, HGT, pp. 240–241.

[27] "Miscellanies," No. 87, HGT, pp. 128–129.

[28] Jonathan Edwards, *Images or Shadows of Divine Things*, ed. Perry Miller (New Haven: Yale University Press, 1948), p. 79.

[29] "Things to Be Considered and Written Fully About," No. 14, WEA, p. 231.

whole—namely, God's own beauty. This is why the "mutual tendency of all bodies to each other" has as its most fundamental meaning the fact that it is a "type of love or charity in the spiritual world."[30] "God created this world," Edwards tells us, "for the shining forth of His excellency and for the flowing forth of His happiness."[31] In practical terms this means that all material entities are "images or shadows of divine things"—that is, images or types of God's deeds in the Christ event and in the history of God's work of redemption. "Indeed, the whole outward creation, which is but the shadows of His being, is so made as to represent spiritual things."[32] The rising and setting of the sun, for example, is "so ordered on purpose" to be "a type of the death and resurrection of Christ." And the "immense magnificence of the visible world in inconceivable vastness" has as "its very end" a representation of the "infinite magnificence, height, and glory of God's work in the spiritual world."[33]

What is noteworthy in Edwards' discussion of natural objects and events as images of divine and spiritual truths is not so much its Platonism but rather its relational ontology.[34] When Edwards speaks about the images and types from the natural world, he is not merely coming up with the corporeal illustrations or analogies of certain spiritual meanings; rather he is pointing to all of the dimensions of the relations that make up the very essence of the being of material objects

[30] *Images or Shadows*, p. 79.

[31] "Miscellanies," No. 332, HGT, p. 130.

[32] "Miscellanies," No. 362; *Images or Shadows*, p. 63.

[33] *Images or Shadows*, p. 134.

[34] For recent discussions of Edwards' theory of typology see, for example, Mason Lowance, "Images and Shadows of Divine Things: The Typology of Jonathan Edwards," *Early American Literature* 5 (1970): 141–181; Ursula Brumm, *American Thought and Religious Typology*, trans. John Hoaglund (New Brunswick: Rutgers University Press, 1970); Sacvan Bercovitch, *The American Jeremiad* (Madison: University of Wisconsin Press, 1978), pp. 93–131; Margaret Batschelet, "Jonathan Edwards' Use of Typology: A Historical and Theological Approach" (Ph.D. diss., University of Washington, 1977). Not to be ignored is Perry Miller's important introduction to *Images or Shadows*, pp. 1–41.

themselves. In other words, a material entity's connection with the spiritual truths of God is not something that the human beholder imposes upon it; such a connection is something to which the law of that material entity itself tends—something that is itself an integral part of the total framework of created laws. So Edwards declares that when Christ said, "The tree is known by its fruits," "these things are not merely mentioned as illustrations of his meaning, but as illustrations and evidences of the truth of what he says."[35] As Perry Miller has pointed out, types and images for Edwards were not mere rhetorical convenience or ornamentation but rather the corporeal embodiments of the spiritual truths themselves.[36] "The beauties of nature," Edwards wrote, "are really emanations or shadows of the excellencies of the Son of God."[37] The natural world, when rightly perceived by the regenerate imagination of the saints, is the corporeal repetition of God's own beauty.

The Actuality of Human Beings and of the Material World. I began this section with the observation that Edwards' definition of the structure of being in terms of laws and habits results in a radically relational conception of being. I have discussed three elements in this relational ontology: that the structure or essence of an individual entity is inseparable from its relations; that an entity's relations determine its existence on the level of Aristotle's substantial form; and, finally, that each entity is a tendency to be related with itself, with others, and with the law of the whole or God's beauty.

When these observations are considered together, they lead to an important conclusion: for Edwards, an entity does not fully exist until all of the three dimensions of its relationships are somehow actualized. Even in Aristotelian metaphysics the essence of an entity is not completely fulfilled until all of its potencies are truly exercised. Forms and qualities are in a

---

[35] *Images or Shadows*, p. 49.

[36] Miller, "Introduction," in *Images or Shadows*, pp. 17–23.

[37] "Miscellanies," No. 108, FAJ, p. 373. See also Paula M. Cooey-Nichols, "Nature as Divine Communication in the Works of Jonathan Edwards" (Ph.D. diss., Harvard University, 1981).

sense final causes that seek the actualization of certain ends, be they actions or events. However, in the Aristotelian framework, an entity actually exists as a substance and as a subject even "before" any of the accidents (e.g., relations) are actualized.[38] In Edwards' ontology, however, an entity does not actually exist in any sense unless its relations actually exist. The relations of an entity are indeed real as real possibles or virtuals even before they are fully actual. But the actual existence of an entity—spiritual or corporeal—is impossible unless all of its essential relationships are moved from their state of being real possibles to the state of being actuals.

A human being is essentially a law of, and a tendency to, a particular sort of relationship with one's own self and others that is congruent with his or her relationship with the whole or God's beauty. Now, a human being's relations can only be the relations of knowing and loving. So it would follow that a human being fully exists only as he or she is knowing and loving God's beauty and all other things in their relationship with that beauty. Only then is his or her essence or law actually exercised in all of its three dimensions. A sinner truly exists, though this is not true of him or her. But he or she does not fully exist as a human being unless this is true. In his important treatise, "The End for Which God Created the World," Edwards equates human beings' intellectual and affectional relationships with their existence itself:

> Understanding and will are the highest kind of created existence. And if they be valuable, it must be in their exercise. But the highest and most excellent kind of their exercise, is in some actual knowledge and exercise of will. And certainly the most excellent actual knowledge and will, that can be in the creature, is the knowledge and the love of God.
>
> And that there should be in them an increasing knowledge of God to all eternity, is an existence, a reality infinitely worthy to be, and worthy to be valued and regarded by him, to whom it belongs to order that to be, which, of all things

---

[38] Substance exists "before" accidents at least in the order of nature if not in the order of time. See Maritain, *An Introduction to Philosophy*, p. 157.

possible, is fittest and best. If existence is more worthy than defect and nonentity, and if any created existence is in itself worthy to be, then knowledge or understanding is a thing worthy to be; and if any knowledge, then the most excellent sort of knowledge, viz., that of God and his glory. The existence of the created universe consists as much in it as in any things: yea, this knowledge is one of the highest, most real and substantial parts of all created existence, most remote from nonentity and defect.[39]

Would the full actuality of material entities also consist of the actualization of all three dimensions of their relationships? The logic of Edwards' discussions indicates that this is the case. A material entity is the activity of resisting according to a particular law that stipulates that this resisting be done in a particular sort of relationship with itself, with other entities, and to the whole or God's beauty. A material entity, in other words, cannot fully exist without those relationships. But what is a material entity's relationship with the whole or the beauty of God? Edwards' answer, as was indicated, is that every material entity is designed by the creator to be an image or shadow of divine things, and ultimately of the beauty of God himself. Two things are required: a material entity is to be an image of *beauty*, and it is to be an image of *God's* beauty. For both of these reasons, Edwards argues that consciousness or intelligence is required for the fulfillment of the essence of a material entity. In other words, God intends that the material universe be "happy." But how can anything be happy without consciousness? How can the beautiful proportion of a material entity's relationship with itself, with others, and with the whole be made explicit and actual except in a consciousness? Here I must refer to a passage that I have already quoted:

Wherefore, if God created the world primarily from goodness, every whit of this goodness must, necessarily, ulti-

[39] "Dissertation concerning the End for Which God Created the World," WC, 2: 205, hereafter cited as "End in Creation."

mately terminate in the consciousness of the creature, for the world is no other way capable of receiving goodness in any measure. But the intelligent beings are the consciousness of the world. The end, therefore, of the creation must necessarily be that they may receive the goodness of God and that they may be happy. It appears also from the nature of happiness which is the perception of excellency. For intelligent beings are created to be the consciousness of the universe, that they may perceive what God is and does.[40]

In an early entry of the "Miscellanies," Edwards also writes:

Men, or intelligent beings, are the consciousness of the creation, whereby the universe is conscious of its own being, and of what is done in it, of the actions of the Creator and governor with respect to it. Now except the world had such a consciousness of itself, it would be altogether in vain that it was.[41]

Involved here is a balanced conception of nature's relationship with human beings—a view in which the two are seen as neither totally discontinuous nor totally continuous with each other. Human beings are both different from nature as well as an integral part of it. The world of perceiving beings is that point in nature where the universe is conscious of its own being. "Intelligent beings are created to be the consciousness of the universe, that they may perceive what God is and does."[42] In short—and this is important—the relational essence of a material entity fully exists only as a perceiving being knows and loves it in its true relational context—that is, in its relation to itself, to other entities, and to God's own beauty. In other words, it is only via the human perception that all the relations to which a material entity itself tends become explicit. So, when Edwards writes about hills, mountains, and the sun as the types and images of certain divine things, he is functioning as a medium through which those material entities reach

[40] "Miscellanies," No. 87, HGT, pp. 128–129.
[41] "Miscellanies," No. 1, HGT, pp. 195–196.
[42] "Miscellanies," No. 87, HGT, pp. 128–129.

their true actuality. Thus, when Edwards saw in everything, as he says in his "Personal Narrative," "a calm, sweet cast, or appearance of divine glory," his perception was the arena in which a portion of nature was achieving its true being.[43]

What, then, is the peculiar nature of the human mind and its workings that enables it to function as the medium through which the relational quality of all things can be given a mental actuality and explicitness? The answer to this question will comprise the content of the chapters on the imagination and aesthetic perception.

The actuality of material things, then, is dependent upon the human mind. And this is perhaps the deepest reason for Edwards' contention that the material universe is "absolutely dependent on the conception of the mind for its existence, and does not exist as spirits do, whose existence does not consist in, nor in dependence on, the conception of other minds."[44] Edwards does not explicitly and systematically cite the three-faceted relational essence of all entities as the argument for his so-called idealism. But the logic of his ontology as a whole, as well as many of Edwards' own statements, seems to support my interpretation. Edwards' view is not that *esse est percipi*; as I have shown, an entity exists virtually as a law apart from perception by any mind. What is dependent upon human perception is a material entity's actual existence in the full sense of its meaning—that is, existence with its full relational content. Perhaps it was in order to distinguish the full actuality from the virtual actuality that Edwards remarks in a late series of philosophical notes that "real existence depends on knowledge or perception."[45]

Furthermore, Edwards explicitly asserts that since it is "goodness," "happiness," and "beauty" that God aims at communicating in and through the material universe, the aesthetic-affectional sensibility of the human mind must be in-

[43] "Personal Narrative," FAJ, p. 60.
[44] "The Mind," No. 51, WEA, p. 368.
[45] "Notes on Knowledge and Existence," WEA, p. 398. Wallace Anderson believes that this series of notes might have been written as late as around 1755. See WEA, p. 395.

volved. "What could this vast universe of matter, placed in such excellent order and governed by such excellent law, be good for?" asks Edwards. "Senseless matter, in whatever excellent order it is placed, would be useless if there were no intelligent beings at all" to "behold and admire" it.[46] Already in "The Mind," No. 27, Edwards argued that it is only in the mind that the relations among things (resistances) could become explicit and actual. "The idea may be resisted, it may move, and stop and rebound," while, Edwards observed, it is difficult to conceive how the resistances outside the mind could resist and relate with one another.[47] In short, the qualities of relations (e.g., beauty, goodness, ugliness, etc.) could become explicit mentally. "Things are neither good nor bad," writes Edwards, "but only with relation to perception."[48] Furthermore, it is the very telos of God's creation of the material world that it "shine forth" and express the divine beauty. So, except via the intellectual-affectional activities of the human mind and its imagination, God's own purpose for the material world could not be achieved. The material world has a level of reality as real possibles even apart from human perception; but the fully actual existence of the material world is unthinkable apart from being known and loved.

It is not, however, only the existence of the material world that becomes fully actual in and through human knowledge and love. In and through such a knowledge and love, the human subject itself is achieving his or her full actuality.[49] As I have already shown, the essence of a human being is nothing else than a tendency to know and love God and all things in relation to him. As a human being knows and loves the hills and mountains as the images of God's beauty, his or her own relational tendencies are achieving full actuality. So it is through the human imagination and the resultant knowledge

---

[46] "Miscellanies," No. "gg," HGT, pp. 236–237.

[47] "The Mind," No. 27, WEA, p. 351.

[48] "Miscellanies," No. 749, HGT, p. 85.

[49] Seen here again is the reason that Edwards' so-called idealism is not subjectivism.

and love that nature, self, and the Absolute come together and become concretely actual in time and space.

HABITS AND LAWS AS THE DYNAMIC PRINCIPLES OF BEING

A general picture of Edwards' conception of reality now begins to emerge. The universe is a divinely established network of laws and habits of knowing/loving relationships. These relationships, which in their individuality embody in varying degrees the transcendent beauty of God, exist virtually as tendencies. At the appropriate points in time and space, and with God's concurrent causal involvement, these relationships are moved from virtuality to actuality. A given knowing/loving relation achieves its true actuality when it is an actual relation "fitting" with the whole—that is, the divine beauty. The knowing/loving relationships of perceiving beings achieve that reference to the whole through their imaginative ability to form and stretch the scope of their perception of relationships. The relationships of nonperceiving entities manifest their inherent reference to the whole, and thus achieve their true actuality in and through the imagination of the perceiving beings. The created beings are dependent and yet abiding because they are essentially the abiding laws and habits. Relationships are not secondary to being and its structure but rather constitutive of them. As habits and laws, entities are in their essence the patterns of, and tendencies to, actual relations. The actual existence of entities, therefore, is the actuality of relationships.

Thus far, it has been shown that for Edwards, habits and laws function as the permanent and structural principles of being. It remains to elucidate the dynamic nature of reality that results from this dispositional reconception of being. Being, as shall be seen, is dynamic in three ways: (1) The most basic character of reality is dispositional—that is, an ordered power of tendency. (2) Being is the act of moving from virtuality to full actuality. And (3) reality is in a process of being increased or multiplied in actuality.

Being Is Essentially an Ordered Power of Tendency to
Actions and Relations

Actions and relations, according to Edwards, are internal to
the being of an entity. Entities do not first exist as substances
and then flow out into operations through their operational
potencies. For Edwards, operational potencies and the substantial form are one and the same principle: dispositional
powers. Entities exist only as they act and are related.

Edwards, one might say, gives a dispositional answer to the
age-old question of whether being or becoming (permanence
or change) is the most basic character of reality. Reality, for
Edwards, is an ordered tendency. To the extent that a disposition has permanence as an abiding real-ness apart from its
actual operation *and* as a structured or ordered power, being
is essentially permanent. At the same time, since a disposition
is a power with causal efficacy, being, defined dispositionally,
is becoming. Edwards' position, therefore, is neither that of
Parmenides nor that of Heraclitus. Being as essentially ordered power combines the dynamic with the permanent.

I should note here that Edwards' conception of the essence
of being as dynamic cannot be fully understood without a reference to the dynamic being of God. Finite dispositions are not
triggered without the direct involvement of God's own exercise of the divine disposition. The ultimate ground of the dynamic character of finite reality, therefore, is the dynamic
character of the divine being. I shall discuss the nature of the
divine being in Chapter 7.

Edwards' dynamic conception of being, it should be added,
was not formulated in complete isolation from the philosophical discussion of his day. In fact, Edwards' identification of
being with power needs to be understood in relation to the
similar proposals in some of the other seventeenth- and eighteenth-century thinkers. Edwards was in some ways anticipated by these thinkers, and he also attempted to provide the
answers to some of the unresolved questions in their discussions. Understanding what Edwards is doing here may therefore be aided by putting his dispositional ontology into its historical context.

Edwards and Some of the Problems in the Development of a Dynamic Conception of Being

Edwards certainly was not the sole originator of the view that power and activity make up the very essence of being. Implicitly or explicitly, such a view was present in many of Edwards' predecessors and contemporaries, including the Cambridge Platonists, Isaac Newton, John Locke, Robert Greene, and Joseph Priestley.[50] Edwards' achievement lies in the creative resolutions he gave to some of the problems those men faced in their efforts to appropriate the categories of power and motion into their systems of thought.

One such problem had to do with the question of how to reconcile the notion of a power-filled cosmos with a strong doctrine of God's sovereign rule over his creation. Working within the voluntarist theological assumption of the radical contingency of the created world upon God's will, Newton explicitly rejected the immanence of the gravitational force in matter. For him, everything in the world is "subordinate to [God], and subservient to his Will," and thus, as Colin MacLaurin represents Newton, God, "equally active and present everywhere," is "the source of all efficacy."[51] Newton seems to have assumed that the inherence of power in the essence of matter would diminish the necessity of God's causal involvement in the world. So, seventeenth-century mechanical philosophy's notion of matter as inert and passive mass with its fellow doctrine of causation by impact persists in Newton's thought in spite of the apparent impression given by his law

[50] Robert Greene and Joseph Priestley were among those eighteenth-century natural philosophers who modified Newton's thought by seeing powers and forces as essential to matter. P. M. Heimann and J. E. McGuire discuss Edwards as well as Greene and Priestley in their account of this new development of thought. See Heimann and McGuire, "Newtonian Forces and Lockean Powers," pp. 251–261. See also P. M. Heimann, "Voluntarism and Immanence: Conceptions of Nature in Eighteenth-Century Thought," *Journal of the History of Ideas* 39 (1978): 271–283.

[51] Isaac Newton, *Opticks*, (4th ed. (London, 1952), p. 403, quoted in Heimann, "Voluntarism and Immanence," p. 273; Colin MacLaurin, *An Account of Sir Isaac Newton's Philosophical Discoveries* (London, 1748), quoted in Heimann, "Voluntarism and Immanence," p. 275.

of gravitation that the force of attraction is part of the essence of matter capable of causation at a distance. Impact causation and distance causation, and matter and force, stand in an unresolved dichotomous disjunction in Newton.[52]

Could not force be immanent in matter without belittling the divine causation in the world? Newton probably believed that such an immanence of force in matter implied an admission of a self-existent and self-active causal principle in the created realm, something his theology would not allow. Newton's own view is probably reflected in the words of his exponent Samuel Clarke, who argued against John Toland's theory of an essentially active universe by saying that matter could not be endowed with a self-existent principle of motion because "self-existence is necessary existence" and necessary existence certainly could not be attributed to matter.[53]

Those who saw force as essential to matter, however, did not see any contradiction between their dynamic view of matter and divine providence. And their strategy was to deny clearly any self-existence or self-sufficiency to the inherently active universe, thereby implying that the inherent force itself is continually dependent upon God's causal agency. Early in the century, Leibniz held that force made up the very essence of the material substance, and insisted that such a view did "not exclude God's providence" and that "the creation wants to be continually influenced by its creator."[54] Then, in 1712, one of Newton's earliest critics, Robert Greene, maintained that "nature is active . . . [and] matter itself is so," insisting at the same time that since activity cannot be self-existent, it must continually be dependent upon divine agency. During

---

[52] See Miller, *Jonathan Edwards*, pp. 86–92; Ernan McMullin, *Newton on Matter and Activity* (Notre Dame: University of Notre Dame Press, 1978), pp. 111–112.

[53] Samuel Clarke, *Discourse concerning the Being and Attributes of God* (London, 1716), 1: 49, quoted in Heimann, "Voluntarism and Immanence," p. 276. See also John Toland, *Letters to Serena* (London, 1704), p. 158 (Toland here claims that "motion is essential to matter").

[54] G. W. Leibniz, "Specimen Dynamicum," *Acta Eruditorum* 14 (1695): 145–157; *The Leibniz-Clarke Correspondence*, ed. H. G. Alexander (New York: Philosophical Library, 1956), pp. 18–19.

the second half of the eighteenth century, Joseph Priestley and James Hutton developed a similar view of the essentiality of force in nature. While Hutton was led to deistic conclusions by his dynamic view of matter, Priestley had no problem in holding on to a strong doctrine of God's causal involvement in the world.[55]

The emergence of the dynamic perspective on nature in the eighteenth century, however, went against only a part of Newton's thought; as indicated already, Newton himself provided much of the impetus for the development of such a line of thought. Modern scholarship on Newton has paid fresh attention to the extent to which a dynamic perspective on nature is a pervasive element in his thought.[56] I have already mentioned the dynamic perspective implied in his law of gravitation. Then there are his ideas of "active principles" and ether. What Newton calls "active principles" are immaterial forces or causes of forces that function not by causation by impact but at a distance. At first, Newton associated these principles closely with divine agency, but later he seemed to consider them an integral part of, and thus immanent in, the fabric of nature. Ether would be an example of such an immaterial active principle that is immanent in nature and functions causally in a way different from impact.[57] P. M. Heimann and J. E. McGuire have argued that it was a small step from "active principles" to "active substances."[58] Such a step is precisely what Edwards took, and he should be viewed as belonging to the group of eighteenth-century thinkers who gave a further development to the dynamic perspective on nature that was inchoately present in Newton himself. Like them, Edwards affirmed simultaneously the essentiality of power and activity in matter and also the continual divine agency in the world.

[55] Heimann and McGuire, "Newtonian Forces and Lockean Powers," pp. 268–295.
[56] See esp. McMullin, *Newton on Matter and Activity.*
[57] Heimann and McGuire, "Newtonian Forces and Lockean Powers," pp. 239–240.
[58] Ibid., p. 236.

Edwards' distinctive contribution, however, must not be ignored. The uniqueness of his view is that with the help of his notion of habits and laws as conditional general laws, he was able to formulate a logical framework for the coexistence of an immediate divine causality in the world with a limited and yet real causal efficacy of the finite creatures. As I pointed out in connection with the abiding nature of finite entities, habits and laws are active powers, but their operation is contingent upon the fulfillment of certain conditions or occasions. So, a material entity is essentially a law that actively demands, so to speak, that there be an actual resisting/relating activity of a sort at a particular point in time and space; yet the propensity of such a law is carried out only on the condition that God is willing and ready to cause an infinite amount of resisting actually to exist in accordance with the law in question. Conceived in this way, the integrity of a sort of causality in the finite entity fully coexists with a direct causality of God. Edwards' language about God's involvement is not coy at all. He does not just speak in a general way about God's causal involvement, as others, such as Greene and Priestley, seem to. For Edwards, the resistance or existence is "the Deity acting," that is, God himself in action. Edwards then qualifies it by saying that resistance is "what immediately *results* from the exercise of divine power."[59] But the direct character of God's involvement is clear. Nothing could be so far removed from the deistic position as Edwards' position at this point. And yet, more than anyone, he wanted to recognize the dynamic element in the created entities themselves, something that Newton and others also had to acknowledge as factual. Edwards' recognition of both the immediate involvement of God in the world and the dynamic nature of the finite entities is particularly evident in his discussion of the actions of human beings. In the following two quotations, Edwards is speaking about the divinely infused habit of grace that functions only in and through the principles of action that make up a human being's natural essence.

[59] "Of Atoms," WEA, p. 215.

It is not intended that the natural faculties are not made use of in it. The natural faculties are the subject of this light: and they are the subject in such a manner, that they are not merely passive, but active in it; the acts and exercises of man's understanding are concerned and made use of in it. God, in letting in this light into the soul, deals with man according to his nature, or as a rational creature; makes use of his human faculties. But yet this light is not the less immediately from God for that; though the faculties are made use of, it is as the subject and not as the cause.[60]

In efficacious grace we are not merely passive, nor yet does God do some, and we do the rest. But God does all, and we do all. God produces all, and we act all. For that is what he produces, viz., our own acts. God is the only proper author and fountain; we only are the proper actors. We are, in different respects, wholly passive, and wholly active.[61]

God "does all" and "produces all," since it is God who originally established the laws of the natural human being and who now establishes the new habit of grace in the regenerate. God "does all" also because God's immediate acts of causing existence and actions in accordance with the established laws and habits are necessary if those laws and habits are to be triggered into actions and relationships. But the regenerate person also "does all" and is the subject of the virtuous acts because the habits and laws of his being actively regulate and govern the manner in which God immediately causes existence and relationships.

R. G. Collingwood has observed that the difference between the Greek and the Renaissance views of nature is that the former regarded the cosmos as a self-moving organism with its inherent principles of causation, while the latter viewed it as a machine, the motions of which are radically contingent upon the causal activity of God himself.[62] The

[60] "A Divine and Supernatural Light," FAJ, p. 109.
[61] "Efficacious Grace," WC, 2: 580.
[62] R. G. Collingwood, The Idea of Nature (New York: Oxford University Press, 1960), pp. 1–9.

Greek view considered the laws of nature as immanent in and intrinsic to nature itself, while the Renaissance view saw them as imposed from the outside by the will of God. For Edwards, the laws of nature are certainly not intrinsic to nature; they are established by God's "arbitrary" (sovereign) will and thus are imposed upon the creation. So Edwards, in his dynamic view of nature, is not returning to the Greek conception, but neither is his view an example of the Renaissance view according to which power and activity are external to matter. For Edwards, power and the laws of nature are in a sense immanent since they constitute the very essence of entities. Edwards' view, one might say, represents a definite move toward a modern synthesis of the Greek and the Renaissance cosmologies—a synthesis that introduces activity and movement into nature. Edwards moved to this modern perspective, however, without compromising God's immediate providential involvement in his creation.[63]

Another question that Edwards had to deal with in working out a dynamic conception of being has to do with the nature of causality itself. This issue was set up for Edwards particularly by the Cambridge Platonists whose writings Edwards read very early in his life. These philosophers' consuming interest was to reintroduce the "final, intending and directive causality" to nature thereby correcting Hobbes' explanation of nature purely in terms of "material and mechanical necessity."[64] Anxious to avoid the excesses of an extreme occasionalism or re-creationism, these men at Cambridge sought to find a teleological principle that would mediate between the creator and the created world.

[63] Collingwood traces the emergence of modern cosmology in an overall frame according to which the Greek organic view was succeeded by Renaissance mechanism, which was then followed by the historical-evolutionary perspective. See ibid., pp. 29–177. For a fine discussion of the role played by the Christian belief in creation in the development of modern cosmology, see Klaaren, *Religious Origins of Modern Science*. See also the various essays collected in D. O'Connor and Francis Oakley, eds., *Creation: The Impact of an Idea* (New York: Charles Scribner's Sons, 1969).

[64] Ralph Cudworth, *The True Intellectual System of the Universe* (London, 1678), quoted in Cragg, *Cambridge Platonists*, p. 237.

Their answer was the idea of "plastic nature" or "the spirit of the world," and it was Ralph Cudworth who gave it the most systematic expression. According to Cudworth, plastic nature, distinct from God, is a "subordinate instrument" which "doth drudgingly execute that part of his providence which consists in the regular and orderly motion of matter." Working as the "inward principles" of things, plastic natures give the cosmos its "reason and art."[65] What is unsatisfactory in Cudworth's theory, however, is that he leaves teleology and mechanism in an unsynthesized dualism. There was something about the mechanical explanation of the world that he admired. As Gunnar Aspelin has pointed out, Cudworth did consider the mechanistic view as useful and valid in its analysis of many aspects of the natural world.[66] He seems to have believed the atomistic conception of matter and the formulation of the order of the world in terms of mathematical laws to be valid ideas in reference to at least portions of the natural phenomenon. Cudworth typically affirms both mechanism and teleology. There is something in nature "besides mechanism"; "there is a mixture of life or plastic nature, together with mechanism, which runs through the whole corporeal universe," writes Cudworth.[67] It is not that he was uninterested in working out a synthesis. He even asserted that "the laws of nature concerning motion are really nothing else but a plastic nature, acting upon the matter of the whole corporeal universe,"[68] and thereby indicated his desire to work out a more unified conception of causality. But Cudworth does not

[65] Ibid., pp. 242, 247. Henry More's term for "plastic nature" is "the spirit of nature." See Henry More, *Enchiridion Ethicum*, the English translation of 1690 (New York: Facsimile Text Society, 1930), p. 36. See also Caroline Collins Hunt, "Plastic Nature: A Study of the Cambridge Platonists" (Ph.D. diss., Harvard University, 1970).

[66] Gunnar Aspelin, *Ralph Cudworth's Interpretation of Greek Philosophy* (Göteborg: Elanders Boktryckeri Aktiebolag, 1943), pp. 12–13.

[67] Cragg, *Cambridge Platonists*, p. 237.

[68] Ibid., p. 240. Gunnar Aspelin observes: "But Cudworth does not arrive at the synthesis of a mechanistic and finalistic explanation of nature which is his goal. He stops at a compromise" (Aspelin, *Cudworth's Interpretation of Greek Philosophy*, p. 15).

explain how laws and plastic natures can be reduced to each other, and confusingly resorts to the compromise that both sorts of causality coexist in nature.

Edwards' contribution was precisely that he worked out a synthesis of the two perspectives that were merely juxtaposed in Cudworth's writings, and the solution lay in Edwards' notion of active tendency as a relational law. Habit or tendency is a teleological principle since it is a striving toward an end and an order; but it is also a law or the relational pattern of the observable phenomena themselves. Edwards' idea of active tendency, therefore, combines into one conception both the teleological category of intentional purpose and mechanistic science's principle of the mathematical laws of motion. In working out such a synthesis, certain elements in both sides had to be abandoned or modified, of course. The Cambridge men's plastic nature was not relational enough; Edwards had to make a clean-cut departure from any vestige of the metaphysics of forms. On the other hand, the causality-by-impact doctrine of seventeenth-century mechanical philosophy had to be dropped in favor of a more relational conception.

To get a full picture of Edwards' teleological-relational conception of power and causality, however, I must mention another source of inspiration—namely, the aesthetic perspective of the third earl of Shaftesbury, whose works Edwards also read very early in his life.[69] Shaftesbury continued the basic tenets of the Cambridge School, but gave the principle of teleology an added dimension. He looked at the world essentially as a work of art, the teleological forces in nature as principles of aesthetic creativity. So, Cudworth's plastic natures now become "the forming forms" or the beautifying beauty. Beauty, for Shaftesbury then, is a power. As he puts it, "The beautifying, not the beautified, is the really beautiful."[70]

[69] Shaftesbury's *Characteristicks*, 3 vols. (London, 1714), was available at the Yale Library during Edwards' student years. Perry Miller believes that Edwards may have read Shaftesbury as early as before Edwards began writing notes on "The Mind." See Miller, *Jonathan Edwards*, p. 238; Anderson, "Editor's Introduction," in WEA, p. 21.

[70] Shaftesbury, *Characteristicks*, 2: 131–132, quoted in Stanley Green,

Shaftesbury's notion of beauty is still conceived too much in the language of particulate forms to suit Edwards' relational perspective. Nevertheless, Shaftesbury's perspective must have played an important role in helping the young Jonathan Edwards find conceptual tools to express what seems to have been his temperamental affinities with aesthetic categories.

So, Edwards' synthesis of teleology and mechanical laws in terms of his idea of active tendency as a general law is worked out in distinctively aesthetic categories. Causality and power, in other words, are conceived as teleological, relational, and aesthetic. Things happen neither by the mechanical transmission of efficient causes by contact nor through the final causality of particulate forms; things happen rather by the mutual implications of relationships. To put it in Edwards' own language, what occurs does occur because of a fitness or harmony of relations, a fitness or harmony of one relational event with other nexuses of relations and ultimately with the whole, which is the beauty of God. When God created the first instances of resistance or existence, he created them "in such parts of space as God thought fit." And thus, "there is no such thing as mechanism if that word is taken to be that whereby bodies act upon each other purely and properly by themselves."[71] Edwards is not here denying that an individual law of relations is an active tendency with a causal influence. What he is denying is that one law of relations would ever function all by itself upon another. All things happen only by being related with all other things. Even the "motion, rest, and direction of the least atom has an influence on the motion, rest, and direction of every body in the universe," writes Edwards.[72] And the ultimate content or quality of all those influences taken as a whole is beauty.

In this way, the teleological principle that had been taken out of the cosmos by seventeenth-century mechanistic philos-

Shaftesbury's Philosophy of Religion and Ethics (Oxford: Ohio University Press, 1967), pp. 253–254.

[71] "Of Atoms," WEA, pp. 215–216.

[72] "Things to Be Considered and Written Fully About," No. 14, WEA, p. 230.

ophy is restored by Edwards. But it is a teleology with a difference; Edwards is not going back to the Greek view of nature as an intrinsically self-moving organism, nor is he simply repeating the final causality of Plato or Aristotle. For Edwards, final causes are not substantial or accidental forms but rather the relational laws of relationships. The energies in nature are not self-existent or self-active, but rather radically dependent upon the creator without being totally passive or lifeless. Furthermore, the distance between being and power, structure and function, is closed, as power and activity are seen as essential to being and structure. Finally, the final causality is given an aesthetic definition, as the active tendency is seen as a law of, and a propensity to, beautiful relations, and also as the end of activity is viewed as the activity itself—the activity of beautifully relating.

Being as a Movement from Virtuality to Actuality

The first way in which being is dynamic in Edwards' ontology is that the most fundamental and abiding character of reality is seen as dispositional—as ordered powers of tendency. The second sense in which being is dynamic follows from the first: If the essence of an entity is an active disposition to a type of action and relation, then that entity would be fully actual when its dispositional essence is exerted in actual actions and relations of a certain type. An entity is real, first of all, in a virtual mode or as a real possibility.[73] When an entity's disposition is exerted, that entity is moved from virtuality to actuality—that is, from its state of being real as a real possibility to a state of being full actuality. Being, in short, is the movement, or the act of moving, from virtuality to actuality. An entity does not fully exist first and then engage in operations. Rather, its existence consists in its operations—that is, its movement from being a real possibility to being an actuality through the operations of its dispositional essence. The existence of the world, in short, is a movement, an action.

[73] For further discussion of Edwards' notion of "real possibility," see above, Chap. 2.

Ultimately the world is an act of God. The dispositions of created beings, as was seen, are not triggered into operations on their own. God's own activity of causing resistance according to his own dispositional essence is required for the exertions of all finite dispositional essences. The dynamic nature of the created existence is ultimately grounded in God's own activity. Nevertheless, the finite habits and laws, though continually dependent upon God, are given a relative and yet real causal function. Once God establishes a system of finite laws and habits, God usually exercises his own disposition *according to* the previously established finite habits and laws. In this way, the created beings govern, though in a limited sense, their own operations and thus their own reality. Creatures are participants in God's own ongoing activity of moving the world from its virtuality to actuality.[74] (Whether God's own life is continually moved from virtuality to actuality, in some limited sense, is an all-important question to which I will return in Chapter 8.)

In this way, Edwards maintains a balance between God's direct and continual involvement in the created world's actual existence, on the one hand, and the created world's relative and yet real contribution to its actuality, on the other. In other words, Edwards avoids deism as well as occasionalism. God's direct involvement precludes deism, and Edwards avoids occasionalism because God's continuous creative activity is in accordance with his preestablished and abiding laws. True, God's continuous activity does move the creation from its virtual reality to its full actuality. In this limited sense, God "creates the world out of nothing every moment."[75] But Edwards' conception of the disposition as a mode of real-ness saves his ontology from an unqualified form of occasionalism. It also follows that the dispositional integrity of the created world also helps Edwards to maintain a relative and yet real integrity

[74] For this reason, Edwards' view is not occasionalism in its usual sense. For further discussion of the dependent and yet real permanence of creatures, see above, Chap. 3.

[75] "Things to Be Considered and Written Fully About," No. 47, WEA, p. 241.

of the creation as a reality distinguishable from the being of God. The world's dynamic being participates in the dynamic character of God's own ongoing involvement in the world.

To say that being is movement and action, for Edwards, does not mean that reality is without permanence, structure, or purpose. Since the movement from virtuality to actuality is the exertion of a disposition or habit, it has an abiding ground that provides a unity of particular movements. The movement from virtuality to actuality also has a particular structure that only exhibits the structure or pattern of the disposition or habit. Since a dispositional power has a propensive thrust toward the actuality of a particular sort of act and relation, the exertion of a disposition makes a modal difference. In other words, such an exertion constitutes a change from real possibility to actuality. An end that at one point did not exist is achieved. There is purposive character in the movement from virtuality to actuality. Being is inherently teleological.

A process of movement, however, calls for an ultimate explanation. Why are there dispositional habits and their exertions? At this point, Edwards' perspective is sharply different from process thought, which also emphasizes movement as the basic character of being. Whitehead, for example, makes a clear distinction between God and creativity.[76] Edwards, on the other hand, sees God as the ultimate source and explanation of creativity and all existence but also as directly and continually involved in the creative process itself. I shall return to this.

Being as a Process of Increase

I have discussed two ways in which Edwards' conception of being, defined as essentially dispositional, is dynamic: first, the very essence of being is an active power of tendency; and second, being is a movement or act of moving from virtuality to actuality. These considerations lead to the third sense in which being, for Edwards, is dynamic—namely, being, defined as es-

---

[76] For a recent critique of Whitehead's conception of the God-creativity relation, see Neville, *Creativity and God*, esp. pp. 3–47.

sentially dispositional, is a continual process of increase through a multiplication of the actuality of relationships. If the essences of entities are dispositional powers, their exercise brings about actual existence—that is, the movement of operational relationships from real possibility to actuality. But a dispositional power remains a disposition even after its exercise and is not exhausted by its exercise. Edwards' dispositional conception of being makes operations and relations internal to, and constitutive of, actual existence; dispositions are abiding and by nature capable of repeated exercise. The consequence of Edwards' view is that being is incremental, and habit or disposition is the principle of an ontological increase.

What I have just said about the ontological productivity of dispositions and habits is a general statement. I need to probe more deeply into the nature of the increase of being that dispositions and habits are capable of. Is any movement from virtuality to actuality an increase of being? What meaning can be attached to the idea of "more" in Edwards' ontology?

There is no doubt that Edwards saw actuality as having a higher degree of being than real possibility, although the latter has a mode of reality as virtuality. In a discussion of the relation between the new disposition of grace in the regenerate and its behavioral outcome, Edwards writes that "the being of a closing with and adhering to Christ lies more in the transitive practical acts of a principle of union and adherence" than in the principle of such "union and adherence" itself.[77] The relationship of "closing with" Christ is a real possibility when a person has the principle or disposition toward such relationship. But when such a disposition is exercised, it is now an actuality; the "being of a closing with and adhering to Christ lies more" in the actuality of it than in the real possibility for it. Actuality is one yardstick for the degree of being.

But being cannot be thought of simply as actuality. For Edwards, being is a structured reality. And habit or disposition that is the propensity to actuality is an ordered power—a propensity to relations of certain specific qualities. For Edwards,

---

[77] "Miscellanies," No. 819, Yale MSS.

being, considered as inclusive of virtuality and actuality, is ultimately governed by the beauty of God. Actualities that the exercise of habits and dispositions brings about, then, would increase being if they are beautiful actualities. When beauty is added to beauty, being is added to being. Now this general contention needs to be unpacked a bit further.

All beauties, according to Edwards, have the common characteristic of being similarities or proportions of relationships taken as wholes. But among the various distinctions Edwards introduces in this regard is the difference between "simple beauty" and "complex beauty." The principle that functions in this distinction is that the more extensive and complex a nexus of relationships is, and if such a nexus taken as a whole is a proportion, the higher and the more intense the beauty is. Extensiveness, then, is a yardstick for the degree of proportion and thus of beauty. "The more extended or limited its system is, the more confined or extended is its beauty," wrote Edwards. In his early writing in "The Mind," Edwards had already noted, "Excellency may be distributed into greatness and beauty: the former is the degree of being; the latter is being's consent to being."[78] Extensiveness and proportion function together to constitute higher forms of beauty.

But Edwards' thought is strictly theocentric and would not allow extensiveness and proportion in themselves to be autonomous principles. Ultimately, God alone is the absolute fountain and measure of beauty and being. What this means functionally is that the extensiveness and proportion of relationships would constitute true beauty only if such extensiveness and such proportion consent to "being in general" or the universality of things.

Extensiveness by itself, therefore, is only a "capacity" for beauty. Unless an extensiveness of relations is agreeable to the ultimate principle of beauty, it can be a greater deformity than a less extensive nexus of relationships.

Not only may greatness be considered as a capacity of excellency, but a being, by reason of his greatness considered

---

[78] "The Mind," Nos. 14, 64, WEA, pp. 344, 382.

alone, is the more excellent because he partakes more of being. Though if he be great, if he dissent from more general and extensive being or from universal being, he is the more odious for his greatness because the dissent or contradiction to being in general is so much the greater.[79]

Extensiveness is a real and valid criterion of beauty and being—but only when it is harmonious with the ultimate principle of beauty.

Proportion or beauty as such is not an autonomous principle, either. "That which is beautiful . . . with respect to itself and a few other things . . . is false beauty and a confined beauty" while "that which is beautiful with respect to the universality of things has a generally extended excellence, a true beauty."[80] Edwards is here acknowledging the presence in the world of many forms of relationships that are proportions and beauties and are capable of being perceived as such. Among these "inferior beauties," Edwards is making the distinction between those which are agreeable in some way to the ultimate principle of beauty (as manifested in Christ and in the history of redemption) and are thus called the "images or shadows" of the divine beauty, on the one hand, and those which dissent from the ultimate principle and thus are in the final analysis "false beauties," on the other.

In short, extensiveness and proportion are valid yardsticks for the degree of beauty when they are used in conjunction with the ultimate criterion of harmony with the beauty of God.

The upshot of my discussion of beauty in this context is that the fundamental requirement for ontological fulfillment and increase is the widening of the imaginative reach of the dispositions of perceiving beings so that their exercise can actualize beautiful relations in a manner harmonious with the divine beauty itself. Such a widening of the habits of mind and heart, as I have shown, requires nothing less than the indwell-

[79] "The Mind," No. 62, wea, p. 381.
[80] "The Mind," No. 14, wea, p. 344.

ing of God's own disposition within the human self.[81] When the dispositions of human minds and hearts are so transformed by God's own disposition, their exercise will result in knowing and loving God's beauty and all things in a manner harmonious to that beauty. When this happens, the actualities of relations that the exercise of the disposition brings about are actualities of true beauty and thus constitute true actualizations of the knowing minds and the known objects. And the repetition of the exercise of a regenerate disposition adds beauty to beauty, and being to being.

Once the human disposition is divinely transformed, it is clear, the increase of the extensiveness of relationships constitutes a real increase or multiplication of beauty and being. Every time a transformed self knows and loves God and all things in relation to God, the actuality of that self, as well as the actuality of the known object, is repeated and thus increased. The knowing self's and the known object's relationships become more extensive and multiplied, and thereby their beauty and their being become "bigger."[82]

The repetition and multiplication I just spoke of is not a simple repetition—"simple" in the sense that there is no variation whatsoever. What one knows in knowing anything is ultimately its fitness to God's beauty, and this ultimate dimension in all acts of knowing and loving remains the same. However, a finite mind has a limited capacity to experience relationships at a given time and at a given place. Human beings live within the duration of temporality and spatial localities. No one act of knowing God, though a true knowledge of God, can comprehend all the variable relational contexts of such knowledge.

Every new act of a regenerate person's knowing and loving increases beauty and being in two ways: it repeats the actuality of knowing and loving God and all things in God, and also it increases and intensifies that actuality through the same knowledge and love of God in ever new relational circum-

[81] See below, Chap. 5, n. 61.
[82] "The Mind," No. 45, WEA, p. 363.

stances and contexts, and in ever new objects of experiences. The multiplication of relationships that brings about an increase of being is both a repetition of the original experience as well as an intensification that takes time and is spread out in duration. In this limited and yet real sense, temporality does matter in the increase of being.

To put the matter somewhat differently, a person with the divine disposition as his or her own human disposition is now a propensive power to reach out to an infinite number of relationships. This is so because God's disposition is the tendency to an infinitely complex and extensive system of relationships. In the disposition of a regenerate person, there is in a virtual mode the real possibility of an infinitely extensive multiplication of experienced relations. The regenerate person is nothing less than a dynamic force that would seek out and know and love an unending number of beings in an unending number of circumstances. A regenerate mind and heart is a dynamic propensity to an unending multiplication of relationships. In an entry in his "Miscellanies," titled "Happiness," Edwards wrote, "And how happy is that love in which there is an eternal progress in all these things, wherein new beauties are continually discovered, and more and more loveliness, and in which we shall forever increase in beauty ourselves."[83]

Since the increase of beauty and being is grounded in the activity of God's own disposition in and through the human dispositions, this increase is none other than the process in and through which God's own beauty and being is repeated and multiplied. The regenerate minds and hearts participate in God's never-ending activity of self-communication.

There are many reasons to think that what God has in view, in an increasing communication of himself throughout eternity, is an increasing knowledge of God, love to him, and joy in him. And it is to be considered that the more those communications increase in the creature, the more it be-

---

[83] "Miscellanies," No. 198, HGT, p. 195. For further discussion of Edwards' conception of the "increase" in the saints' being and the relation of that increase to the divine being, see below, Chaps. 7 and 8.

comes one with God; for so much the more is it united to God in love, the heart is drawn nearer and nearer to God, and the union with him becomes more firm and close, and at the same time the creature becomes more and more conformed to God.[84]

I already alluded to Edwards' contention that the increase of being in the finite world is the process through which God's own disposition is exercised. Does this then mean God's own being is somehow increased? In what sense could the divine life itself be repeated? These are the natural and compelling questions that emerge from the discussion thus far. I shall turn to them in Chapter 7. I turn in the next two chapters to Edwards' conception of the imagination and its role in experience and in the process of ontological increase.

[84] "End in Creation," WC, 2: 210–211. For further discussion of Edwards' conception of God's creation of the world, see below, Chap. 7.

CHAPTER V

Imagination as the Habit of Mind

THE NATURE and meaning of the mind's active role in the cognitive process was one of the most basic epistemological and psychological problems of eighteenth-century thought. Nature was no longer being thought of as a living and inherently active organism, as it had been in Greek philosophy; creativity was now being attributed more and more to the mind itself. Further, the notion of composite substances and substantial forms was no longer available as the explanation of the order in the world; the knowing mind is now confronted with simple "atoms" of experience the relations of which were being increasingly considered as somehow produced by the mind itself. From the period of the Enlightenment down to the twentieth century, the history of Western thinking about knowledge is also a history of the theories of the imagination, or the ordering, shaping power of the human mind.

This was not an easy problem, however, particularly as it emerged in the works of the eighteenth-century empiricists and those who shared their main tenets. The difficulty lay in the tension between sensation and imagination. The most fundamental dictum of the empiricists, and also to a great extent of the age as a whole, was that knowledge is to be obtained through a direct sense contact with the objective world of which the knowledge is a knowledge and not through the innate ideas the validity of which is based upon some otherworldly source, such as God. Knowledge can only be received and not made or created. How can this empiricistic maxim be harmonized with the seemingly inevitable involvement of the mind's own activity in the knowledge process?[1]

[1] See Ernst Cassirer, *The Philosophy of the Enlightenment* (Boston: Beacon Press, 1960), pp. 97–133; C. R. Morris, *Locke-Berkeley-Hume*, pp. 24–31.

Another factor that hampered the development of a coherent theory of the imagination was the lingering Cartesian bias against the practical, nonintellectual side of the human self. If the mental activity in cognition in Scholastic thought was associated with the activities of the intellect, the shaping power of the mind in the eighteenth-century epistemologies was seen as closely related with the inclinations, interests, and affections. The elemental motive force for the imagination was being traced to the directions of the appetites and desires of human beings. The recognition of the primacy of the practical and the moral stood in conflict, however, with the Cartesian and Stoic conceptions of the passions as essentially "perturbations of the mind," negative elements that only disturb and confuse the "clear and distinct ideas."[2] Until this bias was somehow overcome, the mind's activities that are connected in any way with the affections were not to be granted a full-fledged cognitive significance.

Such, then, was the epistemological and psychological problem that Jonathan Edwards inherited from his predecessors. How can the imagination and sensation be brought together? The notion of the habit of mind is the key to Edwards' response to this question. The mind's imaginative activity, conceived of as the propensive activity of the habit of the mind, mediates between sensation and the intentions of the mind. Edwards also works out a broadened conception of sensation according to which the imaginative activity of the mind's habit is an act of immediate and direct reception of the objective information about reality.

Edwards, of course, approaches the construction of a theory of the mind's shaping activity with a relational, aesthetic, and dynamic ontology. In a metaphysical outlook in which being is seen essentially as powers of relationships, the mind's activity of ordering and relating will attain the status of the rational principle with an ontological reach. In a view of reality for which beauty is the fundamental content of relationships, the practical or affective dimension of the self will enjoy

---

[2] See Cassirer, *Philosophy of the Enlightenment*, pp. 104–108.

a primacy over the intellectual and discursive. In Edwards' perspective, therefore, the imagination is "Reason in her most exalted mood,"[3] as well as the agent of the ontological fulfillment and enhancement of reality itself.

That Edwards viewed the mind as playing an active role in cognition is not a novel discovery in Edwards scholarship. But there has not been sufficient attention to Edwards' psychology of the imagination. The epistemological and ontological significance of the imagination in Edwards also has not yet been fully explored.[4] It is true that Edwards nowhere presents a complete account of a theory of the imagination. As with so many other aspects of Edwards' thought, this theory must be pieced together on the basis of discussions scattered throughout his works. My intention here is not to offer a comprehensive discussion of Edwards' epistemology but rather to analyze his conception of the mind's imaginative activity and the imaginative sensibility.

LOCKE AND THE CAMBRIDGE PLATONISTS

The problem of the mind's active role in the knowledge process was crystallized for Edwards by the writings of John Locke and such Cambridge Platonists as Ralph Cudworth and the third earl of Shaftesbury. Locke's empiricistic presupposition was that one should reject any and all doctrines whereby the

---

[3] This phrase comes from William Wordsworth, quoted in Walter Jackson Bate, *From Classic to Romantic: Premises of Taste in Eighteenth-Century England* (New York: Harper and Row, 1946), p. 186.

[4] The basic line of interpretation developed in this and the following chapter was initially presented in my "Mental Activity and the Perception of Beauty in Jonathan Edwards," *Harvard Theological Review* 69 (1976): 369–396. Other recent discussions of Edwards' concept of "imagination" include Robert E. Colacurcio, "The Perception of Excellency as the Glory of God in Jonathan Edwards: An Essay towards the Epistemology of Discernment" (Ph.D. diss., Fordham University, 1972), pp. 258–282; Harold Simonson, *Jonathan Edwards: Theologian of the Heart* (Grand Rapids, Mich.: Eerdmans, 1974), pp. 69–89. Also significant in this connection is Conrad Cherry, *Nature and Religious Imagination: From Edwards to Bushnell* (Philadelphia: Fortress Press, 1980), pp. 26–64.

validity of knowledge is based upon an authority extraneous to the actual sense experience of the world. So he begins his *Essay concerning Human Understanding* with a vehement attack upon innate ideas and then proceeds to demonstrate how knowledge is derived wholly from the simple and unmixed ideas passively received through the external organs of the five senses and the internal sense or "reflection." He runs into difficulties, however, in connection with the relations and order among the presumably simple and unmixed ideas of sensation. Locke deals with this problem in varied and confusing ways. At times he speaks of ideas as bringing along certain other ideas. He also speaks of the mind's ability to "intuit," "notice," and "trace" certain "natural connections" among ideas.[5] These observations are not only left largely unelaborated and unanalyzed in Locke but also would seem to be in conflict with a strictly atomistic doctrine of simple ideas.

Another strategy Locke adopts in an effort to explain the relations among ideas is to resort to the mind's "combining" and "comparing" activities. In fact, Locke is very impressed by the unlimited extent of this ordering activity of the mind which, he said, is "infinitely beyond what sensation or reflection furnished it with." And the number of "complex ideas," the results of the mind's combinatory activity, is "infinite and the variety endless."[6] As H. H. Price has remarked, it is "historically false that the Empiricists thought the human mind passive. It would be more just to criticize them for making it more active than it can possibly be."[7]

Locke's reference to the wide-ranging possibilities involved in the mind's combinatory activity provided an enormous amount of impetus to the development of modern theories of the imagination and aesthetic creativity. But the mechanism of such activity remains almost totally unexplained in the *Essay*,

[5] Locke, *Essay*, bk. 2, chap. 14, no. 1; bk. 4, chap. 2, no. 1; bk. 2, chap. 23, no. 1; bk. 2, chap. 33, no. 5.

[6] Ibid., bk. 2, chap. 12, nos. 2–3.

[7] Quoted in John W. Yolton, "Locke's Concept of Experience," in *Locke and Berkeley: A Collection of Critical Essays*, ed. C. B. Martin and D. M. Armstrong (Garden City, N.Y.: Doubleday, 1968), p. 41.

nor was its conflict with the empiricistic stress upon sensation as the sole foundation of knowledge dealt with at all. If the mind is actively involved, as Locke admits, it does contribute something to cognition. Locke was very reluctant to discuss this matter, probably because he was loathe to attribute any sort of a priori structure to the mind. And he was hesitant to concede such a structure of the mind, probably because he felt that to do so would be to view the mind as innately possessing full-fledged, ready-made ideas and axioms.[8]

Scholars have pointed out that another approach Locke could have considered, but apparently did not, was to endow the mind not with completed ideas but rather with the capacity to do something to or make something of the simple ideas it received, though of course this capacity operates only when it is given impressions upon which to act.[9] Such a view would have enabled Locke to explain the psychological basis and mechanism of the ordering activity of the mind with minimal compromise of his insistence upon sense impressions as fundamental. Such a dispositional conception of the mind's capacity could have reconciled the mind's own activity vis-à-vis sense ideas with the sense ideas passively received through sensation; both the active and passive sides of the mind's cognitive process would thereby be given their proper roles. Jonathan Edwards took up precisely this general approach. Edwards did accept Locke's basic empiricistic maxim that knowledge must be through, and based upon, sensation. But, seeing that this empiricistic principle did not necessitate the doctrine of the mind as a tabula rasa, and also realizing that an appeal to the mind's combinatory activity was unavoidable even in Locke's own account, Edwards set out to formulate a dispositional conception of the mind's capacities.

An inspiration for Edwards' own theory was present in an inchoate way in Locke's *Essay*. Locke, a complex thinker, inspired Edwards not only into empiricism but in a way also out

---

[8] For a discussion of the central problem in Locke's theory of the knowledge process, see ibid., pp. 40–52. See also C. R. Morris, *Locke-Berkeley-Hume*, pp. 50–53.

[9] See C. R. Morris, *Locke-Berkeley-Hume*, p. 26.

of it. In a historically influential chapter called "Of the Association of Ideas," Locke offered a discussion of the connections among ideas that contains the seeds of a dispositional theory of the imagination. The "natural connections" among ideas, he says, are "traced" by what he calls "reason." But ideas are also associated with one another through the presumably nonrational principle of custom and habit. "Ideas, that in themselves are not at all of kin," he tells us, "come to be so united in some men's minds that it is very hard to separate them." These sorts of connections occur with automatic spontaneity, as "the one no sooner at any time comes into the understanding but its associate appears with it." Locke refers to the automatic power involved here as "custom" and the "habits of thinking," and further points out that the directions of their operations are influenced by the "different inclinations, education, interests, etc."[10]

Here, a nonintellectualistic conception of the mind's ordering activity is presented. In the Aristotelian-Scholastic tradition, mental activity was seen as an intellectual act of abstracting the common elements or universals from the composite particulars. The active intellect then directly intuits the universal idea or form. But now Locke is dealing not with composite particulars but rather with unmixed simple ideas, and no common element could be abstracted from them. The mental activity involved in the mind's experience of the relations among simple ideas, then, would have to be different from the process of abstraction.[11] In the chapter on the habitual association of ideas, Locke moves toward such a conception. The connections among ideas are here explained as being based upon their being held together in the mind's view through the force of custom or habit. The universals and the structure of reality are seen here as relations and not forms, and the power involved in the perception of these universals is being viewed as

[10] Locke, *Essay*, bk. 2, chap. 33, nos. 5–6. The influence of Locke's *Essay*, particularly the chapter entitled "Of the Association of Ideas," on the development of modern theories of the imagination is traced in Tuveson, *Imagination as a Means of Grace*, esp. pp. 5–41.

[11] See "The Mind," No. 42, WEA, pp. 360–361.

a nondiscursive principle of habit rather than the passive and active intellect. A dispositional mechanism of the mind's associative activity is thereby suggested—a notion that could explain the mind's active role in cognition without jettisoning either the doctrine of simple ideas or the empiricistic stress upon sensation as fundamental.

The rationalistic side of Locke prevails, however. He calls the habitual associations of ideas a "madness" that produces only the "unnatural" and accidental connections, and does not apply the principle to the mind's combinatory activity in general.[12] Functioning here also must have been the above-mentioned Cartesian bias against the nonintellectual and practical forces within the human self. Customs, habits, and inclinations could not be accorded a legitimate cognitive function. Further, Locke seems not to have been clear in his mind about the status of habits. He wavers between the notion of habits as active forces and the positivistic view of them as mere customs or descriptions of facts. Locke, therefore, was not prepared to see the habitual associations of ideas as being the results of the activity of the mind. More daring and consistent than Locke, David Hume made the habitual associations of ideas the general principle of all the relations among ideas, including the natural or normal ones. In this respect, he moved in the same direction as Edwards. But like Locke, Hume was not prepared to see dispositions and habits as the source of a necessary and true knowledge of the objective world, and his skeptical conclusions could not be diverted.[13]

Locke was not the only thinker whose writings were important to Edwards in his consideration of the problem of mental activity. There was also Cudworth, Shaftesbury, and other Cambridge philosophers whose vigorous defense of a dynamic view of the human mind against Hobbes' mechanistic perspective surely must have exercised a great influence upon Edwards. Cudworth spoke of the mind as "senior to the world,

[12] Locke, *Essay*, bk. 2, chap. 33, no. 3.
[13] See C. R. Morris, *Locke-Berkeley-Hume*, pp. 137–145; Marjorie Grene, *The Knower and the Known* (New York: Basic Books, 1966), pp. 98–102.

and the architect," capable of a kind of "self-activity" in perception itself.[14] The forward-looking element in Cudworth's epistemological discussions, as Basil Willey points out, is that for him "not only every process of abstract thought, but every *perception* contained some element contributed by the mind."[15] Sensation itself, Cudworth says, is not a "mere passion" but a "perception of that passion," thus involving something that the mind itself does.[16] Following Cudworth quite closely, Shaftesbury characterized the mind as a "forming" power that can grasp an organic whole out of particular parts. As Ernst Cassirer has stressed, Shaftesbury saw reality itself as inherently dynamic, and knowledge, not as an act that rests once the end is achieved, but rather as a creative process.[17] These and other Cambridge thinkers must have provided Edwards with much inspiration for his own dynamic view of knowledge and reality.

However, the epistemological view of these men must have appeared to Edwards as insufficient responses to Locke's empiricistic doctrines of sensation and of the simple ideas. Both Cudworth and Shaftesbury still tended to work with the notion that at least potentially present in the mind are some presumably ready-made innate ideas waiting to be made explicit by sense stimuli. Cudworth was decidedly more traditional at this point than the others. He spoke of the mind's creative activity in the cognitive process as one of applying to sense data the "intelligible ideas exerted from the mind itself, that is, by something native and domestic to it."[18] Shaftesbury saw the nature of innate ideas somewhat differently. Innate ideas, such as the idea of God, are "in a manner innate, or such as men

[14] Cudworth, *True Intellectual System*, 1: 420, quoted in Basil Willey, *The Seventeenth-Century Background* (Garden City, N.Y.: Doubleday, 1953), p. 158.

[15] Willey, *Seventeenth-Century Background*, p. 161.

[16] Cudworth, *True Intellectual System*, 3: 62, quoted in Willey, *Seventeenth-Century Background*, p. 160.

[17] See Cassirer, *Philosophy of the Enlightenment*, pp. 326–327.

[18] Cudworth, *True Intellectual System*, 3: 62, quoted in Willey, *Seventeenth-Century Background*, p. 160. For a discussion of the rationalistic dimensions in Cudworth's thought, see Hunt, "Plastic Nature," pp. 99–105.

were really born to and could hardly by any means avoid."[19] Sense stimuli are necessary for the innate ideas to become explicit. To that extent, Shaftesbury tried to take Lockean empiricism seriously. Nevertheless, his innate ideas are still completed, full-fledged ideas, and thus quite different from Locke's simple, discrete "atoms" of sensation. When innate ideas, simple or complex, are seen as full-fledged ideas waiting to be made explicit, the mind could be active only in becoming aware of them or in using them but *not* in forming or formulating them. But if one takes Locke's doctrine of simple ideas seriously, the mind's combinatory and ordering activity must be seen, as it was in Locke's own *Essay*, as involved in the very formation of at least the complex ideas and of their relations.[20] What is the nature of such activity of the mind? How can such an activity be conceived of without undermining the empiricistic stress upon the simple ideas of sensation as the fundamental materials of all knowledge? These questions are not confronted head-on in the writings of Cudworth and Shaftesbury.

Edwards took Locke's empiricism much more seriously than the Cambridge philosophers did, and the questions just mentioned were real questions for him. In an early series of notes called "Subjects to Be Handled in the Treatise on the Mind," Edwards writes:

> Sensation. How far all acts of the mind are from sensation; all ideas begin from thence and there never can be any idea, thought, or act of the mind unless the mind first received some ideas from sensation, or some other way equivalent, wherein the mind is wholly passive in receiving them.[21]

Sensation is fundamental: whatever else there may be in the total content of the cognitive process, sensation is the indis-

---

[19] Shaftesbury, *Characteristicks*, 2: 178, quoted in Grean, *Shaftesbury's Philosophy of Religion and Ethics*, p. 251.

[20] See Locke, *Essay*, bk. 2, chap. 12, nos. 1–2; Yolton, "Locke's Concept of Experience," pp. 40–52.

[21] "Subjects to Be Handled in the Treatise on the Mind," No. 29, WEA, p. 390.

pensable beginning. And, as Edwards' remarks at various places make clear, the ideas of sensation are simple ideas.[22] No complex ideas and relations are received through the senses in their explicit and completed form, nor are there any innate ideas in the mind's own structure just waiting to become explicit. In this way, Edwards accepted the fundamental concerns of Locke's empiricism. Knowledge is to be attained through a direct contact with the world. But then, how can the mind also be active in the knowledge process? Edwards did not soften the issue at all but faced it head-on.

As already indicated, a dispositional theory of the imagination is Edwards' solution to the problem I have been outlining. Unlike Locke, Edwards is working with a newly conceived, realist conception of dispositions and habits. As shall be seen, the imaginative activity, as based upon the active and yet conditional power of habit, will mediate between the mind's own shaping activity and the simple ideas of sensation. Not only does Edwards approach the problem of mental activity with a reworked doctrine of habit, but also, as was indicated, with a reworked metaphysical framework. The effect that Edwards' relational, aesthetic, and dynamic ontology might have upon the significance of the imagination has already been intimated. Two implications of Edwards' ontology for his epistemological considerations may be raised here.

First of all, in Edwards one is dealing with a perspective that does not think dualistically about matter and mind, the known world and the knower. The distinction between them is still there. The mind is intelligent and creative, but matter is not. The mental and spiritual is the more substantial or elemental force in the scheme of reality, while the material is an image of it. Nevertheless, both dimensions of reality are constituted and governed by similar principles—namely, by habits. Thus, in Edwards' perspective, knowledge is in principle a possibility, and the works of the imagination have the capacity to contain what is real.

The second point is the effect that Edwards' radically rela-

---

[22] See, for example, "The Mind," No. 42, WEA, pp. 360–61.

tional ontology has upon the Lockean doctrine of the simple ideas. Being, for Edwards, is essentially relational, and individuality (simplicity) and relations are correlative and overlapping categories.[23] The essence of an entity is a tendency to particular sorts of relationships. Thus, just as the atoms of the cosmos are tendencies to relations, the "atoms" of sensations are also inherently dispositions to be related with one another in particular ways. Unlike Locke, therefore, Edwards saw the simple ideas of sensation as coming into the mind with a readiness for relations.[24] Such a logic must be seen as underlying some of Edwards' comments.

> So that God has not only distributed things into species by evidently manifesting (by His making such an agreement in things) that He designed such and such particulars to be together in the mind; but by making the soul of such a manner that those particulars which He thus made to agree are unavoidably together in the mind—one naturally exciting and including the others.[25]

The relations among ideas, then, have as their basis both the structure of the mind and also the tendencies inherent in the simple ideas themselves. Here again one sees that continuity and not disjunction prevails in Edwards' view of the nature of things. Edwards is thereby equipped with an ontological framework in which the interaction between the mind and the world can have a cognitive import.

THE IMAGINATION OF THE HABIT OF MIND
The Activity and Receptivity of the Imagination

As I now turn to Edwards' view of the imagination, a terminological clarification is necessary. In Edwards' explicit usage, the term "imagination" has a rather narrow meaning. The imagination is, he declares,

[23] For further discussion of this point, see Chap. 4 above.
[24] See "The Mind," No. 43, WEA, pp. 361–362.
[25] Ibid., p. 362.

that power of the mind, whereby it can have a conception, or idea of things of *an external or outward* nature (that is, of such sort of things as are the objects of the outward senses), when those things are not present, and be not perceived by the senses. (Emphasis added)[26]

Edwards' use of the term in this narrow sense probably originates from his reading of the Platonistic and rationalistic thinkers of his time, such as Cudworth. Philosophers of the rationalistic persuasion, with their stress upon the "clear and distinct ideas" and "intelligible forms," were preoccupied with the dangers of the nonrational wanderings of the imagination, and tended to associate the imagination more with the physical or sensual than with the mental or rational.[27] Edwards adopts their usage of the term "imagination," and often points out himself the dangers of erroneous acts of judgment that can result from the imagination.[28] He clearly left the rationalistic world view, however, and in his thought relations, beauty, and affections have the primacy over form, concept, and the discursive intellect. And, as I shall demonstrate shortly, the mind's nondiscursive shaping power plays a central role in his thought. But he did not call this power the

[26] *Religious Affections*, pp. 210–211.

[27] Donald F. Bond has observed, "This aspect of the imagination, as the power whereby the mind is cognizant of external objects without the direct sensory stimulus, is prevalent through the period," i.e., the late seventeenth century. In addition, there was a widespread disparagement of the imagination in this restricted sense due to the strong rationalistic tendencies during this period. Bond also traces, in his essays, the emergence of the romantic conception of the imagination as a creative or synthesizing power through the influence of Hobbes and Locke. Jonathan Edwards develops a modern conception of the imagination as a synthetic power, but tends to use the term "imagination" in the seventeenth century's restrictive sense. Edwards' nomenclature, so to speak, has not caught up with his theory. See Donald F. Bond, " 'Distrust' of the Imagination in English Neo-Classicism," *Philological Quarterly* 14 (1935): 54–69; idem, "The Neo-Classical Psychology of the Imagination," *Journal of English Literary History* 4 (1937): 245–264.

[28] See, for example, "Of Being," wea, p. 204; *Religious Affections*, p. 210; "Some Thoughts concerning the Revival," in *The Great Awakening*, ed. C. C. Goen, vol. 4 of *The Works of Jonathan Edwards* (New Haven: Yale University Press, 1972), p. 460.

imagination. Edwards' language at this point lags behind his thought.

In this study, I shall use the term "imagination" in its modern and broader sense—that is, to refer to the mind's activity of ordering and relating particular ideas of all sorts, external and also mental. I do so because Edwards' conception of mental activity sorely needs to be brought into view and deserves to be accorded an important place in the history of modern theories of creative process along with the theories of such pivotal figures as Shaftesbury, Addison, Kant, and Coleridge.

The fundamental materials of knowledge, according to Edwards, consist of the simple ideas received through the five external senses, and the simple ideas of reflection, that is, the ideas of such acts of the mind as thought, love, fear, and so on.[29] And the relations among these ideas are experienced by the mind as the mind, through the imaginative or ordering activity of its propensive power of habit, responds to those ideas by holding them in a certain way.

> How exceedingly apt are we, when we are sitting and accidentally casting our eye upon some marks or spots in the floor or wall, to be ranging of them into regular parcels and figures and, if we see a mark out of its place, to be placing of it right by our imagination. So we may catch ourselves at observing the rules of harmony and regularity in the careless motions of our heads or feet, and even when playing with our hands, or walking about the room.[30]

In another entry in "The Mind," Edwards makes it clear that the activity of "ranging" our ideas according to the "rules of harmony or regularity" is a propensive activity of the mind's habit:

> The mind perceives that some of its ideas agree, in a manner very different from all its other ideas. The mind therefore is determined to rank those ideas together in its thoughts; and all new ideas it receives with the like agreement it naturally

[29] "Miscellanies," Nos. 123, 238, HGT, pp. 245–248.
[30] "The Mind," No. 1, WEA, p. 336.

and habitually and at once places to the same rank and order and calls them by the same name; and by the nature, determination, and habit of the mind the idea of one excites the idea of others.[31]

Besides the rule of harmony or regularity, there are two other general ways in which the mind orders its ideas: cause and effect, and contiguity. These rules or patterns of relations presumably cover all possible relations among ideas. I will discuss the meaning of these rules in the next section. My point here is that all of these three types of relations are brought about in the mind through the activity of its habit. It has been demonstrated that this is the case with the rule of harmony or regularity. In regard to the cause-and-effect relation, Edwards asserts that there is a "habit of mind" or a "necessary, fatal propensity" whereby when we see "anything begin to be, we intuitively know there is a cause of it."[32]

An example of the mind's ordering activity according to contiguity is the human skill to use language. The connection between certain sounds or letters and what they signify is formed through a habit acquired by a repeated experience of them as contiguous with each other.

> Having learned by frequent experience, our minds in the presence of the sign being habitually led to the relations and connections with other things, the presence of the sign in the mind does by custom as naturally and spontaneously suggest many relations of the thing signified to others, as the hearing of such a certain sound or seeing such letters does by custom and habit spontaneously excite such a thought.[33]

Four aspects of the nature of the mind's imaginative activity become apparent at this point. First of all, the mind responds to the ideas of sensation by ordering them in relation to the initial bias of its habit. The mind completes the initial direction of its habit by construing the order among ideas in rela-

[31] "The Mind," No. 42, WEA, p. 361.
[32] "The Mind," No. 54, WEA, p. 370.
[33] "Miscellanies," No. 782, HGT, p. 117.

tion to that direction.[34] Because of the regulative ideal of its habit, the mind refuses to experience its ideas in meaningless jumbles and insists on "placing" and "ranging" them into "regular parcels and figures," that is, into meaningful wholes. When the mind receives simultaneously a group of ideas that together make up a meaningful pattern (e.g., a regular parcel of marks on the wall), the mind goes over those ideas, as it were, and makes explicit in consciousness the relationship of those marks as a regular parcel. If a mark is out of its place, the mind places it right in order to construe the given ideas as a meaningful pattern. The imagination thus loosens up as well as builds the perceived world. A mark on the wall that is out of its place is taken out of that place, so to speak, and an absent though appropriate mark is brought into view and placed in the proper place in order to fill the gap. The direction given to the imagination by the initial habit, therefore, can influence the mind's apprehension of the relational meaning of a given set of sense data.

But, such an activity of the imagination would not be triggered unless at least some of the sense ideas themselves suggest or demand a particular meaningful pattern. Some of the marks or spots on the wall must at least suggest a particular pattern if the imagination is going to construe them in that particular way. The ideas themselves must suggest a particular sort of agreement, to refer to the second passage quoted above, if the imagination is going to "rank and order" them together. In addition, there is the suggestion in the passages quoted above that a particular case of relatedness may function as what might be called an organizing image or a paradigm for the future activities of the imagination. As Edwards says, once the mind experiences two ideas agreeing "in a manner very different from all its other ideas . . . all new ideas it receives with the like agreement it naturally and habitually and at once

[34] In my analysis of Edwards' conception of the imagination, I have found very helpful the descriptions of various types of theories of the imagination in Ray L. Hart, *Unfinished Man and the Imagination: Toward an Ontology and a Rhetoric of Revelation* (New York: Herder and Herder, 1968), pp. 315–402.

places to the same rank and order." For example, as the mind experiences two particular human beings and their similarities with each other in being human, this particular sort of agreement called human-ness determines the imagination of the mind's habit in such a way that all other human beings it encounters will be placed in the same camp, so to speak, and will be called by the same generic name. Just as the direction of the imagination determines how a given group of ideas are mutually related, the specific ideas and relations that the mind encounters can affect and modify the specific character of the imagination's direction. I shall return to this point when I discuss the process in which the general dispositions of the mind are given specific directions by concrete experiences. My point here is that the direction of the organizing activity of the mind's habit is provided by the initial direction of the habit, and that concrete sense stimuli trigger the propensive imagination and also are sometimes capable of modifying the specific manner of the imaginative activity. There is indeed a two-way commerce between sensation and the imagination.

The second aspect of the mechanism of the imagination is that a given group of concrete ideas must be held together in the mind's view in order for them to be experienced by the mind as making up a significant relationship. " 'Tis certain that the human soul can have two ideas and more at the same moment in time; otherwise, how could the mind compare ideas and judge between them?"[35] Since the mind works not with composite images of things (as in the Aristotelian-Scholastic view) but rather with simple ideas, the structure of the world cannot be experienced through some abstract ideas that are separated from the particulars; the order can be experienced only as the particular simple ideas themselves stand together in a certain way in the mind's consciousness. In order to experience the relational meaning of an idea, one does not put that idea under a more general idea or form and measure against it; one must rather "excite" its fellow ideas and let them stand next to it. So, Edwards states that the strength of

[35] "Miscellanies," No. 81, Yale MSS.

a mind and its comprehension consists in its ability to "excite several ideas at once to that degree as to see their connections and relations."[36] The mind does not move away from the ideas of sensation toward higher levels of universality or abstraction but rather stays with them when it is experiencing the relations of those ideas.

The ultimate relational meaning of a given group of ideas can be apprehended only by seeing those ideas in their relationship with the meaning of the ultimate, God. Such perfecting of vision, however, is to be achieved not through a spiritual ascent that totally transcends the earthly ideas of sensation but rather by setting those very ideas side by side—ultimately, side by side with the meaning of the whole reality as manifested in God's history of redemption. Any mysticism of the sort that would abrogate the essential place of time and history in cognition is fundamentally incompatible with Edwards' conception of the imagination.[37]

The third aspect of the imagination that must be pointed out is its spontaneous, immediate, and nondiscursive manner of operation. The habit's imaginative activity is ordered and structured but works "at once" and without "rationation or any kind of argument."[38] The mind does not have to understand conceptually and logically the particular kind of relation that exists among a given group of ideas; the mind through its habit is simply determined to respond to certain ideas in a cer-

---

[36] "Miscellanies," No. 782, HGT, p. 118.

[37] The term "mysticism" is difficult to define. Edwards is indeed a mystic if one means by that term one who emphasizes the immediate or nondiscursive character of the aesthetic experience. What I am insisting is that the immediacy, for Edwards, does not bypass or supplant in any way the particular sense ideas received through the regular organs of sensation. It is precisely in and through these sense ideas that the ineffable and intuitive experience of the saint happens. Thus, Richard Niebuhr's reference to a "marriage of empiricism and mysticism" in Edwards' religious epistemology is very appropriate. See Richard R. Niebuhr, *Streams of Grace: Studies of Jonathan Edwards, Samuel Taylor Coleridge, and William James* (Kyoto: Doshisha University Press, 1983), p. 35. See also Chap. 6, n. 16, below.

[38] See "The Mind," Nos. 42, 59, WEA, pp. 46, 56–57; "Miscellanies," No. 268, HGT, pp. 78–79.

tain way. The mind's propensive and nonintellectual activity of ordering its ideas is not to be guided or controlled by some superior faculty of the self; the rationality of the imagination is determined by the direction of the mind's habit itself. And it is through the activity of the habit's imagination that the human mind can cognitively reach the inner structure of reality. The habit and its imagination, in other words, know something that conceptual understanding by itself can never know. Habit functions automatically, in a nondiscursive way. But in this automatic character lies its power and influence. Habits and dispositions, as Edwards writes in *Religious Affections*, determine the direction of all the intellectual and moral functions of the human self. The habit and its imagination do not constitute an esoteric faculty operating separately from the total economy of the human personality, nor do they abrogate the regular workings of the mind and heart. Habit functions in, under, and with the intellect and the affections in its work of establishing the alignment of the total person with the nature of things.[39] In this way, the mind's imagination, or its propensive and nondiscursive activity of ordering its ideas, determines the health or the corruption of the manner in which a person understands, feels, and acts.

The highest possible cognitive and moral function accorded here to the imagination stands in contrast to the more secondary role assigned to it in the intellectualistic doctrines of knowledge. In Thomistic epistemology, for example, the function of the imagination is one of mediating between sensation and the active intellect. The imagination holds still, so to speak, the images received through sensation so that the active intellect can abstract the forms from them, divesting them of all other elements. So knowledge consists in the intellectualization of form, and it is the active intellect, and not the imagination, that can extricate the conceptual essence from sense impressions. The intellect, in short, is the mind's ability to discern the pattern and structure of reality, and the imagination serves the subordinate role of making available the initial

[39] *Religious Affections*, p. 206.

mental contents for the active intellect.[40] In Edwards, there is a rather different situation. It is the habit and its imagination, not the discursive intellect, that possesses the ability to detect or discern the structure within sense impressions. Further, the imagination, for Edwards, does not merely hold sense impressions together but puts them into certain relationships, and to these relationships the activity of discursive and conceptual reason will be bound. As the conception of the structure of reality moves from the realm of intelligible forms and abstract ideas to the realm of the relations among particulars, the locus of the rational power in the human self also shifts from rationation to imagination. As a person imagines, so will she or he perceive, understand, love, and act.

I now come to the fourth aspect of Edwards' psychology of the imagination: the function fulfilled by its creativity, and the active/passive nature of this creativity. The mind's ordering activity is creative not only in its ability to make explicit the relations among simple ideas but also in its capacity to place those relations into a context larger than what is given in sensation at a particular moment. The mind is able to recall or excite some absent and yet appropriate ideas in order to place the presently given ideas into some coherent pattern. Such creativity is particularly important for Edwards because of his view that the ideal knowledge of things requires a perception of them "in their true relations and respects to other things, and to things in general."[41] And the reference to the "things in general" or the whole system of being can be made by relating everything to the superlative beauty manifested in Christ and in the history of redemption. At any rate, as the mind orders its ideas into a particular type of relationship, the mind must gauge and weigh that relationship with respect to its harmony with the beauty of God. This widening of vision, which makes the true apprehension of the essence of things possible, is the creative contribution that the imaginative activity of the mind's habit makes to the cognitive process. This creative out-

---

[40] Hart, *Unfinished Man and the Imagination*, pp. 318–334.
[41] "Miscellanies," No. 408, HGT, p. 249.

reach of the imagination, then, constitutes the rationality of the habit and its imagination.

It is important to note, however, that the mind does not make or impose order upon its ideas, but rather asserts it in the mind by making explicit the relations to which the ideas themselves already tend. As I have already indicated, the simple ideas in Edwards' view must be seen as also essentially relational—that is, as being tendencies to certain sorts of relationships. For this reason, Edwards often speaks of the mind's propensive activity of holding together its ideas in certain relations, and the attraction of ideas toward one another, as two dimensions of one and the same phenomenon.

> For it is to be observed, that one thing which contributes to the beauty of the agreement and proportion of various things, is their relation to one another; which connects them, and introduces them together into view and consideration, and whereby one suggests the other to the mind, and the mind is led to compare them, and so to expect and desire agreement.[42]

So the mind can be said to "expect and desire" to hold together those ideas which agree with one another, but it is equally true to say that "one [idea] suggests the other to the mind." In a passage previously quoted, Edwards can say in the same breath that the mind "habitually places to the same rank" those ideas which agree with one another and also that "the idea of one excites the idea of others."[43] In "The Mind," Edwards once commented that the ideas of all things are in a sense within a single idea because they "necessarily suppose it."[44] All ideas, then, suppose one another and tend to be mutually related. Therefore, when the mind is actively placing its ideas into a relational context larger than what is immediately given in sensation, it is not making any relations ex nihilo but is actualizing in consciousness the relational possibilities inherent within the ideas themselves.

[42] *True Virtue*, p. 29.
[43] "The Mind," No. 42, WEA, p. 361.
[44] "The Mind," No. 34, WEA, p. 354.

Here is a conception of the imagination in which activity and passivity, creativity and receptivity, coalesce into one process.[45] The imagination's ordering and broadening activity is the very vehicle through which the structural tendencies of the world are made mentally explicit. The point is that without the creativity of the imagination, the relations of ideas cannot be in the mind's consciousness at all. But then the world that the mind experiences is a network of relational tendencies, and it is these objectively real relational meanings that become explicit through the imagination's creativity. Habit is a conditional power that has its own end and design but works only by being stimulated by appropriate occasions. The imagination with habit as its motive power, therefore, is conditioned in its operation by both the idealizing power of the mind's habit and also the character of the sense impressions themselves. The mind and the world are both networks of relational tendencies, and it is in the creative activity of the mind's imagination that both networks of tendencies are exercised and thereby actualized.

Here then one begins to see how Edwards brings together sensation and mental activity—two elements that stood in an uneasy juxtaposition in Locke. This analysis of Edwards' synthesis of activity and receptivity is not complete, however, without an explication of his contention that the simultaneously creative and receptive activity of the imagination is an activity of *sensing* and that the mind's habit or the power of such an imagination is a power of *sensation*. To prepare fully to understand this further step Edwards takes, one should first look at what I call the rules that are followed by the imagination.

The Three General Rules of the Imagination. Locke believed that the connections of ideas formed by the force of habit were all the results of the repeated experiences of accidental asso-

---

[45] Edwards here anticipates Coleridge, who described the imagination as "an intermediate faculty which connects the active with the passive powers of our nature, the intellect with the senses" (quoted in Bate, *From Classic to Romantic*, p. 185).

ciations.[46] For Edwards, however, all the connections among ideas, including the natural ones, are formed by the mind's habit, and the imaginative activity of the habit is not by chance but according to the three general, innate patterns or rules.

Connections of Ideas. Concerning the Laws by which Ideas follow each other, or call up one another, in which one thing comes into the mind after another, in the course of our thinking. How far this is owing to the Association of ideas; and how far, to any Relation of Cause and effect, or any other Relation. And whether the whole may not be reduced to these following: *Association of Ideas; Resemblance of some kind*; and that *Natural Disposition* in us, when we see any thing begin to be, to suppose it owing to a Cause.[47]

Although Edwards does not say so in this passage, he contends at other places that all three sorts of relations are brought about by the activity of the mind's habit or disposition. The first of the three laws is the "association of ideas." Unlike most other eighteenth-century thinkers, Edwards uses the phrase "association of ideas" to refer to only one of the connections of ideas.[48] And the phrase actually refers to the rule of *conti-*

[46] Locke, *Essay*, bk. 2, chap. 33, nos. 1–5.

[47] "Subjects to Be Handled in the Treatise on the Mind," No. 43, WEA, pp. 391–392. There is a striking similarity between this passage and David Hume's list of the kinds of connections among ideas, although Hume and Edwards were working with quite different views of the ontological and epistemic significance of the relations among ideas. Hume wrote, "To me, there appear to be only three principles of connexion among ideas, namely, *Resemblance, Contiguity* in time or place, and *Cause or Effect*" (*Enquiries concerning the Human Understanding and concerning the Principles of Morals*, ed. L. A. Selby-Bigge [Oxford: Clarendon Press, 1951], sect. 3, no. 19). There seems to be little chance, however, that Edwards is in any way indebted to Hume on this matter. Paul Ramsey has observed that Edwards "probably read Hume as late as 1755, or nearly two years after finishing the *Inquiry*," i.e., *Freedom of the Will* (Ramsey, "Editor's Introduction," in *Freedom of the Will*, p. 15).

[48] See Martin Kallich, "The Association of Ideas and Critical Theory: Hobbes, Locke and Addison," *Journal of English Literary History* 12 (1945): 297.

guity of time or place. Whenever Edwards uses "association of ideas," he has in mind the connections of ideas that are formed through the repeated experiences of certain ideas as temporally or spatially contiguous. The mind, in other words, possesses by nature the initial direction of associating together the ideas that have been experienced as next to each other. This capacity of the mind's habit, according to Edwards, is very useful to human beings because many of their skills and abilities depend on it. The ability to use language, for example, has as its source the habit of associating certain sounds and signs with certain ideas and things.[49] The connections of this kind, however, do not represent the essential relational structure of things; they merely point to the temporal and spatial circumstances of those ideas in their immediate, and thus limited, context. For this reason, these kinds of connections can be false representations of the relations among ideas.[50] And the habit involved here can be the source of many incorrect and prejudicial judgments of the nature of things.

The other two ways in which ideas come to be connected with one another in the mind are *resemblance* and *causality*. These sorts of relations, unlike circumstantial contiguity, do represent the connections to which sense ideas themselves have a natural tendency. But even of these two, it is the relation of resemblance that can most directly refer to the essence of things. This is so because the structure of being is beauty, and resemblance or similarity is the general characteristic of all forms of beauty. It is, therefore, the habit to order ideas according to various forms of resemblance, and not the habit to order ideas in terms of contiguity and causality, that makes an experience of the true nature of things at least in principle a possibility.[51]

In light of this centrality of beauty in Edwards' view of the nature of things, it is also not surprising that he sees the habit

[49] "Miscellanies," No. 782, HGT, pp. 115–118; see also, "The Mind," No. 59, WEA, pp. 373–375.
[50] "Subjects to Be Handled in the Treatise on the Mind," No. 2, WEA, p. 387.
[51] See "The Mind," No. 1, WEA, pp. 332–338.

to order ideas in resembling relations as the basic structure of the human self (what Edwards calls "self-love" or the "inclination" which is the ability to be pleased by what is beautiful).[52] It is the movement to beauty that gives the life of the self an integration and unity. The activities of ordering ideas in contiguous or causal relations can be very superficial and peripheral operations of the human mind. The habit to order ideas in resembling relations, however, functions only by engaging both of the two essential powers of the self—the understanding and the inclination. The understanding is involved because there must be some actual ideas that may be ordered into resembling relations. And the inclination (i.e., the ability to be pleased or displeased by the beauty or deformity of the object) is also involved since the mind unavoidably would be pleased by the relation of resemblance that the mind's imaginative activity makes explicit. As I have mentioned, Edwards writes in *Religious Affections* that habits and dispositions do not make up a separate faculty alongside other regular functions of the self. The habit of ordering ideas in resembling relations, then, is a "manner or kind of exercise" of both of the essential powers of the self and thus of the whole person.[53] In short, it is through the functioning of this habit that the relational tendencies of both the knowing mind and the known objects can be given their fullest expression.

These three general laws of ordering ideas, according to Edwards, are subject to modifications through experience. In other words, the mind's inborn general directions of habit and imagination acquire more specific directions through the stimuli of concrete experiences. Such a conditioning process is implicit in Edwards' discussion of all three directions of habit, and one example is his discussion of the way the mind acquires the ability to order ideas into various species and genera.

If a person, a stranger to the earth, should see and converse with a man and a long time after should meet with another

[52] *True Virtue*, p. 42.
[53] *Religious Affections*, p. 206.

man and converse with him, the agreement would immediately excite the idea of that other man, and those two ideas would be together in his mind for the time to come, yea, in spite of him.[54]

And the following portion of a passage already quoted completes Edwards' point:

And all new ideas [the mind] receives with the like agreement it naturally and habitually and at once places to the same rank and order and calls them by the same name; and by the nature, determination, and habit of mind the idea of one excites the idea of others.[55]

The mind's habit to relate together all resembling ideas led the "stranger to the earth" to rank together the ideas of the first two men. But through his experience of the similarity between the first two human beings, he would develop the specific habit of relating together all beings who have the characteristics of being human. The specific habit thus formed is not another habit alongside the general habit of relating all resembling ideas together, but is simply a specific way in which a general habit would function. Through the actual experience of certain ideas that resemble one another in a particular way, the general habit learns to hold together those once-experienced resembling ideas and all other similarly resembling ideas. The sense stimuli are the instigators of the conditioning process as well as what triggers the specific habits.

The three general habits are the a priori element in the imagination and in the knowledge process. All *specific* ideas and the *specific* directions of the general habits are not a priori but come from sensation. The experience of the relations, then, is very much the product of the collaboration between what is a priori and what is sensation originated. In other words, in the mind's experience of the relations of ideas, the inborn propensities of the mind and what is received through sensation mesh into one integrated process.

[54] "The Mind," No. 43, WEA, pp. 361–362.
[55] "The Mind," No. 42, WEA, p. 361.

While the general directions of the imagination are in the mind independent of experience, they are also substantively open to the influences of the experience. The general rules of the imagination's operations cannot be changed in their innately given directions, but the specific directions and functions are shaped and molded by the sense ideas and sense images that the mind encounters. But, at the same time, erroneous connections of ideas could also be "beat[en] into us by every act of sensation" that they are "so incorporated with our very minds that whatsoever is objected to them, contrary thereunto, is as it were different to the very constitution of them."[56]

A question now arises. In order for the perception of the relationship among a particular set of sense impressions to influence the imagination and give its direction a specific content, the mind would first have to be able to order that particular set of sense impressions in the proper way. And to order those ideas in their proper relationship, the mind would first have to have the proper habit or the proper direction of its habit and imagination. Presumably, the mind's general habits of ordering ideas according to the rules of contiguity and causality are sufficient for the mind to "recognize" and order all contiguously and causally related ideas as so related in the mind's *first* encounter with them. But is this true for the habit of ordering ideas according to the rule of "resemblance of some kind"? Is that general habit the sufficient capacity to recognize all forms of "resemblance" including the proportion in God's transcendent beauty? As shall be seen below, human beings, according to Edwards, are not capable of attaining, through their own resources, the specific habit of recognizing the divine sort of beauty due to their fallen condition. The general analysis I gave to the mind's inborn dispositions and their conditioning process via concrete sense stimuli, then, requires qualification and refinement in reference to the rule of resemblance. Nature is not going to be sufficient; grace will be needed.

[56] "Of the Prejudices of Imagination," WEA, p. 196.

The Possibility of the Knowledge. It is not that the fallen humankind's experience of all beauty is totally invalid. Edwards does recognize that men and women do have the capacity to delight in many things as beautiful. But, he says, these are of secondary or natural beauty. A sort of "regularity, order, uniformity, symmetry, proportion, harmony, etc.," is involved in such inanimate as well as animate things as the various sides of a square, or an equilateral triangle, the beautiful proportion of the various parts of a human body or countenance, the mutual consent of various notes of a melodious tune, or the human conscience and sense of social justice. And the reason that these secondary beauties appear to be beautiful to human beings, Edwards asserts, is "a law of nature which God has fixed, or an instinct he has given."[57] In other words, the mind's general inborn habit to order ideas according to the "resemblance of some kind" is by nature capable of recognizing and of appropriately ordering the ideas of the relationships of the secondary or natural beauty.

What human beings are not naturally capable of seeing is the proportion involved in the divine beauty and in the universal system of beings. Thus, unregenerate persons are not capable of knowing God on their own, neither are they able to know all things in their true and ultimate relational context—that is, their innermost essence. The ultimate reason that secondary beauty is beautiful, Edwards declares, is "that there is in it some image of the true, spiritual, original beauty . . . consisting in being's consent to being."[58] The true beauty in the finite realm is an intelligent being's consent to or love of God's beauty and to all beings in relation to God's beauty. If a person does not know this, he or she is not capable of truly apprehending the true meaning of even the secondary beauty. The fallen humankind does experience the secondary beauty as beautiful. But such a perception without an apprehension of its ultimate meaning and context is not a true and full knowledge of the secondary beauty. Thus all human knowl-

[57] *True Virtue*, pp. 28, 32.
[58] Ibid., p. 30.

edge, though not totally lacking in a limited validity, is in need of being completed and transformed by the humankind's knowledge of God.

Edwards' conception of beauty allows him to maintain both the discontinuity and continuity between God and the finite reality—that is, between the true or divine beauty and the natural beauty. God's beauty is "infinitely diverse"[59] from all other forms of beauty; nonetheless, "all beauty consists in similarness," and God's beauty, too, would have to be seen as a form of similarity. In possessing the general habit of ordering all resembling or similar ideas together, human beings indeed have in the fabric of their nature an opening for the transcendent; nature is not totally discontinuous with supernature.

However, as the result of the Fall, the "superior principles" that had enabled Adam to know God have ceased to exist. And the "inferior principles," or the ability to experience the secondary beauty, which were meant to be regulated by the superior principles, became the "absolute masters of the heart." Fallen humankind, in other words, is governed by a "corrupt and evil disposition." As a consequence, human beings now take delight in that which serves their private interests. After the Fall, "man did immediately set up himself, and the objects of his private affections and appetites, as supreme; and so they took the place of God."[60] Human beings not only lack the specific capacity to know and love the divine beauty, but they have also elevated inferior beauty to the position of their highest value. Because of the corruption of the disposition, all human knowledge and experience have been vitiated.

How, then, can the mind attain the specific habit or the specific direction of the imagination whereby it can respond to the divine sort of similarity by receiving it as transcendently beautiful? To put it differently, how can the mind's general habit to order ideas according to the rule of "resemblance of

[59] *Religious Affections*, p. 298.
[60] *Original Sin*, pp. 381–383.

some kind" receive the specific ability to appreciate the divine kind of resemblance?

At this point, Edwards' philosophical epistemology and theological soteriology merge into one doctrine. Objectively, God became incarnate in Jesus Christ, making visible the transcendent beauty of the divine being. This manifestation of God's beauty also involved Christ's work of the atonement for human sin. Subjectively, God's Spirit comes to dwell in the depth of the human mind and heart, transforming the imagination. Edwards asserts that the Spirit of God must be "infused" in the minds of the elect and dwell in them as a new direction of their habit.[61] Edwards takes pains to deny that such a presence of the divine in the human violates or supplants the regular functioning of the human self. God's grace does not simply act upon the human psyche or bypass it but rather becomes "united to human faculties" as the foundation of a new direction of their operation. God's Spirit in the elect "acts very much after the manner of a natural principle or habit."[62] "God, in letting in this light into the soul, deals with man according to his nature, or as a rational creature; and makes use of his human faculties."[63] To express Edwards' point here within the context of the present discussion, one can say that the new habit of grace is, so to speak, a new mode of the functioning of the human being's inborn general habit of ordering ideas according to the rule of resemblance. This divine act of conditioning (sanctifying) the direction of the habit and its imaginative activity, then, lays the foundation for a perception of the sort of resemblance or similarity involved in the beauty of God. As Conrad Cherry and Paul Ramsey

[61] *Religious Affections*, p. 197; "Miscellanies," Nos. 1, "P," 73, 818, Yale MSS. As Conrad Cherry has pointed out, although Edwards uses the Scholastic notion of "infused grace," he is careful to distinguish it from the Thomistic "created grace." For Edwards, the infused grace, while acting as a real principle of the regenerate person's mind and heart, still does not become wholly a natural possession of such a person. See Conrad Cherry, *The Theology of Jonathan Edwards: A Reappraisal* (Gloucester, Mass.: Peter Smith, 1972), pp. 34–39.
[62] "Treatise on Grace," PH, pp. 74–75.
[63] "A Divine and Supernatural Light," FAJ, p. 109.

have pointed out, the traditional categories of "infusion" (referring to the grace in the will) and "illumination" (referring to the grace in the understanding) merge into one reality with the help of Edwards' notion of the habit of mind as the direction or character of the entire human self.[64]

If the sanctified habit functions only by engaging the regular human powers of understanding and inclination, this habit would be triggered into exercise only if the appropriate ideas are received through the usual channels of sensation. And the appropriate ideas for the divinely sanctified habit and imagination can only be the sense ideas about the divine being. Thus, God's beauty becomes visible in time and history via the person and work of Jesus of Nazareth and the redemptive history of which Jesus is the center. Now, by beholding those concrete manifestations of the divine beauty, the regenerate can grasp the ultimate form of beauty; by relating all other things to that beauty, he or she can apprehend them as the images or shadows of divine things, that is, in their true relational structure. So, through the operation of the sanctified form of the human imagination, not only is the perception of the divine beauty and truth made possible, but all human acts of knowing and loving now become events of knowing and loving God. "A natural man may love others, but 'tis some way or other as appendages and appurtenances to himself; but a spiritual man loves others as of God, or in God, as some way related to Him."[65]

Thus, it is the indwelling of the divine habit in the human mind and heart that makes it possible for the human imagination to make fully and truly explicit in consciousness the relational tendencies which, as has been seen, constitute the structure and the essence of all created entities. And truth is "the consistency of our ideas with those ideas or that train and series of ideas that are raised in our minds according to God's

[64] Ramsey, "Editor's Introduction," in *Freedom of the Will*, pp. 42–43; Cherry, *Theology*, p. 26. For a good discussion of Edwards' relation to the Reformed theologians Peter van Mastricht and Francois Turrettini, on the issue of the role of grace in regeneration, see Cherry, *Theology*, pp. 34–39.

[65] "Miscellanies," No. 821, HGT, pp. 240–241.

stated order and law"—that is, "in having perfect and adequate ideas of things."[66]

By invoking the theological category of the Holy Spirit, however, Edwards is not avoiding a philosophical analysis of the validity of knowledge. Edwards has given a further development to Locke's and Hume's treatment of the problem of the "necessary connections" among ideas. As I noted above, Edwards, unlike either Locke or Hume, approaches the problem of knowledge with a relational ontology wherein the simple ideas of sensation are seen as essentially relational and thus capable of conveying to the mind the structure of reality. In addition, as my interpretation in the present chapter indicates, Edwards also bases the possibility of knowledge upon the a priori structure of the mind's disposition and upon the imaginative activity of that disposition. Locke left largely unanalyzed the inborn structure of the knowing mind, although he saw the mind as actively engaged in the cognitive process. Hume held that it is the principle of habit by which the connections of ideas are formed in the mind in a regular fashion— that is, according to certain specifiable rules. But Hume, at least in his explicit statements, did not view the habits of the mind as the original equipment of the knowing subject, nor did he see the associative activity of these habits as resulting in inseparable and necessary connections of ideas.[67]

For Edwards, however, habits are abiding and active realities, and they constitute the original structure of the human mind and the power of the imagination. And, since the relations that the habit's imaginative activity makes explicit refer to what is inherent in the ideas themselves, the mind's perception of those relations is founded upon the nature of the knowing mind as well as upon the nature of the world itself. With respect to true beauty, it is true that the mind's inborn general capacity to apprehend beautiful relations is not sufficient. But with respect to secondary beauty, considered in itself without any reference to its connection with the true

[66] "The Mind," No. 10, WEA, p. 342.
[67] See C. R. Morris, *Locke-Berkeley-Hume*, pp. 136–145.

beauty, the mind's a priori structure is adequately equipped and is thus capable of apprehending inseparable and necessary sorts of relationships.

Thus, the primary way in which Edwards moved beyond the Lockean empiricism was through his elaboration of the mind's active (imaginative) role in the knowledge process. It is also true, however, that Edwards in a sense did not reject the Lockean empiricism but rather expanded its meaning. Edwards viewed the perception of reality that is now made possible through the indwelling divine disposition as an imaginative *sensation*—an intuition that constitutes an act of *receiving* the objective structure of reality into the mind's consciousness, though involving the full activity of the imagination. Edwards did affirm, in his own way, the Lockean principle that knowledge must be a knowledge gained through the experience of the objective world. I now turn in the next chapter to Edwards' notion of the imaginative power of the mind's habit as a power of sensation.

CHAPTER VI

Imagination as Aesthetic Sense

I BEGAN the preceding chapter with an elaboration of my thesis that the issue for Edwards in epistemology was how to integrate his acceptance of the Lockean stress upon the direct sense reception of the raw data about the world as the foundation of knowledge with his (as well as Locke's) view of the mind as playing an active role in the cognitive process. I have shown how Edwards explains the mind's imaginative activity as the function of the propensive power of habit that is an abiding power at once active and also dependent upon occasions (sense stimuli). I have tried to show how the imagination as a function of habit mediates between the mind's a priori dispositions and the simple ideas of sensation. The rules of the dispositional imagination, which make explicit in consciousness the relational structure of the simple ideas themselves, have also been analyzed.

In the course of my discussion, I noted how in Edwards' notion of the mind's dispositional imagination creativity and receptivity merge into one process. The ordering activity of the mind's habit vis-à-vis sense ideas is the very process through which the relational tendencies inherent in sense ideas themselves are made mentally explicit and thus received and sensed by the mind. I shall now examine Edwards' conception of the simultaneously creative and receptive imagination as *sensation*. Through this conception, Edwards' integration of knowledge as sense reception and knowledge as construction reaches a greater depth.

In the very earliest pages of his writings, Edwards viewed the mind's dispositional activity of ordering ideas as an act of judgment and thus an act of cognition.[1] The mind's habit, as was noted, does not require the guidance of any higher ra-

---

[1] See, for example, "The Mind," No. 59, WEA, pp. 373–374.

tional power. Though an automatic power, habit is an ordered propensity that knows, as it were, how to respond to sense ideas. Thus, the mind's dispositional activity of ordering sense ideas according to the rules of contiguity, causality, and resemblance is a cognitive activity. In the case of the mind's experience of the relation of resemblance or beauty, however, Edwards carried further the general notion of ordering activity as an activity of judgment and characterized the ordering activity involved therein as an activity of *sensing*, and the power of such ordering activity as a *sense*.

Such a move by Edwards is congruent with his very early view that the self-evident and certain knowledge is a "sensible knowledge" received through a direct contact with the world. In an early note, Edwards wrote, "When we see grass, the idea of green is excited by it; and this we know self-evidently."[2] But the sensation of the greenness of grass is an experience that involves only a simple idea, and all simple ideas are received through sensation and thus known sensibly and self-evidently. But when the relations among the plurality of ideas, such as the relation of beauty, are involved, something other than the sensation through the five external senses and the internal or reflexive sense is involved—namely, the mind's own ordering activity. So the critical question is, How can an experience that necessarily involves mental activity be an event of sensation? Here it can be seen that in Edwards, empiricism runs deep. And his final integration of sensation with mental activity through an enlarged concept of sensation that is at once receptive and active was necessary to meet the demand that the self-evident knowledge must be a sensible knowledge.

The Habit of Mind and the Sensation of Beauty

The Identification of the Habit of Mind as the Aesthetic Sense

The first thing one must do to understand the distinctiveness of Edwards' conception is to notice that he identifies the habit

---

[2] "The Mind," No. 19, WEA, p. 346.

of mind itself as the sense of beauty. He sometimes speaks ambiguously of habit and sense as "attending" each other.[3] But, pushed to clarify his meaning, he explains.

> You enquire whether it is not inconsistent to say that a sense of the divine Beauty arises from a good Temper, and a good Temper arises from a sense of the divine Beauty. I answer yes, as the expression may be understood. If by a sense of the d. [divine] Beauty, you mean an habitual sensibility of moral Beauty. I say in this sense a sense of d. B—— [divine Beauty] don't arise from a good Temper for an habitual sensibility of moral Beauty (or an habitual good Taste of mind) and a good Temper of mind are the very same thing.[4]

And, especially in *Religious Affections* and *True Virtue*, Edwards' contention that the habit of mind is a sort of sense is clearly indicated. Speaking about the difference between the sense of secondary beauty and the sense of true beauty, for example, Edwards writes:

> There appears to us to be a natural agreement, proportion, and adjustment between these things; which is indeed a kind of *moral sense*, or *sense of beauty* in moral things. But, as was before shown, it is a moral sense of a secondary kind, and is entirely different from a sense or relish of the original essential beauty of the true virtue; and may be without any principle of true virtue in the heart. Therefore, doubtless, it is a great mistake in any to suppose, that the moral sense which appears and is exercised in a sense of desert, is the same thing as a love of virtue, or *a disposition and determination of the mind* to be pleased with true virtuous beauty. (Emphasis added)[5]

In a notebook later used in writing *Religious Affections*, Edwards writes:

> Hence it follows that a man that is not a truly godly [man] can really have no manner of idea of that *sensation or dis-*

---

[3] *Religious Affections*, pp. 282–284.
[4] Letter to Joseph Bellamy, in FAJ, p. 390.
[5] *True Virtue*, pp. 50–51.

position or affection or kind of acting of soul wherein the
essence of true godliness [consists] any more than a blind
man has of colors. (Emphasis added)[6]

So, the mind's aesthetic sense does not refer to only the saint's
new sense of the divine beauty; there is an aesthetic sense for
the inferior beauty also. Further, aesthetic sense is not a separate faculty but rather the active tendency of the entire self
that determines the direction of all the functions of the human
person. Often Edwards refers to the aesthetic sense as the
"sense of the heart," thus emphasizing the involvement of the
inclinational aspect of the self.[7] But he also calls it a "sense or
taste of the mind," for example, in "Miscellanies," No. 397.[8]
There is no mistaking that the aesthetic sensation, for Edwards, is a function of the integrated unity of the entire human
person.

To identify the aesthetic sense with the habit of mind is to
conceive of that sense as activity. In "a true sense of the divine
excellency," writes Edwards, the mind's faculties "are not
merely passive, but active."[9] "The first act of the Spirit of God,
or the first that this divine temper exerts itself in, is in spiritual
understanding or in the sense of the mind, its perception of
glory and excellency, etc.—in the ideas it has of divine
things."[10] The mind's sensation of beauty then is in its essence
an active exerting of the mind's habit. And in view of my previous discussion of the imaginative activity of the mind's habit
vis-à-vis resembling or beautifully related ideas, one would expect the habit's active exertion in the sensation of beauty to be
primarily the propensive activity of the imagination. In other
words, the mind would sense beauty as it holds together beautifully related sense ideas and also excites similarly beautiful
though absent ideas to hold them in the same rank and order.

[6] "Note Book Used in the Religious Affections," No. 7, pp. 1–3, Yale MSS.
[7] See, for example, *Religious Affections*, p. 272.
[8] "Miscellanies," No. 397, HGT, p. 249. For a good discussion of Edwards'
holistic concept of the self, see John E. Smith, "Editor's Introduction," in *Religious Affections*, pp. 11–15.
[9] "A Divine and Supernatural Light," FAJ, pp. 108–109.
[10] "Miscellanies," No. 397, HGT, p. 249.

And since the mind's habit works immediately, the activities of ordering and sensing would occur simultaneously: they would constitute one process. Aesthetic perception then is an imaginative sensation.

"One alone cannot be excellent, inasmuch as, in such case, there can be no consent," writes Edwards.[11] Two or more ideas, either as parts of one complex idea or as separate ideas, must be in the mind at once if any perception of relations is to occur. One aspect of the mind's imaginative activity in its sensation of beauty, then, is that of holding together or asserting a plurality of ideas.

> When the ideas themselves appear more lively and with greater strength and impression, as the ideas of spiritual things do [to] one that is spiritually enlightened, their circumstances and various relations and connections between themselves and with other ideas appear more; there are more of those habitudes and respects taken notice of, and they also are more clearly discerned. And therefore, hereby a man sees the harmony between spiritual things, and so comes to be convinced of their truth.[12]

Edwards once noted that the idea of the cognitive process would have to contain "an actual idea of consciousness, an actual idea of a disposal of ideas in the mind, an actual idea of a consequent perception of relations and connections between them, etc."[13] The imagination's disposal of ideas, in other words, involves the act of holding together certain ideas so that their relations "appear more" and are more clearly "taken notice of." And the mind's habit knows how to respond to which ideas immediately and nondiscursively and without rationation.

Involved in the mind's sensation of beauty also is the propensive activity of exciting certain appropriate though absent

[11] "Miscellanies," No. 117, HGT, p. 258.
[12] "Miscellanies," No. 408, HGT, p. 249.
[13] "Miscellanies," No. 782, HGT, p. 114.

ideas so that their relations with certain other ideas can be apprehended.

> A holy disposition and spiritual taste, where grace is strong and lively, will enable a soul to determine what actions are right and becoming Christians, not only more speedily, but far more exactly, than the greatest abilities without it. This may be illustrated by the manner in which some habits of mind, and dispositions of heart, of a nature inferior to true grace, will teach and guide a man in his actions. As for instance, if a man be a very good-natured man, his good nature will teach him better how to act benevolently amongst mankind, and will direct him, on every occasion, to those speeches and actions, which are agreeable to rules of goodness, than the strongest reason will a man of a morose temper. . . . Yea its holy taste and appetite leads it to think of that which is truly lovely, and naturally suggests it.

And further:

> But a spiritual taste of soul, mightily helps the soul, in its reasonings on the Word of God, and in judging of the true meaning of its rules; as it removes the prejudices of a depraved appetite, and naturally leads the thoughts in the right channel, casts a light on the Word of God, and causes the true meaning, most naturally to come to mind, through the harmony there is between the disposition and relish of a sanctified soul, and the true meaning of the rules of God's Word. Yea, this harmony tends to bring the texts themselves to mind, on proper occasions; as the particular state of the stomach and palate, tends to bring such particular meats and drinks to mind, as agreeable to that state.[14]

The mind's aesthetic taste or sense, as it is the function of active tendencies, "directs" and "leads" the mind to think of the ideas of harmoniously related actions and rules. Again, one can see that the mind's aesthetic sense or taste functions only

---

[14] *Religious Affections*, pp. 283, 285.

as it acts imaginatively to rank and order together a plurality of ideas.

As it is the imaginative power of the mind's habit that non-discursively but accurately recognizes and judges the relations among ideas, so it is that the imaginative activity is the most essential activity involved in the mind's sensation of beauty. But the habit of mind, as I have shown, is the manner of the operation of the entire self. Thus, the mind's sensation of beauty could not function without also engaging both the understanding and the inclination. The necessary involvement of the understanding can be seen in Edwards' insistence that there must be some ideas before the mind's habit as aesthetic sense can function:

> The matter which the principle acts upon is those notions or ideas that the mind is furnished with of the things of religion. . . . If there could be a principle of grace in the heart without those notions or ideas there yet, it could not act, because it could have no matter to act upon.

Edwards then continues:

> Therefore, here is the advantage of clear convincing instructions of setting forth divine things in a clear light. Here is the advantage of divine eloquence, in instructing warning counselling, etc. . . . They serve as they give more strong and lively impression of the truth. The stronger reason and argument are offered to confirm any truth or to show the eligibleness of any practice, it serves as it gives those ideas that are the matter that grace acts upon and disposes them in such order, sets them in such light that grace if in the heart shall have the greater opportunity to act more fully and more according to its tendency.[15]

The sense of beauty, as Edwards conceives of it, then, is not a separate sense organ that receives from the world some information with which the regular powers of the self have nothing

---

[15] "Miscellanies," No. 539, Yale MSS.

to do. It rather works with those very ideas which are received through the regular channels of sensation.[16]

The habit of mind, functioning as aesthetic sense, also engages the heart or the mind's inclinational and affectional dimension. In Edwards, the connection between beauty and the mind's inclination has a metaphysical basis. That is, all things, for Edwards, essentially tend to be mutually related, and the cognitive event is the medium through which a mind and all other entities come to be mutually related. Moreover, a mind's proper relation to beautifully related entities can only be its taking pleasure in those entities. The mind's own relation to the relation of beauty occurs in the form of pleasure or delight. Furthermore, Edwards held that "all sorts of ideas of things are but the repetitions of those very things over again."[17] Thus, the mind could not have an idea of beauty without having something beautiful in the mind—namely, the mind's own agreement to the object, that is, the mind's pleasure. As Herbert Richardson has argued, Edwards seems to have believed that a beautiful relation between ideas is concretely present in the mind in the form of the felt pleasure.[18] So, Edwards distinguishes "sensible knowledge" from mere "notional knowledge":

When the mind is sensible of the sweet beauty and amiableness of a thing that implies a sensibleness of sweetness and delight in the presence of the *idea* of it: and this sensibleness of the amiableness or delightfulness of beauty, carries in the very nature of it the *sense of the heart.*

[16] For contrasting interpretations, see David J. Lyttle, "The Sixth Sense of Jonathan Edwards," *Church Quarterly Review* 167 (1966): 50–59; Morton White, *Science and Sentiment in America: Philosophical Thought from Jonathan Edwards to John Dewey* (New York: Oxford University Press, 1972), pp. 29, 294. For a discussion of the recent debate on this issue in Edwards scholarship, see Bruce Kuklick, *Churchmen and Philosophers: From Jonathan Edwards to John Dewey* (New Haven: Yale University Press, 1985), pp. 31–32.

[17] "The Mind," No. 66, WEA, p. 383.

[18] Richardson, "The Glory of God," pp. 245–246.

And further:

> All knowledge of this sort, as it is of things that concern the heart, or the will and affections, so it all relates to the good or evil that the sensible knowledge of things of this nature involves; and nothing is called a sensible knowledge upon any other account but the sense, or kind of *inward tasting* or feeling, of sweetness or pleasure, bitterness or pain, that is implied in it, or arises from it.[19]

Edwards does sometimes (as in the above quotation) use the term "sense" to refer to the actual feeling of pleasure that occurs in the mind's encounter with beauty. In this usage of the term, to "sense" beauty is to be pleased by beauty. However, as Edwards indicates in this quotation, a sensible knowledge of beauty is more than a feeling of pleasure. The latter, he says, is "implied in [the sensible knowledge], or arises from it." But the term "sense," in Edwards' overall conception of aesthetic sensibility, has a broader meaning as well as the more strict reference to the heart's feeling of pleasure. The sense of beauty is the habit of mind, the direction of the whole self. And, as I have already mentioned, Edwards calls the aesthetic sense the "sense of the mind" as well as the "sense of the heart." The inclination's taking pleasure must be, and can only be, involved in the perception of beauty. But the aesthetic sensation, as it is a function of the mind's habit, includes other activities of the self—namely, the reception of ideas through the understanding, and the imaginative activity.

The inclination, or the heart (the whole mind as it inclines toward or away from something), and the mind's habit are so closely related in Edwards' way of thinking that the distinction between them is not an easy one. Both of them move the entire self in one direction or another, as the category of love does in Augustine's psychology.[20] But the habit of mind is the more comprehensive category of the two. The mind's habit (or

---

[19] *Religious Affections*, p. 272; "Miscellanies," No. 782, HGT, p. 120.
[20] See Smith, "Editor's Introduction," in *Religious Affections*, p. 32.

temper) refers to the direction of the entire self, while the inclination (or the heart) refers more specifically to the mind's ability to be pleased or displeased by something. What, then, is the difference between the imagination and the inclination? The direction of both of them is determined by the mind's habit or disposition. And they both move the self toward beauty and value. But the imagination refers to the mind's propensive activity of responding to sense ideas by ordering them in certain specific ways, while the inclination is more specifically the mind's ability to be affectively pleased or displeased. Consequently, the imagination makes a beautiful relation explicit and visible in consciousness so that the inclination can take pleasure in it. Thus, the imagination would be logically prior to the inclination, although they function in an integrated unity.

The Aesthetic Sensation as an Active, Receptive, and Organic Process

The mind's sensation of beauty, then, is the imaginative and inclinational activity of the habit of mind. It must now be asked, How can such a purposive and multifaceted activity be a sensation? How can the active power of the habit be a sense organ? The answer to this question was implicit in my previous discussion of the nature of habit and its imaginative activity. Habit itself is a power that is at once active and also receptive in that it exerts its own direction and design and yet functions only in response to the occurrence of the appropriate occasion.

The imaginative activity, conceived of as the function of the mind's habit, exerts its own creativity in setting sense ideas into the relational patterns that are larger than immediately perceived, and yet in that very creativity the imagination is only making mentally explicit the relational potentialities inherent in the ideas themselves. In the propensive activity of the imagination, activity and receptivity coincide. The imagination of the habit of mind and the accompanying involvement of the heart, then, discover and receive the objective information about the world, just as other sense organs do. Just as each of the other sense organs, the habit of mind receives into the mind something that no other sense organ can. The taste of honey, for example, can be apprehended only by the palate; in a similar manner, the relation of beauty can be experienced only through the exercise of the mind's habit.[21] Edwards' interest in working out a dynamic theory of the mind's imagination without undermining the Lockean view of knowledge as reception rather than creation was fundamentally satisfied in his conception of the creative activity of the dispositional imagination as an act of receiving. Now, in calling the mind's habit and its imagination a sense, that conception of Edwards is simply brought to its logical conclusion.

The appropriateness in calling habit of mind a sense can also be looked at from another angle—in light of the nature of beauty. The beauty or proportion of relations, for Edwards, is a whole, not a sum or aggregate, and has its own unitary and irreducible meaning that cannot be explained in terms of the parts. So, a complex nexus of relationships may contain partial irregularities which, when considered as a whole, nevertheless constitute a proportion with its own singular character. Now, one reason that Locke believed the "passive" sensation of ideas to be fundamental was that it is only through such a direct and receptive contact with the world that the irreducible or objective characteristics of that world can be conveyed to the mind. The sensory ideas (i.e., simple ideas) can never be fabricated out of other ideas. Thus Locke held that "it is not in the power of the most exalted wit, or enlarged understanding, by any quickness or variety of thought, to invent, or frame one new simple idea in the mind."[22] The sensation of beauty, for Edwards, of course, involves the imaginative activity of the mind, and thus is quite different from the five "passive" senses that Locke had in mind. But the habit's imaginative creativity, in Edwards' conception, is capable of discerning the irreducible singular meanings of beautiful groups of relationships taken as wholes.

[21] *Religious Affections*, p. 209.
[22] Locke, *Essay*, bk. 2, chap. 2, no. 2.

What the habit's imagination makes visible in consciousness is a particular datum that cannot be apprehended by any other sense organ. The habit of mind, of course, needs the ideas received through the regular sense organs as the materials it can work on. For instance, to experience the beauty of a beautiful face, the mind must first receive several simple ideas of various parts of that face through the sense of sight. But unless the habit puts together those several ideas into a whole, the distinctive beauty of that face cannot become visible in the mind. It is, then, appropriate for Edwards to call the habit of mind a sense because the beauty that its imaginative activity receives into the mind is a singular datum that cannot be reduced to, or explained by, the several ideas received by other sense organs.

One would, then, expect Edwards to use the Lockean terminology of "simple ideas" in reference to aesthetic perception. In fact, Edwards does explicitly use the phrase "a new simple idea" in reference to the saint's experience of the divine beauty.[23] To the best of my knowledge, Edwards does not refer to the perceptions of inferior beauty with the same terminology. But he nevertheless analyzed all forms of beauty as unitary wholes, and clearly understood the psychological mechanisms involved in the perception of both the divine and other forms of beauty as being similar. It would not, therefore, be inconsistent with his thought if one interpreted the perception of all kinds of beauty as involving simple ideas.

Further, the simple idea of beauty, for Edwards, is not something that a person merely has in his or her mind, but rather something that a person in the totality of his or her self-hood *becomes*. The sense of beauty is, as I have noted, the habit of mind or the direction of the entire self. The sensing of beauty, therefore, involves all the following activities: the reception of ideas through the understanding; the imaginative response to those ideas; and the inclination's feeling of pleasure in the beautiful relation among those ideas. Thus, the simple idea of beauty refers to the irreducible quality of all the

<hr/>

[23] *Religious Affections*, p. 205.

active and receptive dimensions of the mind and heart in their amalgamated totality. The whole person is really the channel or power through which a beautiful relation is actively repeated; the perceiver becomes, in effect, a simple idea of beauty. The perceiver becomes an action, a "lightsome body" or "the image of God's own knowledge of himself."[24]

If the content of aesthetic sensation is the unitary relational meaning of a plurality of ideas, then the imaginative activity involved in such a sensation must be a synthesizing and organic process capable of construing a plurality of particulars in such a way that their singular meaning as a whole becomes explicit and visible. One is then led to notice yet another important aspect of the psychological mechanism of the imagination. Thus far, I have discussed the following elements in the nature of the imagination: a propensive activity of ordering ideas according to the patterns already present in the mind's dispositions; an activity of holding a plurality of ideas so that their relations can become explicit or visible; an immediate, nondiscursive, yet rational activity; and an activity that is at once creative and receptive.

Now I must point to the imagination as an organic power. M. H. Abrams has observed that the crucial shift from the aesthetic theory of many eighteenth-century thinkers to that of such figures of romanticism as Coleridge and Wordsworth can best be seen as the replacement of a mechanistic model of the imagination by an organic one.[25] The mechanistic conception defines the nature of creative process as an activity of adding and combining ideas into various groupings. In contrast, Coleridge saw the imagination as a "blending," "fusing," or "coadunating" power that enables a plurality of ideas "to grow into one."[26] The imagination is an insight into the total nature of its objects, a power of integration and coalescence,

[24] Ibid., p. 201; "End in Creation," WC, 2: 210. See also Niebuhr, *Streams of Grace*, pp. 12–35.
[25] M. H. Abrams, "Mechanical and Organic Psychology of Literary Invention," in *English Literature and British Philosophy*, ed. S. P. Rosenbaum (Chicago: University of Chicago Press, 1971), pp. 136–167.
[26] Ibid., p. 150.

later referred to as "mental chemistry" by John Stuart Mill and others.[27] Edwards nowhere announces that he means to hold such a theory. But such a conception is clearly called for by his doctrine of beautiful relations as wholes as well as by his definition of the power of aesthetic perception as a sense. And, more important, an organic theory of the imagination is very much implicit in the way Edwards actually analyzes certain aesthetic experiences and aesthetic realities.

In his "Personal Narratives," Edwards describes his own perceptions of the transcendent beauty of God:

> Not long after I first began to experience these things, I gave an account to my father of some things that had passed in my mind. I was pretty much affected by the discourse we had together; and when the discourse was ended, I walked abroad alone, in a solitary place in my father's pasture, for contemplation. And as I was walking there, and looking up on the sky and clouds, there came into my mind so sweet a sense of the glorious *majesty* and *grace* of God, that I know not how to express. I seemed to see them both in *a sweet conjunction*; majesty and meekness joined together; it was a sweet, and gentle, and holy majesty; and also a majestic meekness; an awful sweetness; a high, and great, and holy gentleness. (Emphasis added)[28]

God's majesty and grace, the two categories Edwards had particular trouble in reconciling with each other from a logical standpoint, are now seen in a "sweet conjunction." They are "joined together" into the one singular whole with its own irreducible meaning of being inexpressibly "sweet." The particular ideas of majesty and grace are not transcended or left behind but rather are firmly held at the forefront of the mind's view. But they are so coalesced into each other that Edwards can only speak of the majesty as a "sweet, and gentle, and holy majesty," and grace as a "high, and great, and holy gentle-

[27] Edwards anticipates the eighteenth-century English romantic criticism that saw the imagination as a capacity to experience "the total nature of its object" (Bate, *From Classic to Romantic*, p. 118).

[28] "Personal Narrative," FAJ, p. 60.

ness." Edwards can be said to have had the sanctified habit of mind that enabled him to hold together the ideas of God's seemingly contrasting qualities in such a way that their true harmony is made explicit and is immediately sensed.

Another important locus in Edwards' writing in which an implicitly organic conception of the imagination can be seen is his discussion, "The Excellency of Christ." In a sermon with that title, he analyzes the divine beauty of Christ as consisting of a union of opposites. The qualities that are "very diverse" meet in "a conjunction" in the person of Christ. In him, there are "infinite highness and infinite condescension" and "infinite justice and infinite grace." But, viewed with a sanctified habit of mind, those "very diverse" qualities appear "admirable" together in "a conjunction."[29]

Edwards discusses the same point in a letter to a woman who has tragically lost her daughter:

> [Christ] is indeed possessed of infinite majesty, to inspire us with reverence and adoration; yet that majesty need not terrify us, for *we behold it blended with humility*, meekness and sweet condescension. We may feel the most profound reverence and self-abasement, and yet our hearts are drawn forth, sweetly and powerfully, into an intimacy the most free, confidential and delightful. The dread, so naturally inspired by his greatness, is dispelled by the contemplation of his gentleness and humility; while the familiarity, which might otherwise arise from the view of the loveliness of his

[29] "The Excellency of Christ," FAJ, pp. 121–122. Edwards' view here represents a broadening of the classical notion of aesthetic value. In Edwards' time, there was a tendency on the part of many thinkers to move away from the classical definition of beauty as the rationally explainable quality of harmony and regularity to a recognition of the diversity in the objects of aesthetic appeal. What is apparently irregular, indefinite, or unusual, they noticed, could be experienced as in some way aesthetically appealing. Edwards kept the criterion of harmony in his conception of beauty but enlarged the meaning and scope of harmony. In this, Edwards utilized a development in the aesthetics of his time for his philosophical and theological reconstruction. See my "Mental Activity and Perception of Beauty," pp. 383–385; Jerome Stolnitz, "Beauty: Some Stages in the History of an Idea," *Journal of the History of Ideas* 38 (1961): 185–204.

character merely, is ever prevented, by the consciousness of his infinite majesty and glory; and the sight of *all his perfections united fills us with sweet surprise,* and *humble confidence, with reverential love, and delightful adoration.* (Emphasis added)[30]

So Christ's majesty is experienced as "blended" with the meek or humble side of his nature. In the saint's sensation of God's beauty, all of the divine perfections are "united," making up a coalesced unity with its own meaning. And here again, as in his "Personal Narrative," Edwards indicates the integrated unity in the saint's sensation of God's beauty by interfusing two terms into one category. God's majesty and meekness are experienced as "humble confidence," "reverential love," and "delightful adoration."

In this way, Edwards' integration of receptive sensation and imaginative activity is rounded out by his organic conception of the imagination. Habit's dual character as an active and also conditional power makes the imagination's creativity a process of receiving. The habit of mind is then explicitly designated and described by Edwards as the aesthetic sense. In this way, the organic nature of the imaginative process explains how the content of the aesthetic sensation is something similar to the content of any other sort of sensation—namely, a simple idea.

The idea of a sense through which mental and moral, not just physical, objects are perceived was in the air in the seventeenth and early eighteenth centuries. Locke spoke of the "internal sense" of "reflection" through which the mind receives the simple ideas of mental operations and thus by implication the ideas of beauty and goodness. It is well known that the British moral philosophers, such as John Smith, Henry More, Shaftesbury, Francis Hutcheson, and others, all held the view that the mind's apprehension of beauty is an act of immediate sensation.[31]

---

[30] "Letter to Lady Pepperell," WG, 1: 482.

[31] The history of the idea of an "internal sense" of moral and aesthetic value in the seventeenth and eighteenth centuries is quite complex. See Tuveson,

The great issue, however, was what exactly was meant by this internal sense—more specifically, what sort of mental processes are involved in the operation of this sense. Especially under the influence of Locke's *Essay*, there was a desire among many thinkers of this period to see the internal sense as an act of receiving the data directly from the perceived objects without resorting to any innate or preconceived ideas of beauty or moral value. Further, there was a gradual movement away from the view that the internal sense functioned apart from the regular operations of the other five senses of the human mind. Locke himself was rather confusing at this point, however, when he wrote about the possibility to imagine creatures with "a sixth, seventh, or eighth sense."[32] Nevertheless, Locke's own stress upon the usual sense data and the mind's operation about those data as the primary and only foundation for knowledge militates against any conceptualization of an esoteric, separate sense medium. Thus, the associationist school, for example, attempted to develop a view according to which the mind's experience of moral and aesthetic values is seen as the consequence of the mind's activity of relating the ideas received through the regular sense organs.[33] Edwards carried further this associationist project and integrated it with the intuitionist element in the idea of an internal sense.

Edwards has clearly left behind him the older separatistic conception of a moral or aesthetic sense. In him, the imagination, affections, and the understanding converge in an integrated event of an immediate sensation. Edwards' view, therefore, must be seen as an anticipation of the later eighteenth- and the early nineteenth-century English romanticism

---

Imagination as a Means of Grace, esp. chap. 2; Martin Kallich, "The Associationist Criticism of Francis Hutcheson and David Hume," *Studies of Philology* 43 (1946): 644–651; idem, "The Arguments against the Association of Ideas in Eighteenth-Century Aesthetics," *Modern Language Quarterly* 15 (1954): 125–136.

[32] Locke, *Essay*, bk. 2, chap. 1, no. 4; bk. 2, chap. 2, no. 3.

[33] Kallich, "The Associationist Criticism," p. 645; Clarence DeWitt Thorpe, "Addison and Hutcheson on the Imagination," *Journal of English Literary History* 2 (1935): 215–234.

that attempted to bring together the Cambridge Platonists' moral and aesthetic sense and dynamic view of the mind, the empiricistic stress upon sensation and the association of ideas, and the increasing recognition of the importance of feeling. Describing this holistic conception of aesthetic discernment in romanticism, Walter Jackson Bate has written:

> "Discernment," whatever the elements that constitute it, is a single and integrated intuition: in seizing upon the interior workings of the mind and feelings of the person with whom it has become identified, it follows them "through all their windings, and the effects arising from each, however complicated," with an automatic immediacy; and it achieves a coalesced unity which cannot be grasped rationally or "by considering separately each particular part, however necessary to constitute the whole."[34]

The interfusion of the various psychological elements into the immediacy and unity of aesthetic sensation is achieved by the structured yet automatic power of the mind's habit that functions as the organizing and controlling principle of the entire self.

It must be noted here that through the mediation of this habit of mind, a connection is established even between aesthetic sensation and discursive knowledge. The sense of beauty does have primacy as the rational power in Edwards' conception of knowledge. However, the aesthetic sense is none other than the habit of mind itself that also functions as the direction of the discursive understanding. Thus, a person who is capable of sensing the beauty in a group of ideas is, for that very reason, also able to have a greater logical and conceptual understanding of those ideas and their relations with one another. Aesthetic sensibility "not only removes the hindrances of reason, but positively helps reason." "The ideas themselves, which otherwise are dim and obscure, by this

[34] Bate, *From Classic to Romantic*, p. 138, quoting John Ogilvie, *Philosophical and Critical Observations on the Nature, Characters, and Various Species of Composition* (1774), 1: 220–221.

means have a light cast upon them, and are impressed with greater strength; so that the mind can better judge of them."[35] So, the elevating of the sensation, imagination, and the affections above the discursive and logical does not by any means make Edwards an anti-intellectualist or a mystic.[36] In Edwards' epistemology, nothing is violated or totally transcended.

THE ONTOLOGICAL FUNCTION OF THE IMAGINATION

Thus far I have analyzed the epistemic function of the imagination. I must now briefly point to its ontological productivity. The essence of the matter is that the imaginative activity of the mind is the expression of the very being or essential disposition of the human self. There is no substantial form to which operational habits and tendencies belong; the operational habits themselves constitute the permanence and structure of the human being. It is not that a person fully exists and then imagines, knows, and loves; it is rather that a person is real as a system of habits and is brought to full actuality or existence through the exercise of those habits. And it is through the mind's imaginative activity that those habits are exercised. For this reason, the imagination completes the actuality of a person. The imagination is ontologically productive.

I have already had occasion to note the close connection between knowing and being in Edwards' thought. If knowing is an exercise of the habit of the mind, knowledge then is an act in which the knower's being becomes an actuality. I also set forth the interpretation that the full actuality of the nonperceiving aspect of the universe (the material existence) is achieved via the perceiving being's knowledge of it in its total relational context—that is, in its full relational meaning to which its essence (habit) tends.[37]

[35] *Religious Affections*, p. 307. See also n. 16 above.
[36] See Chap. 5, n. 37 above.
[37] My interpretation of Edwards at this point implies a view of nature according to which nature and humanity are closely related. Nature and per-

What must be pointed out now is that knowledge can grasp the true structure of reality and thereby enhance its actuality only through the imagination. This is so because being is relational (beautiful) in its structure, according to Edwards, and it is the imagination that brings the relations into view. Further, knowledge is a true expression and actualization of the inmost essence of the knower only as the imagination is involved. This is so because the essence of the knower is relational (tending toward beautiful relations), and it is the imagination that makes explicit that very relational tendency by ordering the components of experience according to it. In this way, when the imagination is involved, the act of knowing is an act of relating—relating to the relations that are experienced as objects of knowledge. In short, being and the knowledge of being are both essentially relational, and the imagination is the relating faculty. So being and knowledge are constituted and fulfilled through the imagination.

How then does the imagination accomplish its ontological task? The discussion in this chapter has been in preparation for the answer to this question. Imagination makes explicit the relations to which the known things themselves tend by holding together the mind's sense ideas of those objects in a manner harmonious with the law of the totality of being. I have also noted the synthesizing activity of the imagination—an activity whereby a plurality of particular ideas and their mutual relations are coalesced into something new with its own integrated, unitary meaning. Imagination, then, actuates the relational tendencies of the objects of knowledge by asserting or mentally repeating those relations which already exist, though only virtually, within the habits and tendencies of the objects of knowledge.

A kind of creativity is involved in the psychological mecha-

---

ceiving beings are certainly distinguished by Edwards, but he does not see them in a sharp disjunction. For Edwards, the attainments of the full reality of both nature and humanity are *mutually* dependent. For discussions of Edwards' view of nature, see Cooey-Nichols, "Nature as Divine Communication"; George A. Tattrie, "Jonathan Edwards' Understanding of the Natural World and Man's Relation to It" (Ph.D. diss., McGill University, 1973).

nism of the imagination. Imagination not only holds sense ideas together, but it also widens the mind's attention to the relational meaning among ideas. Further, imagination grasps the unitary relational quality among a plurality of ideas. But these creative acts of the imagination do not make or produce relationships; imagination only makes mentally actual what is already virtually there. This is precisely why the creative activity of the imagination *receives* and *discerns* the information about the objective structure of the world.

So, imagination does not create something ex nihilo. What it accomplishes is the movement of being from virtuality to actuality. Imagination does this by asserting or making explicit in consciousness the relational structure of reality. The manner of the imagination's creative function is essentially a multiplication or repetition of relationships.

Edwards' experience of God and nature as described in his "Personal Narrative," therefore, is more than a cognitive event; it is also a new state of being. "The appearance of everything was altered," wrote Edwards. "God's excellency, his wisdom, his purity and love, seemed to appear in everything; in the sun, moon, and stars . . . and all nature."[38] In this consenting response of Edwards to the beauty of God and the beauty of nature in relation to God, the relational potencies and thus the ontological destinies of both humanity and nature were being made explicitly actual. Edwards himself declares the close connection between knowing and being:

> Knowledge or understanding is a thing worthy to be; and if any knowledge, then the most excellent sort of knowledge, viz., that of God and his glory. The existence of the created universe consists as much in it as in anything.[39]

And again:

> Men, or intelligent beings, are the consciousness of the creation, whereby the universe is conscious of its own being, and of what is done in it, of the actions of the Creator and

---

[38] "Personal Narrative," FAJ, pp. 60–61.
[39] "End in Creation," WC, 2: 205.

governor with respect to it. Now except the world had such a consciousness of itself, it would be altogether in vain that it was.[40]

In other words, through the regenerate person's consciousness of the universe in relation to God, the universe achieves a "consciousness of itself." And through this process, "the existence of the created universe" or the being of nature and of the perceiving persons is actualized. The ontological import of knowledge for the knowing subject is also asserted by Edwards in one of his sermons on the saint's apprehension of Jesus Christ:

> The glory of Christ is such that it is of a transforming nature. It's of a powerful [sic] when it changes all that behold it into the same Image. . . . They see the excellence[sic] holiness of Christ and that changes them into the same Image. They also become holy, their hearts are purified from their filthiness.[41]

The imagination, then, is the instrument through which God continues his creative activity—an activity in which the being of the world, and as I shall show, in a sense the very being of God, is expanded. As the imagination fulfills its function it welds together the human self, nature, and God. In the human knowledge of God and of the natural world in its relation to God, both humanity and nature become what they essentially tend to be—namely, living images of God's beauty. Such knowledge and becoming are the temporal embodiments and extensions of God's own being. And it is the imagination through which the absolute is in the finite, and the finite in the absolute. Imagination can do this because it always insists upon placing everything in its eternal context and yet does this without ever taking temporal particulars away from their temporality.

As I have shown, in the intellectualistic metaphysics in which universals and forms are the categories of the real, the

---

[40] "Miscellanies," No. 1, HGT, pp. 105–106.
[41] "Sermon on II Cor. 3:18 (1)," Yale MSS.

mind grasps the essence of things as the active intellect abstracts the universal and intelligible elements from the particulars. In Edwards, however, the mind experiences the essence of things through a quite different procedure—through the activity of the imagination that holds together the particulars in such a way that their relationship among themselves and with the totality of being becomes explicit. The imagination does not abstract any thing away from nature; it rather helps nature's own relatedness become visible. So, as Edwards himself says, through the intelligent beings' knowledge of the world, "the universe is conscious of its own being."

CHAPTER VII

The Increasing Fullness of the Divine Being

THE BOLD RESHAPING that Edwards gave to traditional Western conceptions of reality and knowledge presupposed an equally bold reconception of the very nature of God. I have argued that Edwards thought of the nature of reality no longer in terms of substance and form but rather in terms of disposition and habit, thereby introducing a dynamic element into the very fabric of being. Now, if this interpretation is correct, and if ontological categories are to some extent applicable to God, is the divine being himself essentially dispositional and thus inherently dynamic? Does God in some sense comprehend in God's own being an element of becoming?

I have also argued that the sanctified imagination of the mind's habit adds to being and beauty through a multiplication of relations, and that the activity of the imagination is the focal point or medium through which the being of the created world is moved from virtuality to full actuality and also continually increased. Now, it is the Holy Spirit indwelling in the saints as the divine disposition that makes possible the ontological productivity of the imagination. If this is so, is God's own being in some way affected by what happens in time?

Up to this point, I have cursorily indicated that Edwards answered both of these questions in the affirmative. It is the burden of this chapter to take a closer look at Edwards' conception of the dynamic character of the divine being with the particular focus on the function of disposition in that conception.

The question of exactly what sort of dynamic movement Edwards intends to attribute to God's own being is a critical issue in understanding Edwards' thought. This is so because Edwards speaks about God as at once eternally complete and perfect and also as inherently creative, self-communicating, and even self-enlarging. If there is one thing about which Edwards scholars have agreed, it is his deep personal conviction in the absolute sovereignty of God and the fundamental role this principle plays in his philosophical theology.[1] My own analysis up to this point has also shown that although the created reality is granted a dependent but real permanence, its actuality is constantly and directly dependent upon the creative and sustaining activity of God. God, for Edwards, is absolutely prior to the world in completeness and perfection. "God is infinitely, eternally, unchangeably, and independently glorious and perfect," and "stands in no need of, cannot be profited by, or receive anything from the creature."[2]

This absolutely perfect God, however, is also described by Edwards as inherently creative. "It is God's essence to incline to communicate Himself," writes Edwards.[3] Further, in and through his self-communication, God "as it were enlarges himself in a more excellent and divine manner."[4] In short, God is both completely perfect and also creatively self-expansive.

When the matter is put in this way, the natural question is, How can God be both completely perfect and also self-enlarging? How could a perfectly complete God be moved to create the world and even to enlarge God's own life? Interpreters of Edwards have usually found the answer to this question in the idea of creativity as self-communication—that is, an activity of giving rather than receiving, and thus an activity of an already complete and perfect being.[5] Since God only gives of himself out of "fullness," God's completeness and actuality presumably are not compromised. Scholars have also shown that this self-giving God of Edwards is an *inherently* self-com-

[1] Anderson, "Editor's Introduction," in WEA, pp. 26–27.
[2] "End in Creation," WC, 2: 200
[3] "Miscellanies," No. 107, Yale MSS.
[4] "End in Creation," WC, 2: 220.
[5] See, for example, Douglas J. Elwood, *The Philosophical Theology of Jonathan Edwards* (New York: Columbia University Press, 1960), pp. 90–112; Delattre, *Beauty and Sensibility*, pp. 168–184; John E. Smith, "Jonathan Edwards as Philosophical Theologian," *Review of Metaphysics* 30 (1976): 314–319.

municating being, which would imply that God's self-communicating act in creating the world is consistent with God's own internal being. Roland Delattre has further strengthened this point by arguing that God's being for Edwards is essentially beauty that by virtue of its own nature must "appear, shine forth, manifest, and communicate itself." God is an inherently beautifying" and not just a beautiful being.[6]

This answer to the question I have posed is correct as far as it goes and is faithful to Edwards' own view. These discussions of Edwards' dynamic idea of God as self-communicating have also served well in correcting some previous portrayals of Edwards' doctrine as primarily static.[7] However, the question needs to be pushed further in order to get to the inner logic of idea of the self-communication of God. One must inquire, How does Edwards conceive of God's self-communication so that it is not only an overflowing out of fullness but also in some sense self-expansive?

The interpretation of God's self-communication in terms of the idea of God's self-giving out of his eternal fullness does indeed protect God's perfection and self-sufficiency. But this analysis still does not explain the sense in which Edwards believes God is "enlarged" and "increased" by divine activity in time. The idea of self-communication, which Edwards often describes in such emanationistic metaphors as "overflowing," "diffusing," and "shining forth," lends itself to a thoroughly Neoplatonic interpretation of Edwards. But, contrary to "the One" of Plotinus, the God of Edwards has "the more delight and pleasure" in self-communication.[8] Further, Edwards mixes his emanationistic language with a teleological one in his discussion of God's self-communication. Edwards' God aims at a goal or an end in creating the world. Therefore, the movement of human history has a real meaning to God. The urgent question is, What is the inner logic of Edwards' notion

[6] Delattre, *Beauty and Sensibility*, p. 169.

[7] For an example of the portrayal of Edwards' doctrine of God as primarily "static," see Arthur Lovejoy, *The Great Chain of Being: A Study of the History of an Idea* (New York: Harper and Row, 1936), pp. 43–44.

[8] "End in Creation," WC, 2: 213.

of the self-communication of God, a logic according to which God is seen as both perfectly sufficient and also really involved in history, and as both possessing an absolute prior actuality and also capable of self-enlargement?

My thesis is that one does not fully understand the dynamic character of Edwards' conception of God unless it is seen in the light of Edwards' dispositional ontology. God, for Edwards, is the absolutely sovereign disposition of true beauty that is in an eternally complete exercise. Dispositions, as was shown, are abiding principles the reality of which is not exhausted by its exercise. Thus, God, conceived as essentially a disposition, is capable of being a perfect actuality *and* an eternal disposition to repeat this actuality through further exercises. God, for Edwards, is at once both actual and dispositional.

It is within the framework of the doctrine of the Trinity, as I shall discuss in detail below, that Edwards articulates the implications of his dispositional conception of God's essence. And it is Edwards' central concern to view the divine being as inherently dynamic without compromising God's absolute prior actuality and aseity. The First Person of the Trinity is seen as essentially actual as well as essentially dispositional. God the Father is where both God's absolute aseity and his inherently dynamic character are located. Through the ontologically productive exertion of the Father's dispositional essence, the Father's primordial actuality is repeated in the Son and the Holy Spirit. Thus, the immanent Trinity is the eternal exertion of God's dispositional essence and, therefore, the eternally perfect increase or the fullness of God's primordial actuality.

The inner-Trinitarian fullness of the divine being, however, does not exhaust the divine disposition. The exercise of this disposition ad extra, according to Edwards, constitutes God's creation of the world. Created existence, then, is the spatio-temporal repetition of God's inner-Trinitarian fullness, a process which, as shall be seen, will be everlasting in duration. In this way, God is really involved in time and space without being in any way deficient or in need. And God's creative activity in time and space has its foundation in the dynamic life of the immanent Trinity.

In this way, God's self-communication, both within himself and ad extra, according to Edwards, is to be analyzed in terms of the ontological productivity of the divine disposition. Disposition is ontologically productive or communicative since it is an active tendency toward a movement from virtuality to actuality and toward a multiplication or repetition of this movement. In God's case, the disposition is ontologically productive or communicative in a sovereign and self-sufficient way—that is, God brings about more of what is already completely actual, and he does this in such a way that he does not depend upon any other being for the exercise of the divine disposition. In short, for God, the disposition is properly the principle of *self*-communication, both internally and also ad extra.

In a nutshell, the above is the thesis I shall elaborate upon in the remainder of this chapter. I may note here, however, that what is found in Edwards is nothing less than a basic reconception of the Western philosophical theism that was heavily dependent upon the categories of Greek philosophy. For Edwards, God is no longer Plato's timeless "Idea," Aristotle's "Unmoved Mover," or Plotinus' "the One." Edwards does continue the Western philosophical and theological stress upon God's aseity or prior actuality. But God, for Edwards, is also essentially an active and relational Power. And it is Edwards' conception of God's essentially dispositional character, together with the doctrine of the Trinity, that mediates between God's aseity and God's creativity. Arthur Lovejoy, in *The Great Chain of Being*, points to the two mutually inconsistent ideas of God that have dominated Western metaphysics: God as the absolutely self-sufficient "Idea of the Good" and God as the absolute "Goodness" from which all things originate.[9] It could be said that what Edwards attempted was a creative synthesis of these two ideas. It is a synthesis, however, which replaces Plato's abiding and self-sufficient Idea

[9] Lovejoy, *Great Chain of Being*, pp. 43–50.

with the abiding and self-sufficient Divine Dispositional Actuality. And through such a notion of the divine being, Edwards attempted to bring together the idea of God as the absolute and self-sufficient ultimate reality and God as the inherently creative originator of all existence and meaning.

GOD AS DISPOSITION AND ACTUALITY
The Dispositional Character of the Essence of God

Before I discuss Edwards' articulation of the dynamic fullness of the inner-Trinitarian life of God, I need to raise Edwards' dispositional conception of the divine being as well as some of the limitations that Edwards specifies in his attribution of the dispositional category to the divine being. "It is God's essence to incline to communicate Himself," writes Edwards.[10] And this "disposition to communicate Himself" is what "we must conceive of as being originally in God as a perfection of his nature."[11] Edwards goes on to resolve the communicative disposition of God into "a disposition effectually to exert Himself, or to exert Himself in order to an effect."[12] God's disposition to operate as God, in other words, is the essence of the divine being.

Edwards expresses the same point at times by associating the divine being closely with the divine power. The following observations occur in Edwards' discussion of the distinctions among the three Persons of the Trinity:

If it shall be said that there are power, wisdom, goodness, and holiness in God, and that these may as well be proved to be distinct persons, because everything that is in God is God, [I answer], as to the power of God, power always consists in something—the power of the mind consists in its wisdom, the power of the body in plenty of animal spirits and toughness of limbs, etc.—and as it is distinct from those and other things, 'tis only a relation of adequateness and

[10] "Miscellanies," No. 107, Yale MSS.
[11] "End in Creation," WC, 2: 207.
[12] "Miscellanies," No. 1218, HGT, p. 152.

sufficiency of the essence to everything. But if we distinguish it from relation, *'tis nothing but the essence of God.*

'Tis evident that there are no more than these three, really distinct in God—God, and His idea, and His love and delight. We can't conceive of any further real distinctions. If you say there is the power of God, I answer, *the power of a being, even in creatures, is nothing distinct from the being itself besides a mere relation to an effect.* (Emphasis added)[13]

In "Miscellanies," No. 194, power is again mentioned as a primary characteristic of the divine being:

We ought to conceive of God as being *omnipotence, perfect knowledge, and perfect love,* and not extended any otherwise than as *power, knowledge, and love* are extended, and not as if it were a sort of unknown thing that we call substance, that is extended. (Emphasis added)[14]

In light of Edwards' dispositional conception of the essence of the divine being, the prominence given to the category of power in these passages is not surprising.

I am not forgetting here that the category of beauty also plays, as Roland Delattre has ably demonstrated, a central role in Edwards' articulation of being and of the divine being. "God is God, and distinguished from all other beings, and exalted above 'em, chiefly by his divine beauty," writes Edwards.[15] If both beauty and disposition are essential to the divine being, they are then coordinate categories. The essence of the divine being is the beautiful disposition and the dispositional beauty. The category of disposition articulates the inherently dynamic character of the beauty of God.

To say that the essence of the divine being is the disposition of divine beauty is also to affirm the essentially personal character of the being of God. All beauty is a relation of consent, but the consent in its "prime and proper sense," is the consent

[13] "Miscellanies," Nos. 94, 259, HGT, pp. 257–258, 259.
[14] "Miscellanies," No. 194, HGT, p. 184.
[15] *Religious Affections*, p. 298; Delattre, *Beauty and Sensibility*, p. 117.

between sentient beings—that is, between beings who understand and love.[16] The essence of the divine being is, then, the supremely personal disposition to be beautifully or consentingly related through knowing and loving.

There is a likeness between God and creature, according to Edwards. The abiding essence of a created entity is defined by Edwards as a dispositional law according to which God causes resistance. Similarly, the essence of the divine being is a disposition, not a substance or pure form. But there is a discontinuity as well between God and created beings. The category of disposition, when attributed to the eternally actual and sovereign creator, cannot be in every way the same as the dispositions of created entities. I should now point out some of the limitations or qualifications of the category of disposition as this category is applied by Edwards to the being of God.

The "Peculiarity" of the Divine Disposition

Emphasizing both the discontinuity and continuity between the divine being and the finite creatures, Edwards writes:

> Tho we cannot conceive of the manner of the divine understanding, yet if it be understanding or any thing that can be any way signified by the word of ours, it is by Idea. Tho the divine nature be vastly different from that of the created spirits, yet our souls are made in the Image of God, we have understanding & will, Idea & Love as God hath, and the difference is only in the Perfection of degree and manner.[17]

Explaining further the "Perfection of degree and manner" of the divine being, Edwards writes that in God there is no distinction between "Power or habit and act," or between "will, Inclination, & love," but "it is all one simple act." Edwards then immediately qualifies what he has just said: "But the divine Perfection will not Infer [i.e., imply] that his understanding is not by Idea and that there is not Indeed such a thing as Inclination & Love in God."[18] Edwards' contention is that

---

[16] "The Mind," No. 45, WEA, p. 362.
[17] "An Essay on the Trinity," FAJ, p. 375.
[18] Ibid., p. 376.

words referring to the human self can properly be used in reference to God except that in God intellectual and inclinational powers are infinitely perfect in their nature and infinitely perfect in their operation. So the difference between God and human beings is one of "Perfection in degree and manner." Edwards' statement that in God "it is all one simple act," therefore, means that in God, in contrast to creatures, all the powers of his essence are forever perfectly and fully engaged.

One can, then, understand in a similar way Edwards' use of the term "disposition" in his conception of the divine being. The properties of ordinary dispositions must be applicable to God except that the divine disposition must be conceived as "Perfect in degree and manner." But what, more specifically, are the ways in which the divine disposition is "Perfect in degree and manner"?

First, Edwards applies the category of disposition to God in such a way that God's prior actuality is not compromised. God's prior actuality, for Edwards, has two dimensions. God as the First Person of the Trinity, as I shall demonstrate in more detail below, is primordially the actuality of true beauty as well as primordially a disposition to repeat this actuality. In creatures, actuality is achieved through the exercise of disposition. In God, there is a dimension in which actuality is primordial and not arrived at. Further, God has a prior actuality in the sense that the inner-Trinitarian exercise of the divine disposition is eternal and complete. In created beings, the exercise of their dispositional essence, and thus the actualization of their being, are fragmentary. But the repetition of the divine actuality through the inner-Trinitarian exercise of the divine disposition is not subject to the finite conditions of space and time. The movement in the inner-Trinitarian life that is the exertion of the divine disposition is an eternal movement. In these two ways, the relationship between disposition and actuality in God, according to Edwards, is different from that relationship in finite creatures.

Second, unlike ordinary dispositions, the disposition that is God's essence is not acquired but eternal. Edwards typically refers to the divine disposition as the "eternal disposition" and "infinite propensity." The self-communicative disposition of God is a "perfection" and an "original property of his nature."[19] God's disposition is not only unacquired, but it also never ceases being what it eternally is. As shall be seen below, even its full exercise within God's internal life does not change it from being what it is: an active tendency to exercise. As the essence of God who has neither beginning nor ending, therefore, the divine disposition is absolutely unacquired and unchanging.

Another way in which the divine disposition is "Perfect in degree and manner" is that it is the disposition of the true, ultimate beauty. God's disposition is an "excellent disposition" whereby God is "disposed to do everything that is fit to be done," that is, everything beautiful.[20] Roland Delattre has shown that beauty is "the first principle of being, the inner, structural principle of being-itself," and thus the "measure and objective foundation of the perfection of being—of excellence, goodness, and value."[21] And God is "infinitely the most beautiful and excellent" being and also the "foundation and fountain of all being and all beauty . . . of whom, and through whom, and to whom is all being and all perfection."[22] For God, then, as for all other beings, beauty is a fundamental principle of being and life. Disposition and beauty, as I have already noted, are coordinate categories; they refer to one and the same thing in different ways. God is the divine disposition of beauty, or the divinely beautiful disposition. In this way, beauty articulates the character of the divine disposition and gives it concreteness while disposition articulates the dynamic or expansive character of the divine beauty.

God as the true beauty, according to Edwards, is the objective and ultimate criterion and basis of what is beautiful and thus of what is real. Beauty is proportion, but God is the ultimate criterion of what is truly proportional. The dispositional laws of all entities are created by God in such a way that they

[19] "End in Creation," WC, 2: 206–208.
[20] Ibid., pp. 200, 206.
[21] Delattre, *Beauty and Sensibility*, pp. 1–2.
[22] *True Virtue*, pp. 14–15.

are fitting with the beauty of God—that is, in such a way that their true actualities are not achieved until their fitness to the beauty of God is made manifest.[23]

The conclusion of this is that it is only the divine disposition of beauty that is in the proper sense ontologically productive. The dispositions of finite beings can be ontologically productive through their exercise only when infused by the disposition of God. This is so because only the divine disposition is the disposition of the true beauty that is the general law governing the essential destinies of all entities.

It should also be recalled that God, whose essence is the supremely beautiful disposition, is a supremely personal or spiritual being. All beauty is a relation of consent. But Edwards makes an important distinction between the primary beauty or the cordial consent of conscious love, on the one hand, and the secondary beauty or the far simpler relation of agreement as found in material objects and spiritual beings, on the other. And the simple agreements are beautiful only because they resemble to some degree the higher form of consent—the knowing and loving relation of consent.

> When we spake of excellence in bodies we were obliged to borrow the word "consent" from spiritual things. But excellence in and among spirits is, in its prime and proper sense, being's consent to being. There is no other proper consent but that of minds, even of their will; which, when it is of minds toward other things, it is choice. Wherefore all the primary and original beauty or excellence that is among minds is love; and into this may all be resolved that is found among them.[24]

The divine disposition, then, is a disposition of a mind and heart that knows and loves in the truly beautiful way. It is a power of loving knowledge and of knowing love. The divine disposition is a personal principle. As has been seen, all dispositions or habits are general laws that prescribe that a type

[23] See, for example, "Miscellanies," No. 1196, HGT, p. 184.
[24] "The Mind," No. 45, WEA, p. 362.

of event or action should occur whenever a certain type of occasion arises. The laws of nature are, therefore, in a sense dispositions or habits. But for Edwards the dispositions of minds and hearts are capable of cordial consent, or love, and have a metaphysical priority over the dispositions of nonsentient things. The category of disposition as applied to God must, therefore, be distinguished from the disposition of material things. And this is because the divine disposition is the disposition of true beauty as cordial consent. In short, God, whose being is essentially the disposition of the highest beauty, is the supremely personal power. And when this God self-communicates himself, such an act consists of a communication of the divine knowledge and the divine love.

The fourth way in which the divine disposition is to be distinguished from ordinary dispositions has to do with its absolute sovereignty and sufficiency. Dispositions and habits are the conditional general laws that "such actions upon such occasions should be exerted." The exercise of dispositions is dependently related to the appropriate occasions. Now, God's most basic disposition, according to Edwards, is God's disposition to delight in God's self—that is, to delight upon the occasion of seeing his own beauty. This disposition, which is the essence of the divine being, as shall be seen below, is fully exercised within the inner Trinity. God has a perfect Idea of God's own self, which God infinitely loves. God's internal self-knowledge and self-delight, according to Edwards, are the absolutely perfect exercises of the divine disposition "wherein the Godhead acts to an Infinite degree and in the most Perfect manner Possible."[25] Thus, so far as the internal being of God is concerned, the sufficiency of God's disposition is God's ability to know God's primordial actuality perfectly and to love what God knows "to an Infinite degree."

When one considers the exertion of the divine disposition in God's creation of the world, the absolute sovereignty and sufficiency of that disposition appears in a more radical way. The divine disposition seeks to delight in God's self as expressed in

[25] "An Essay on the Trinity," FAJ, p. 377.

time and space, but there is nothing other than God prior to the creation of the world. There is no temporal or created occasion for the exercise of the divine disposition. How then can the divine disposition find the appropriate occasion to delight in God's own beauty *ad extra*? Edwards answers this question:

> But now goodness, or an inclination to communicate good, has merely possible being as much its proper object as actual or designed being. *A disposition to communicate good will move a being to make occasion for the communication*; and indeed giving being is one part of the communication. If God be in Himself disposed to communicate Himself, He is therein disposed to make the creatures to communicate Himself to, because He can't do what He is in Himself disposed to without it. *God's goodness is not an inclination to communicate Himself as occasion shall offer, or a disposition conditionally to communicate Himself, but absolutely.* (Emphasis added)[26]

In the "End for Which God Created the World," Edwards describes the "self-moved" character of the divine disposition:

> There is something in that disposition in God to communicate goodness, which shows him to be independent and self-moved in it, in a manner that is peculiar, and above what is on the beneficence of creatures. Creatures, even the most gracious of them, are not so independent and self-moved in their goodness, but that in all the exercises of it, they are excited by some object that they find; something appearing good, or in some respect worthy of regard, presents itself, and moves their kindness. But God, being all and alone, is absolutely self-moved. The exercises of his communicative disposition are absolutely from within himself, not finding any thing, or any object to excite them or to draw them forth; but all that is good and worthy in the object, and the

[26] "Miscellanies," No. 445, HGT, p. 132.

very *being* of the object, proceeding from the overflowing of his fullness.[27]

Thus, in creating the finite world, especially the sentient beings in whose knowledge and love the beauty of God can be temporally embodied, the divine disposition creates the very occasions for its own exercise. And this is one more way in which the divine disposition is radically different from created dispositions.

So Edwards uses the category of disposition to conceptualize the essence of the divine being, only with some important qualifications. The divine disposition, unlike ordinary dispositions, is never without the primordial and eternal divine actuality, is unacquired and everlasting, is the absolutely beautiful and truly exercised disposition and thus capable of communicating being and beauty through a communication of divine knowledge and love, and finally, is an absolutely self-moved disposition that creates even its own occasions for exercise. These are, then, the "peculiar" or unusual senses in which the category of disposition is to be understood when Edwards uses it to refer to the divine being.

However, this distinction between the dispositions of God and of created things is not an ontological disjunction. There is, again, a real continuity, and on this basis, many of the ordinary meanings of the concept of disposition do apply to God in a positive (though modified) way.

The Meaning of a Dispositional Conception of the Divine Being

What then does it mean to conceive of the divine being as essentially dispositional? First, since disposition is a principle of existence as well as of operation, operation or activity is internally related to existence. God, in other words, does not first exist and then know and love, but rather he exists in and through knowing and loving. God's being consists of the primordial actuality of divine knowing and loving and of the

[27] "End in Creation," WC, 2: 221.

eternal inner-Trinitarian repetition of this primordial knowing and loving.

Second, to define God's essence as a disposition is to affirm
the inherent relationality of the divine being. Disposition is a
law of relations—that is, a law governing the character of actions or events and the character of their occasions. In God's
case, disposition is a law of beautiful relations; God's actions
and their occasions are fitting or beautiful. God's being is essentially an active tendency to beautiful relations, and, therefore, God as the triune being *is* only *as* God in his internal life
is related beautifully. Relations are internal to God's existence. And God's beautiful disposition is exercised in the form
of consent, that is, knowing and loving. So, God as the Trinity
exists only as God in his Trinity is related through knowing
and loving. This is another way in which Edwards has left the
tradition of substance metaphysics. Substances and forms are
principles of inherence and self-containment, and thus relations are not internal—that is, they do not affect an entity's
being. God's being, for Edwards, is not a substance but a disposition of beauty. There is then a plurality in God, and God's
unity or simplicity would consist of the irreducible and unitary
meaning of the beauty of that plurality of relationships taken
as a whole.[28]

Finally, Edwards' dispositional definition of the divine
being means that God is inherently a tendency toward an increase or enlargement of God's own being. God, in other
words, is truly actual, but he is also inherently disposed to
achieve that actuality again and again as the divine disposition
is further exercised.

Now, God remains essentially a disposition even while this
disposition is eternally in its full exercise. Thus, God whose
actuality is primordial and eternal would still be tending toward further exertions of his disposition and thus toward repeated actualizations. God would still be tending toward further relationships of knowing and loving in a truly beautiful
manner. The fully actual God, therefore, is inherently inclined

---

[28] "Miscellanies," No. 117, HGT, p. 258.

to enlarge, increase, and multiply his own self through a multiplication of beautiful relations. God can add beauty to
beauty and being to being. Not that God's being is still in the
process of becoming, but God's primordial and eternally completed actuality can be still tending toward an expansion of
relationships.

The Fullness of God

I offered above a schematic discussion of an essentially dynamic conception of God that results from Edwards' dispositional definition of the essence of divine being. This analysis
needs to be made more concrete. God, for Edwards, is primordially and completely actual as well as dispositional. And
it is through Edwards' doctrine of God as the triune being that
Edwards articulates the way God's dispositional essence is
fully exerted. Thus, God is seen not only as the primordially
actual being but also as the eternal and complete repetition or
increase of this actuality. God is at once the absolute and infinite being and also the supremely living fullness of all being.
I now turn to Edwards' discussion of the immanent Trinity.

In articulating the doctrine of the Trinity, Edwards combines the logic of the self-communication of the divine being
through the exercise of the divine disposition *with* the analogy
of the human self with two basic functions: knowing and willing or loving. Edwards also utilizes Locke's concept of the
self's reflexive or introspective experience of its internal acts.[29]
So, the three Persons of the Trinity are understood as (1) the
primordial actuality of the divine beauty that is also the eternal disposition to know and love, and thereby repeat, this actuality; (2) the reflexive knowledge of God's internal life that
results from the divine disposition's repeated exertion of re-

[29] See Locke, *Essay*, bk. 2, chap. 1, nos. 1–5; "Miscellanies," No. 238, HGT,
p. 247. For Edwards' view of the self, see *Religious Affections*, pp. 96–98.
Edwards follows Locke in his holistic view of the human self. It is the whole
self that understands, and the whole self that is inclined. So the basic distinctions are: the self, the self as it understands, and the self as it inclines or wills.
For God, the understanding is his reflexive understanding of his own self.

flexively knowing himself; and (3) God's love of his reflexive knowledge that results from the divine disposition's repeated exertion in reflexively loving what he knows. So the full exertion of the divine disposition constitutes: "God, the idea of God, and the love of God."[30]

The First Person of the Trinity refers traditionally to the unoriginated (not begotten) and absolutely primordial reality of God as God. Thus, God the Father could not be thought of only as the divine disposition since a disposition would still lack in the full actuality toward which a disposition is disposed. How, then, does Edwards conceive of the Father? Edwards writes in "An Essay on the Trinity" that "the F. (Father) is the Deity subsisting in the prime, unoriginated & most absolute manner, or the deity in its direct existence."[31] It is clear here that Edwards sees the Father as the deity in his unoriginated and absolute actuality. The Father is the "direct existence" of God as God and thus "the Godhead in its first subsistence."

What, then, according to Edwards, is the content of this primordial divine actuality? On the basis of other things Edwards says about God, one can expect that God in his primordial actuality is the actuality of knowing and loving the divine beauty — namely, God's "delight" or "happiness." Edwards explains:

> The knowledge or understanding in God which we must conceive of as first is His knowledge of every Thing possible. That love which must be this knowledge is what we must conceive of as belonging to the essence of the Godhead in its first subsistence.[32]

It is not that God the Father is constituted by or is arrived at as the result of his knowing and loving. The Father *is* the primordial divine knowing and loving of the true beauty. Neither temporal nor logical distinction is allowed between

---

[30] "Miscellanies," No. 308, HGT, p. 260.
[31] "An Essay on the Trinity," FAJ, p. 379.
[32] "An Essay on the Trinity," PH, p. 130.

the Father as actuality and the Father as knowing and loving. Thus, Edwards says in the above passage, in the Father's knowledge and love belongs "*essence* of the Godhead in its first subsistence" (emphasis added). The Father is essentially (that is, in what the Father is) actuality.

But, what of the divine disposition? Is not the divine disposition also the essence of the divine being, according to Edwards? God's "disposition to communicate Himself" is what is "originally in God as a perfection of his nature."[33] Speaking about God's power, Edwards wrote that "'tis nothing but the essence of God."[34] Further, "It is God's essence to incline to communicate Himself."[35] And, in "Miscellanies," No.94, Edwards clearly identifies the power of God with the Father himself.

> If it shall be said that there are power, goodness, and holiness in God, and that these may as well be proved to be distinct persons, because everything that is in God is God, (I answer), as to the power of God, power always consists in something — the power of the mind consists in its wisdom, the power of the body in plenty of animal spirits and toughness of limbs, etc. — and as it is distinct from those and other things, 'tis only a relation of adequateness and sufficiency of the essence of everything. But if we distinguish it from relation, 'tis nothing else but the essence of God. *And if we take it for that which is that by which God exerts Himself, 'tis no other than the Father; for the perfect energy of God, with respect to Himself, is the most perfect exertion of Himself,* of which the creation of the world is but a shadow. (Emphasis added)[36]

The category of "power," as shown earlier, is given a dispositional definition by Edwards.[37] Thus, the gist of the above

[33] "End in Creation," WC, 2:207.
[34] "Miscellanies," No. 94, HGT, p. 258.
[35] "Miscellanies," No. 107, Yale MSS.
[36] "Miscellanies," No. 94, HGT, pp. 257–258.
[37] "The Mind," No. 29, WEA, p. 352.

passage, as I read it, is that the Father *is* the divine disposition.

What Edwards is affirming, I believe, is that God the Father is at once the divine primordial actuality of true beauty *and* the divine disposition to exert himself—that is, the disposition to repeat the divine primordial actuality. The Father is essentially actual and essentially dispositional. In the Father, the divine actuality is a disposition, and the divine disposition is an actuality.[38]

But this coincidence of actuality and disposition cannot be true only for the Father. The Father is God, according to Edwards' Trinitarian logic, only together with the other two Persons of the Trinity. This would mean that actuality and disposition coincide for God *as the Trinity* and, therefore, for each of the Three Persons of the Godhead. Speaking of the divine being as a whole, Edwards wrote that

> there is no distinction to be made in God between power and habit and act . . . [although] this will not infer [i.e., imply] that His understanding is not by idea and that there is not indeed such a thing as inclination and love in God.[39]

As we shall see below, the coincidence of actuality and disposition is affirmed by Edwards for the entire divine being — that is, for the Son and the Holy Spirit as well as for the Father.

Edwards' insistence on this point is significant because it enables him to conceive of God as essentially dynamic without sacrificing the prior actuality and self-sufficiency or aseity of the divine being. God is inherently creative, in other words, without needing such creative activity for God's internal self-realization. And this is true for each of the Three Persons of the Trinity so that they are equal in their divinity. St. Thomas Aquinas affirmed God's aseity by maintaining

[38] I have benefitted from my conversation with Gregory Boyd of Bethel College about the coincidence of actuality and disposition in Edwards' doctrine of God.

[39] "An Essay on the Trinity," PH, pp. 99–100.

that God's essence *is* his existence.⁴⁰ In a similar manner, Edwards is saying that God's dispositional essence and his existence coincide. God is a disposition only by being also a primordial actuality; God is a primordial actuality only by being the eternal disposition to repeat this actuality in new forms.

It should be noted here that Edwards' conception of the coincidence of actuality and disposition in God as the Trinity is the point where his thought is most profoundly different from that of contemporary process theologians. Like process thinkers, Edwards tried to see the divine being as dynamic. However, in asserting the convergence of primordial actuality and eternal disposition in God, Edwards, unlike process thinkers, affirms God's essential actuality and aseity and also the Christian conception of God as the ultimate principle of all creativity as well as of all being. There is no tendency in Edwards, as there is in process thought, to separate the principle of creativity from the divine being.⁴¹ God as the Trinity, for Edwards, is essentially the creative ground of all being and becoming.

Now, since the Father is essentially dispositional as well as actual, the Father is essentially inclined toward further exertions and thus the repetition and communication of his essential actuality. And this repetition or communication of the Father's eternal actuality occurs in two ways: in the Father's reflexively knowing himself and in his reflexively loving what he knows.

Those ideas which we call ideas of reflection, all ideas of the acts of the mind . . . are, indeed, repetitions of these very things, either more fully or more faintly. . . . Now if this be certain, as it seems to me to be, then it's quite clear

⁴⁰ Thomas Aquinas, *Summa Contra Gentiles* (Garden City, N.Y.: Doubleday, 1955), bk.1, chap. 22, pp. 118–120.
⁴¹ For a critique of Whitehead's concept of God precisely on the issue of God's relation to the principle of creativity, see Neville, *Creativity and God*, esp. pp. 21–47. See also chap. 1, n. 3, above.

that, if God doth think of Himself and understand Himself with perfect clearness, fullness, and distinctness that Idea He hath of Himself is absolutely Himself again. . . . So that by God's thinking of Himself, the deity must certainly be generated.[42]

So there is

a Reflex act of Knowledge and his viewing Himself, knowing himself and so knowing his own Knowledge and the Son is begotten. There is such a Thing in God as knowledge of knowledge, and an Idea of an idea. Which can be nothing else than the Idea or the Knowledge repeated.[43]

Thus, the Second Person of the Trinity is a repetition, via reflexive knowledge, of the Father's actuality, and this repetition of the first subsistence is the result of the ontologically productive activity of the divine disposition. "In the Son the deity, the whole deity and glory of the Father, is as it were repeated or duplicated. Every thing in the Father is repeated, or expressed again, and that fully."[44]

I should note here that Edwards argues for the divinity of the Son both on the basis of his view that a perfect idea of a thing is a repetition of that very thing and from his view that the perfect exertion of the divine disposition is ontologically productive — that is, self-communicative. As Herbert Richardson has emphasized in his interpretation of Edwards, "all sorts of ideas of things are repetitions of those things over again."[45] Thus, ideas in general are repetitions in the mind of the very things of which the ideas are ideas. But God the Father's idea of himself must be infinitely and eternally perfect and thus the perfect repetition of his being. "Therefore

[42] "Miscellanies," No. 238, HGT, p. 247.
[43] Jonathan Edwards, *An Unpublished Essay of Edwards on the Trinity*, ed. George P. Fisher (New York: Charles Scribner, 1903), p. 132.
[44] "Observations Concerning the Scripture Oeconomy of the Trinity," PH, p. 77.
[45] "The Mind," No. 66, WEA, p. 383; see Richardson, "The Glory of God," chap. 2.

as G. (God) with Perfect Clearness, fullness & strength, understands himself, views his own essence . . . that Idea which G. (God) hath of himself is absolutely himself."[46] In other words, any exercise of the deity's disposition can only be an infinitely perfect exercise and thus perfectly self-communicative of his being. The Father's self-understanding, therefore, eternally generates the perfect repetition of the Father's being as the Father's "Idea" of himself. "The Father's begetting of the Son is a complete communication of all his happiness, and so an eternal, adequate, and infinite exercise of perfect goodness that is completely equal to such an inclination in perfection."[47] This is why the Father's exertion of his disposition in reflexive knowledge, even "before" (or, as distinguished from) reflexive love, can be a full repetition or communication of God's actuality.

The Son, then, is the full actuality of the divine being repeated as God's Idea of himself. But the Son's actuality is also the divine disposition to repeat that actuality through further exercises. Edwards writes:

[T]he Son is the adequate communication of the Father's goodness, and is an express and complete image of him. *But yet the Son has also an inclination to communicate himself in an image his person, that may partake of his happiness, and this was the end of the creation.* (Emphasis added)[48]

So, the Son is at once actuality and disposition, and in the above quotation, Edwards speaks of the exercise of the Son's disposition in his activity *ad extra* (i.e., in creating the world). But, as we shall see below, Edwards also refers to the mutual act of love between the Father and the Son, thus implying that the Son's disposition is exercised within the immanent Trinity as well as *ad extra*.

Now, the Father repeats the divine actuality not only by reflexively knowing himself but also by reflexively loving

[46] "An Essay on the Trinity," FAJ, p. 377.
[47] "Miscellanies," No. 104, THA, app. 1, p. 37.
[48] Ibid.

what he knows. Edwards, as I noted above, follows the analogy of the self as the self, the self as knowing, and the self as loving. And the act of the Father's loving what he knows is a further exercise (this time, affectional) of the Father's disposition. So, "the Father loveth the Son as a communication of himself as begotten in *pursuance of his eternal inclination to communicate himself*" (emphasis added).[49] Through God's love of his Idea of himself, God's self-communication is accomplished affectionally. The Father is already eternal loving as well as eternal knowing. But now the divine disposition is exercised in a *reflexive* affection for God's self-knowledge.

> The Deity becomes all act, the Divine essence itself flows out and is as it were breathed forth in love and joy. So the Godhead stands forth in yet another manner or subsistence, & there Proceeds the 3rd Person in the Trinity, the Holy Spirit, viz. the deity in act, for there is no other act but the act of the will.[50]

Edwards, however, does not stop at describing the Holy Spirit as the consequence of the Father's affectional exercise of the divine disposition. Following the Augustinian tradition of affirming the *filioque* (the doctrine that the Holy Spirit proceeds from the Father *and the Son*), Edwards maintains that "the Holy Spirit is the act of God between the Father and the Son, infinitely loving and delighting in each other." Thus, God's affectional self-repetition or self-communication is the "mutual love and delight" between the Father and the Son.[51]

Further, just as in the case of the First and the Second Persons of the Trinity, Edwards sees the Holy Spirit as essentially both actuality and disposition. Edwards writes:

[49] Ibid., p. 38.
[50] "An Essay on the Trinity," FAJ, p. 377.
[51] "Miscellanies," No. 94, HGT, p. 256; "An Essay on the Trinity," PH, p. 108.

So I suppose when we read of the Spirit of God who we are told is a spirit, it is to be understood of the disposition or temper or affection of the divine mind. . . . Now the sum of God's temper or disposition is love, for He is infinite love and, as I observed before, here is no distinction between habit and act, between temper or disposition and exercise.[52]

The Holy Spirit, in short, is at once both the full affectional repetition or "flowing out" of the divine actuality and also the divine disposition toward further repetitions through further exercises.

The full actuality of the divine being *ad intra* can also be seen in terms of the inner-Trinitarian actualization of the divine beauty. As was shown, God essence is the divine disposition of true beauty or excellency, and beauty is a relation of consent. For the divine beauty actualized within the Godhead, then, there has to be a relatedness and thus a plurality within God. "One alone cannot be excellent, inasmuch as, in such case, there can be no consent. Therefore, if God is excellent, there must be a plurality in God."[53] In other words, "there must have been an object from all eternity which God infinitely loves."[54]

In the following quotation Edwards further explains the intra-divine plurality itself as being brought about by the exercise of the dispositional and self-communicative character of the divine beauty. Edwards writes:

It appears that there must be more than a Unity in infinite and eternal Essence; Otherwise the Goodness of God can have no perfect exercises. To be perfectly Good, is to incline to, and delight in, making another happy in the same proportion as it is happy itself: that is, it delights as much in communicating happiness to another as in enjoying it himself, and (is) an inclination to communicate all his hap-

[52] Ibid., pp. 109–110.
[53] "Miscellanies," No. 117, HGT, p. 258.
[54] Ibid.

piness . . . God must have a perfect Exercise of his Goodness, and therefore must have the fellowship of a person
equal to himself.[55]

If we put the above statements together with our earlier
discussion of Edwards' articulation of the Trinity, we can
interpret Edwards' discussion of the Trinity in terms of the
divine beauty, as follows: There is first the Father or the "direct existence" of the divine beauty with its disposition to
know and love beauty, and he repeats his beauty in the Son
through the exercise of his disposition to communicate
beauty and then loves and delights in the Son in a "perfect
exercise" of the divine goodness.

The Father, who is already the primordial divine knowing
and loving and, thus, the primordial divine happiness and
beauty, is seen as the first subsistence of the divine beauty. It
is the Son who introduces to the divine being the proper
Other or "plurality" in relation to whom the Father's disposition to delight in beauty is properly exercised. And the
beautiful consent between the Father and the Son is the Holy
Spirit. In short, the divine beauty with its disposition to
beautify (i.e., to self-communicate and self-repeat through
exercises) and to delight in beauty exists in the fullness of its
actuality and its repetition in the beauty and beautifying in
God the Trinity *ad intra*.[56] So, in Edwards' own words:

God is glorified within Himself these two ways: 1. By appearing or being manifested to Himself in His own perfect
Idea; or in His Son, who is the brightness of his glory. 2. By
enjoying and delighting in Himself, by flowing forth in infinite Love and delight towards Himself, or in his Holy Spirit.[57]

One question that our discussion of Edwards' Trinitarian
articulation of the full actuality of God *ad intra* raises is the
nature of the role of the Holy Spirit in that fullness. In a way

---

[55] "Miscellanies," No. 96, HGT, p. 194.

[56] For an excellent discussion of Edwards' idea of beauty and the doctrine
of Trinity, see Delattre, *Beauty and Sensibility*, pp. 148–161.

[57] "Miscellanies," No. 448, HGT, p. 133.

typical of the Augustinian tradition, the Holy Spirit for Edwards is the relation or act between the first two Persons of the Trinity. The Father and the Son "do" things: the Father self-repeats himself in the Son, and the Son delights in and loves the Father in a mutual love between them. What does the Third Person "do" within the immanent Trinity? Edwards' usual answer is that the Holy Spirit is the loving act itself. But, in a hitherto unpublished manuscript called "Fragment on the Trinity" (dated in the early to mid-1740s) Edwards writes that the Holy Spirit "as it were reigns over the Godhead and governs his heart, and wholly influences both the Father and the Son in all they do."[58]

The intent of Edwards' discussion of the immanent Trinity is clear: In and through the inner-Trinitarian dynamic, the divine selfhood is self-realized and alive in the fullness of its actuality *plus* self-repetition "to an Infinite degree and in the most perfect manner."

The conclusion of the discussion in this section, which is of fundamental importance to my interpretation of Edwards' philosophical theology, is this: For Edwards, God *ad intra* is at once fully actual and also essentially disposed to communicate himself. Thus, Edwards introduces a dynamic dimension to the divine being without compromising God's aseity and prior actuality. And this conception of God as a continuing dispositional thrust is capable of functioning, as we shall see, as the ontological ground for the movement in time in such a way

---

[58] Quoted here by courtesy of the Trustees of the Boston Public Library. See Robert W. Jenson, *America's Theologian: A Recommendation of Jonathan Edwards* (New York: Oxford University Press, 1988), p. 97; Amy Plantinga Pauw, "The Supreme Harmony of All: Jonathan Edwards and the Trinity" (Ph.D. diss., Yale University, 1990).

that time is in some sense genuinely significant even to God himself.[59]

GOD'S SELF-ENLARGEMENT AD EXTRA
God's Creation of the World as the Exercise of God's Dispositional Essence

"God made the world that He might communicate, and the creatures receive, His glory," writes Edwards.[60] But, has Edwards not already stated that the inner-Trinitarian self-communication of God is a self-communication "completely equal to" the eternal divine disposition? Edwards answers:

> 'Tis true that there was from eternity that act in God, within Himself and toward Himself, that was the exercise of the same perfections of His nature. But it was *not the same kind of exercise* of His perfection. God, who delights in the ex-

---

[59] James A. Hand, in his comparative study of Edwards and Paul Tillich, finds Edwards' ontology of consent and emanation lacking in a truly teleological movement, while Tillich's dialectic of being's eternal overcoming of nonbeing implies a dynamic ontology that "provides the archetype for the temporality or the historical character of being." Tillich's perspective, according to Hand, "changes the vision of the divine aseity from that of God eternally loving and delighting in himself to that of God continually 'creating himself.'" In interpreting Edwards' category of emanation in terms of the relational concept of consent, Hand correctly avoids a purely Neoplatonic reading of Edwards that sees no teleology in Edwards' God. However, Hand has not gone far enough. God, for Edwards also, is continually "creating himself" in the sense of self-communication. The self-communication of the Father through the inner-Trinitarian life is of course an eternal movement. Nevertheless, the Father's self-repetition within the Trinity is a teleological activity of the divine disposition. Therefore, God as he is in himself, according to Edwards, is an inherently dynamic reality within which lies the ultimate reason and pattern of the becoming of the created existence. For further elaboration of this point, see the remainder of this chapter and also Chapter 8. See James A. Hand, "Teleological Aspects of Creation: A Comparison of the Concepts of Being and Meaning in the Theologies of Jonathan Edwards and Paul Tillich" (Ph.D. diss., Vanderbilt University, 1969).

[60] "Miscellanies," No. 448, HGT, p. 133.

ercise of His perfection, delights in *all kinds of its exercise*. (Emphasis added)[61]

By the different "kinds" of the exercise of the divine disposition, Edwards is referring to the ad intra/ad extra distinction. God's creation of the world, according to Edwards, is the exertion of "an inclination in God to cause His *internal* glory to flow out *ad extra*" (emphasis added).[62]

God, in other words, now desires to find himself in temporality so that he may delight in himself ad extra. The divine disposition "seeks occasion to exercise" itself ad extra[63]—that is, an occasion in temporality to delight in the divine beauty. But there can be no preexisting entity outside of God that can function as that occasion. So the divine disposition brings about the occasion itself for its own exercise. The giving of existence to the created realm itself, then, is part of the exercise of the divine disposition—that is, part of the self-communication or self-enlargement of the divine being. So the creatures "are made that God may in them have occasion to fulfill His pleasure in manifesting and communicating Himself."[64]

Now, God is a dynamic and personal being whose internal life consists in the perfect knowledge and love of the divine beauty. Thus, the repetition or communication of God's internal fullness in time and space requires sentient creatures who can repeat in time God's dynamic internal life. For this reason, "God has made intelligent creatures capable of being concerned in these effects, as being the willing active subjects, or means; and so they are capable of actively promoting God's glory."[65] In other words, God's "communication is really only to intelligent beings."[66]

---

[61] "Miscellanies," No. 553, HGT, p. 136.

[62] "Miscellanies," No. 448, HGT, p. 133.

[63] "Miscellanies," No. 1218, HGT, p. 149.

[64] "Miscellanies," No. 448, HGT, pp. 133–134.

[65] "Miscellanies," No. 1218, HGT, p. 152.

[66] "Miscellanies," No. 332, HGT, p. 130. This does not mean, however, that God does not communicate himself in and through nonperceiving beings. God does communicate his glory through nonintelligent beings, but this proc-

> In the creature's knowing, esteeming, loving, and rejoycing in, and praising God, the glory of God is both exhibited and acknowledged; his fullness is received and returned. Here is both an *emanation* and *remanation*. The refulgence shines upon and into the creature, and is reflected back to the luminary.[67]

The nonsentient parts of the cosmos are also meant to be the "images or shadows of the divine things," and thus God's self-communication of his glory. But the fulfillment of their destiny is dependent upon the consciousness of the sentient creatures.[68]

The process of God's self-repetition in time, according to Edwards, takes an infinite amount of time since God's internal fullness is infinitely perfect. As I have shown, God's internal fullness is his primordial actuality *plus* its infinite increase or repetition through the inner-Trinitarian relationships. All this now has to be repeated in the realm of finite, temporal beings. Thus, God's self-communication ad extra will take an "eternal duration, with all the infinity of its progress, and infinite increase of nearness and union to God." Indeed, "the time will never come when it can be said it has already arrived at this infinite height."[69]

It should be noted that in discussing God's self-communication in creating the world, Edwards freely mixes emanationistic and teleological languages. In creating the world, God "aims at," and "seeks" to achieve, some end. Edwards also asserts that the creation is a "flowing forth" or emanation of God's internal fullness.[70] Edwards, I believe, is not being careless with his words here but speaks as he does because he sees

---

ess, as I have shown, is dependent upon the saints' perception of them in their ultimate relational context. "The state of the inanimate, unperceiving part of the world is nothing regarded any otherwise than in a subserviency to the perceiving or intelligent parts," writes Edwards. See "Miscellanies," No. 547, HGT, p. 136.

[67] "End in Creation," WC, 2: 255.

[68] See n. 66 above.

[69] "End in Creation," WC, 2: 256.

[70] Ibid., pp. 219, 220–221.

the creation as both a purposive act and also an emanation. And it is Edwards' dispositional conception of God that enables Edwards to combine the categories of emanation and teleology. The logic behind this wedding of the two usually unrelated concepts is to be traced to the idea of disposition and its ontologically productive character. Since it is an ontological as well as an operational principle, its exertion brings about the actuality of being as well as a multiplication of that actuality. At the same time, disposition is also a teleological principle in that it is a tendency toward the end of bringing about a certain sort of actual event or activity. That to which a disposition tends is a real possibility, and this real possibility becomes an actuality when the disposition is exercised; thus, there is a real teleological movement involved here, a movement from virtuality to full actuality. On this basic point, Edwards' conception of the divine creativity must be distinguished from that of either Plotinus or Spinoza, for whom the category of a necessary emanation excludes any room for teleology. For Edwards, God's emanation of himself is a purposive activity. God is involved in a motion that is real even to himself. God's creation of the world is both a "flowing forth" or self-communication and also a purposive activity with a goal.

It is extremely important here to point out Edwards' contention that God's motive in creating the world is the further exertion of his *original dispositional essence*, which is already fully exercised within God's internal being. "The disposition to communicate himself, or diffuse his own FULLNESS, which we must conceive of as being originally in God as a perfection of his nature, was what moved him to create the world."[71] So Edwards traces God's disposition to communicate himself ad extra to God's communicative disposition per se or God's "communicative disposition in general."[72] But this communicative disposition, which was "originally in God as a perfec-

[71] "End in Creation," WC, 2: 206.
[72] Ibid.

tion of his nature,"[73] is none other than God's very essence—that is, God's disposition to delight in himself or the disposition the exertion of which constitutes the internal life of the Trinity. As Edwards puts it in "Miscellanies," No. 1218, God's communicative disposition is none other than his "disposition effectually to exert Himself, and to exert Himself in order to an effect." And "the effect is the communication of Himself *ad extra*."[74] As seen above, the exercise of the divine disposition is self-communicative because of the ontologically productive character of the exercise of the divine disposition. At any rate, God's original dispositional essence is what is involved in God's creation of the world. Again, as Edwards summarizes the point himself:

> It is a regard to himself that disposes him to diffuse and communicate himself. It is such a delight in his own internal fullness and glory, that disposes him to an abundant effusion and emanation of that glory. *The same disposition, that inclines him to delight in his glory*, causes him to delight in the exhibitions, expressions and communications of it. (Emphasis added)[75]

The same point is elaborated further in an important way at another place in "The End for Which God Created the World":

> A respect to himself, or an infinite propensity to, and delight in his own glory, is that which causes him to incline to its being abundantly diffused, and to delight in the emanation of it. Thus that nature in a tree, by which it puts forth buds, shoots out branches, and brings forth leaves and fruit, is *a disposition that terminates in its own complete self*. And so the disposition in the sun to shine, or abundantly to diffuse its fulness, warmth and brightness, is only *a tendency to its most glorious and complete state*. So God looks on the communication of himself, and the emanation of the infinite

[73] Ibid., p. 207.
[74] "Miscellanies," No. 1218, HGT, p. 152.
[75] "End in Creation," WC, 2: 215.

glory and good that are in himself to *belong to the fulness and completeness of himself; as though he were not in his most complete and glorious state without it.* (Emphasis added)[76]

So it is the same divine dispositional essence that was already fully exercised within God's internal being that is involved in God's creation of the world. The point that emerges unmistakably here is that God's creation of the world, as Edwards conceives it, is, at least in some limited sense, a further self-realization of God's own being "as though he were not in his most complete and glorious state without it." If God is eternally "most complete and glorious," what sense could there be in which God is further actualized through this creation of the world?

In What Sense Is the Divine Being "Enlarged" through the Creation of the World?

The consequence of Edwards' conception of God's creation of the world as the exertion of God's original dispositional essence itself is that the world is in some sense a further actualization of God's own being. Thus, Edwards says that in God's act of creating the world, " 'tis Himself exerted and Himself communicated."[77] Through God's creative act, according to Edwards, God's own happiness is "enlarged."[78] God's self-

---

[76] Ibid., pp. 208–209. Edwards' conception of God's creation of the world as an exercise of God's essential disposition makes creation in some sense necessary. For a critique of Edwards on this point, see Patricia Wilson-Kastner, "God's Infinity and His Relationship to Creation in the Theologies of Gregory of Nyssa and Jonathan Edwards," *Foundations* 21 (1978): 314. The interpreter of Edwards must remember, however, the distinction he makes between moral necessity and "natural necessity," the former being the sort of "necessity" that is involved in the actions of the intelligent and voluntary beings. See, for a good discussion of this distinction, Ramsey, "Editor's Introduction," in *Freedom of the Will*, pp. 34–47. For an analysis of Edwards' notion of moral necessity as a conception of "internal self-consistency," see Smith, "Edwards as Philosophical Theologian," p. 317.

[77] "Miscellanies," No. 1218, HGT, p. 152.

[78] "End in Creation," WC, 2: 210, 253.

communication in creating the world, then, in some sense aims at "the fullness and completeness of himself."[79]

Further, if the world in some sense "enlarges" and "completes" God's own life, the world is internally related to God's *own* life. What happens in time and space does matter to God himself. God has a "real and proper delight" and even "more delight" as God's essential disposition is further exercised in creating the world. "God would be less happy if He were less good, or if it were possible for Him to be hindered in exercising His goodness or to be hindered from glorifying Himself."[80]

On the other hand, however, it has already been shown that God is completely actual as God. Edwards denies in the strongest possible terms that God's self-communication in creating the world in any way implies a deficiency in the divine being. God is "self-existent from all eternity, absolutely perfect in himself, in the possession of infinite and independent good," and, therefore, is "above all need and all capacity of being added to and advanced, made better and happier in any respect."[81]

But, having said this, Edwards goes right back to his affirmation of the world as internally and really related to the divine being. "And yet," Edwards writes, "*in some sense* it can be truly said that God has the more delight and pleasure for the holiness and happiness of his creatures."[82] And, drawing out the implications of the world's internal relationship to God, Edwards says that God "really loves the being honored by them [creatures], as all try to be well thought of by those they love. Therefore, we are to seek the glory of God as that which is a thing *really* pleasing to Him" (emphasis added).[83]

The question, then, is the meaning of the phrase "in some sense." What is the exact meaning of the "sense" in which the eternally actual and perfect God is still "enlarged" and made

[79] Ibid., p. 209.
[80] "Miscellanies," No. 679, HGT, pp. 138–139; "End in Creation," WC, 2: 212–213.
[81] Ibid., pp. 211–212.
[82] Ibid., p. 213.
[83] "Miscellanies," No. 208, HGT, p. 129.

"happier" through the creation of the world? Now Edwards' ad intra/ad extra distinction becomes important. And Edwards' dispositional conception of the divine being according to which God can be fully actual and yet remain essentially disposed toward further exercises and toward further self-actualizations functions as the key. God, in other words, needs no self-realization ad intra; however, God, through the *external* exercise of his inexhaustible dispositional essence, is capable of further self-actualizations ad extra. Since God ad intra is fully actual, God's further self-actualization ad extra can only be a *repetition* of what is already actual ad intra. Self-communication as *self-repetition*, then, is the positive meaning of Edwards' phrase "in some sense." Thus, Edwards speaks of God's self-communication through the creation of the world as "an increase, repetition or multiplication" of his internal fullness.[84] What one might call an "external fullness" of God's internal fullness is what is aimed at through God's act of creation. In short, God's self-communication in creating the world does indeed "add" to his *own* fullness since this self-communication by God is the exertion of God's original dispositional essence. However, this act of God's self-enlargement through the creation of the world is *not* God's self-realization as God but rather his *external* repetition of his *internal* actuality. The created world, then, is not internally related to the triune God in the sense that the world adds to God's self-realization ad intra. But, the world is internally related to the triune God in the sense that the world repeats God's internal prior actuality through God's external exercise of his original dispositional essence.

The dispositional conception of the divine being and the ad intra/ad extra distinction, then, are the conceptual vehicles through which Edwards attempts to protect God's absolute prior actuality and self-sufficiency and at the same time replace the older notion of God as the absolutely self-contained actus purus with the dynamic conception of God as at once eternally actual and inherently and inexhaustibly self-enlarg-

---

[84] "End in Creation," WC, 2: 206.

ing. The inside/outside distinction in reference to God has been the traditional way in which orthodox Western Christian theology has tried to preserve God's transcendence (God as he is in himself) while at the same time affirming God's immanence in the world (God as he is related to the world). The novel element in Edwards is his conception of God ad extra not only as God's relation to the world but as *God's external repetition of his own being*.[85] And the fundamental logic underlying Edwards' novel contribution is his conception of the divine being as at once essentially actual and also essentially dispositional. God's essential actuality together with Edwards' doctrine of the immanent Trinity and the ad intra/ad extra distinction enables Edwards to remain faithful to the orthodox doctrine of God's absolute prior actuality and aseity. And Edwards' doctrine of God as essentially the disposition to repeat this actuality in all kinds of the disposition's exercise enables Edwards to see God's own life as inexhaustibly repeatable—even in the form of God's self-repetition in time and space.

Now that I have broached the positive and yet peculiar sense in which God's own being is capable of an ontological self-enlargement, it may be helpful to summarize the various senses in which God, according to Edwards, is incapable of being added to, thereby to achieve an even greater clarity

---

[85] A concept strikingly similar to Edwards' idea of God's repetition of his own being appears in Karl Barth's conception of God and God's self-revelation in Jesus Christ. Like Edwards, Barth tries to see God as inherently dynamic in his being without compromising God's aseity. In God's self-revelation in Jesus Christ, God is himself in time although God is not temporal. Barth conceives of this activity of the already actual God in terms of God's "reiteration" or "repetition" of himself in time (*Wiederholung Gottes*). And this reiteration of God in time is grounded in God's eternal reiteration within the immanent Trinity, a "*repetitio aeternitatis in aeternitate.*" In spite of this very interesting similarity, Barth and Edwards hold quite different views on the scope of God's reiteration. For Barth, this temporal becoming (as reiteration) is very much focused in God's action in Jesus Christ. Edwards, however, holds the more theocentric view that God's temporal self-enlargement (as repetition) encompasses the entire cosmos and temporal existence. See Jüngel, *The Doctrine of the Trinity*, pp. 100–101, n. 152. See also Gunton, *Becoming and Being*, esp. pp. 117–224.

about the specific sense in which God, according to Edwards, is enlarged through the creation of the world.

First of all, God's actuality in his internal being is absolutely complete and thus cannot be added to. The internal life of the Trinity is God's primordial actuality *plus* an increase of that actuality "to an Infinite degree and in the most Perfect manner Possible." God is already God in God's actuality ad intra.

It is true that the essence of this internally actual God remains a disposition and thus inclines toward an external exercise. God's self-repetition ad extra in time and space is yet to be completely actualized. However, the temporal extension of God's actuality repeats in time God's internal actuality and does not improve it.

This complete actuality of God ad intra means, I may further note, that God's self-realization ad intra could not be the aim in God's creation of the world. What, then, does God intend to achieve through the creation? Edwards discusses this question in the early parts of "The End for Which God Created the World." He begins by noting that God by virtue of the excellence of his nature could not pursue any aim that is of a lesser value than the very highest. But God himself by definition, according to Edwards, is the highest value. And if God is the highest value, then, "it is reasonable to suppose that [God] had respect to *himself* as his last and highest end in his work." In other words, God can only "make himself his end" in creating the world.[86]

But, if God ad intra is fully actual and could not be added to, how can God be that which God aims at in the creation? "Thus, *God's existence and infinite perfection*, though infinitely valuable in themselves, and infinitely valued by God, yet cannot be supposed to be the end of any divine operation" (emphasis added).[87] God's existence or self-realization as God, in other words, cannot be what God intends to achieve through the creation. It still remains true, however, that God cannot aim at anything of less value than himself. How, then,

[86] "End in Creation," WC, 2: 200, 207.
[87] Ibid., p. 200.

can God aim at himself without aiming at his self-realization as God? Edwards' answer, as I have shown, is that God aims at an external repetition and communication of God's internal fullness. The end of creation cannot be God himself in a simple sense. God's aim, rather, is God himself repeated externally—God, "existing *ad extra*."[88] "His own glory was the ultimate, Himself was His end—that is, *Himself communicated*" (emphasis added).[89]

Second, God cannot be improved in character. God ad intra is already the fully actual true beauty. God's "infinite beauty" is the "foundation and fountain of all being and all beauty."[90] Through the infinitely perfect relationship of consent within the Trinity, "God has beauty within Himself."[91] God ad intra is the highest good and as such cannot be made more beautiful.

Again, it is true that God's internal beauty is to be expressed in time and space through the external exertion of the divine disposition. The temporal articulation of the divine beauty is not yet completed. And the temporal character of the external repetition of the divine beauty is something that is new even to God ad intra. But the temporal events are truly beautiful *only* as they conform to the already actualized beauty of God ad intra. It is true that the newness of the temporal repetition of God's internal beauty is real, and this repetition is yet to be achieved. The temporal enfleshment of God's beauty will be God's beauty in a new mode. But still, this temporal enfleshment considered in its total meaning is intended to be a repetition or type of God's eternally actual beauty.[92] Thus, God's beauty *in itself* cannot be made more beautiful.

The first two specific senses in which God cannot be added to were in terms of God's actuality and character. The third

[88] Ibid., p. 253.
[89] "Miscellanies," No. 247, HGT, p. 130.
[90] *True Virtue*, p. 15.
[91] "The Mind," No. 45, WEA, p. 365.
[92] Edwards wrote, "The Son of God created the world for this very end, to communicate Himself in an image of His own excellency" ("Covenant of Redemption: Excellency of Christ," FAJ, p. 373).

way God cannot be added to has to do with God's sufficiency in power. God, both in internal and in external life, is not dependent upon any entity that exists and acts independently of God. God, writes Edwards, "cannot be added to or diminished by the power or will of any creature; nor is in the least dependent on any thing mutable or contingent."

> Though he has real pleasure in the creature's holiness and happiness; yet this is not properly any pleasure which he receives from the creature. For these things are what he gives the creature. They are wholly and entirely from him. Therefore they are nothing that they give to God by which they add to him. His rejoicing therein, is rather a rejoicing in his own acts, and his own glory expressed in those acts, than a joy derived from the creature. God's joy is dependent on nothing besides his own act, which he exerts with an absolute and independent power.[93]

It is true that God's self-communication ad extra will require the creation of intelligent and voluntary beings who can actively "remanate" or return God's glory back to God thereby in a sense participating in God's own activity. But the creaturely activity is thoroughly dependent upon God's, and, therefore, their act of glorifying God "is not properly any pleasure which he [God] receives from the creature. . . . It is only the effect of his own work in, and communications to the creature, in making it, and admitting it to a participation of his fulness." Thus, "we have nothing of our own, no stock from whence we can give to God; and that no part of his happiness originates from man."[94] As previously shown, the intelligent creatures do possess a measure of autonomous reality as voluntary agents. And God needs the involvement of the intelligent creatures for his self-enlargement ad extra, but their being and activities are thoroughly dependent upon God's continuing and immediate involvement. The creatures' acts of knowing and loving God are indeed real to God, but they do

[93] "End in Creation," WC, 2: 212–213.
[94] Ibid.

not perform these activities out of their own resources. They do so only by being empowered by God to participate in God's own activity of self-communication ad extra.

> The emanation or communication of the divine fullness, consisting in the knowledge of God, love to God, and joy in God, has a relation indeed both to God, and the creature; but it has relation to God as its fountain. . . . In the creature's knowing, esteeming, loving, rejoicing in, and praising God, the glory of God is both exhibited and acknowledged; his fullness is received and returned. Here is both an *emanation* and *remanation*. The refulgence shines upon and into the creature, and is reflected back to the luminary. The beams of glory come from God, and are something of God, and are refunded back again to their original. So that the whole is *of* God, and *in* God, and *to* God, and God is the beginning, middle and the end in this affair.[95]

There can be, then, according to Edwards, no addition to God as the immanent Trinity that is the true beauty and the absolutely sovereign source of all being and all creativity. By way of a summary of this chapter I should note here, however, that Edwards has significantly broadened the meaning of God's actuality through a dispositional conception of the divine essence. For one thing, the divine actuality, for Edwards, is a dynamic actuality. A teleological principle is introduced into the divine being. It is true, as I have noted, that God, for Edwards, is essentially actual as well as essentially dispositional. Further, God's dispositional essence is in an eternal and complete exercise ad intra. Thus, actuality as a mark of divine perfection is preserved. However, God's actuality, for Edwards, is different from the actus purus as Saint Thomas conceived of it.[96] Edwards' God is not a totally undifferentiated actuality without any sort of movement. Even for Edwards,

[95] Ibid., p. 255.
[96] For a discussion of the categories of actuality and self-sufficiency in Western conceptions of the divine perfections, see Frederick Sontag, *Divine Perfection: Possible Ideas of God* (New York: Harper, 1962), pp. 104–116.

God is an actus purus in the sense of a perfect actuality. But the perfect actuality of Edwards' God is an eternal movement as well as an essential actuality. The essentiality of the divine actuality is located in the First Person of the Trinity. And God's actuality as an eternal movement is the eternal repetition of the Father's actuality within the Trinity. God's actuality, for Edwards, one can see, is a dynamic actuality, a dynamic fullness.

Edwards has broadened the meaning of God's actuality in another way. God remains essentially a disposition even in his fullness, and the external exercise of this disposition brings about the world—that is, the temporal repetition of the divine fullness. God's actuality in its broadened sense, therefore, includes God's eternal fullness ad intra and his external repetition of that fullness. And God's external self-repetition is still an ongoing process. God's actuality as God and his self-sufficiency, however, is still preserved because God as the immanent Trinity is an essential and eternal actuality and also because God's self-repetition in time is God's own activity of repeating his own prior actuality. Nevertheless, the created existence is the exertion of God's own dispositional essence. Therefore, what happens in time and space is really and internally related to God's own life—not in the sense of adding anything to God's being ad intra but rather in the sense of constituting the external extension of God's internal fullness. In this limited and yet real sense, the created world affects God's own being. Through this broadened sense of the divine actuality, Edwards attempts to view God as both eternally self-existent and also capable of being really involved in the temporal process of the world.

Edwards expresses this broadened sense of God's actuality by pointing to the Biblical meaning of the phrase "God's glory." The glory of God (God's "fullness" or "greatness or abundance"), Edwards declares, has two dimensions. God is glorious within himself and also in his self-communication ad extra. Edwards concludes, "They both of them may be called

His glory *in the more extensive sense of the word*, viz., His shining forth or the going forth of His excellency, beauty, and essential glory, *ad extra*" (emphasis added).[97] In short, God's glory is a self-enlarging glory. God's fullness of actuality is a fullness that becomes fuller.

[97] "Miscellanies," No. 448, HGT, p. 133. See also "End in Creation," WC, 2: 246–252.

CHAPTER VIII

God and the Becoming of the World

THE ACHIEVEMENT of Edwards' dispositional reconception of the divine being is that God is conceived as inherently and continuously creative as well as truly actual and absolutely sufficient. And the main implication of this reconception for the nature and meaning of the world is that the creation is viewed as God's external exercise of God's own dispositional essence, an exercise that brings about the extension or repetition in time and space of God's internal fullness.

Time is a return to the eternal as well as a movement to a goal yet to be achieved.[1] History moves not merely back to its Origin, but rather to the temporal repetition of the Origin. And the temporality of this repetition is real and taken seriously; it requires duration. Further, what is to be repeated in time is the infinite being of the Origin, God. Therefore, the duration of such a repetition can only be everlasting. As Edwards himself says, "there never will come the moment" when this process is absolutely completed.[2] There are, and have

[1] Mircea Eliade speaks about the ontology of the "premodern" or "primitive" societies as having as its chief characteristic the notion of time as repetition of, and participation in, the eternal archetypes. In this essentially Platonic world view, everything has reality only to the extent that it is a temporal repetition of eternal exemplars. See Mircea Eliade, *The Myth of the Eternal Return* (Princeton: Princeton University Press, 1974), pp. 5–35. Temporality for Edwards is also a repetition of the eternal. But, for him, this repetition is not simply a participation of time in the eternal but also the self-extension of the eternal itself *within time*.

[2] Edwards may have gotten this idea of an unending future of history from the Cambridge Platonist Henry More. See Lovejoy, *Great Chain of Being*, p. 246. George S. Hendry has commented on the significance of Edwards' use of this idea: "Edwards avoids this 'fearful symmetry' (the dissolution of the creature in the Creator) and strives to construe the moment of return to God in a manner which is compatible with man's continuing creatureliness and entails a real future for him as man . . . and when he thought of the perfection of the glory in its return to God, he saw this perfection, not as annulling the relation,

been, many events in which the repetition of God's fullness is truly, though partially, accomplished. History is a series of such actualizations. The complete repetition in time of God's infinite being, however, will have no ending.

This interpretation of Edwards' doctrine of God and of God's creation of the world provides the theological underpinnings for my earlier discussion of the nature of being and knowing. The end in God's creation is the repetition in time of the dynamic inner life of the triune God: it is the repetition of God's own inner-Trinitarian activity of knowing and loving his own beauty. God thus requires a world of intelligent beings through whom he can exercise his disposition to know and love the divine beauty. In the chapters on habit and being, I showed how the created world is a network of divinely established and active habits and dispositions that possess a dependent and yet abiding permanence and integrity of their own. These habits and dispositions have a mode of reality apart from their operation, but they also require for their continued existence and operation God's immediate involvement. Since Edwards takes time seriously, he holds that the temporal repetition of God's inner life needs to be mediated by finite beings that are distinguishable from, though thoroughly dependent upon, the divine being.

In the chapters on imagination and aesthetic sense, I discussed the habit of mind as the power of imagination that makes possible the apprehension of the relationships among ideas and thus the inner structure of reality. The imagination does not create relationships but still is creative in the sense that, when it is divinely sanctified, it holds up, so to speak, the immediate sense data in their ultimate relational contexts, thereby enabling the mind to discern the ultimate meaning of things. The imagination *repeats* before the mind's view the true structure of reality. This imagination is also the power of the dispositional essence of the knower's being. Thus, the ac-

---

but as raising it to a higher and ever higher perfection." Hendry points out that Edwards differs from Barth on this point. See George S. Hendry, "The Glory of God and the Future of Man," *Reformed World* 34 (1976): 155–156.

tivity of the imagination actualizes and increases the knower's actuality. But then, the veridical functioning of the human imagination is possible only when the disposition of God is exercised in and through the imagination—that is, when the conversion of the human self has occurred. If this is true, then God is extending or repeating his inner glory in and through the regenerate human mind's knowledge and love of that divine glory. Human imagination is ontologically productive and does count even to God in the specific sense that, through its activity, not only the being of the knower, but also indeed God's own life is repeated and increased. Both the significance and limitation of the imagination can be understood correctly only in light of Edwards' contention that the created existence adds to the divine life in the peculiar sense of repeating what is already actual.

As this brief recapitulation indicates, the primary purpose of this study has been to explicate the fundamental logic of Edwards' dispositional reconception of reality with a specific focus on the nature of being, knowing, and God. What I have not discussed is the implications of my interpretation for Edwards' doctrinal formulations of the actual history of the becoming of the world, although I have unavoidably made some references to them throughout my discussion. A full and systematic exposition of Edwards' soteriology, Christology, ecclesiology, and eschatology is beyond the scope of the present study and clearly calls for another volume. I shall, however, attempt a schematic discussion of two of the most fundamental implications of Edwards' dispositional conception of God for the meaning and destiny of created existence in this chapter. First, through a brief discussion of Edwards' postmillennialism, I will illustrate the way his doctrine of God enables him to take temporality with a radical seriousness and without undermining God's prior actuality and transcendence over the world. Second, I will outline the rhythm of actuality and increase in the becoming of the world—a rhythm through which the world participates in God's own work of self-enlargement ad extra.

THE TEMPORALITY OF THE SELF-ENLARGING GOD AND THE MEANING AND DESTINY OF HISTORY

On the question of human history, Jonathan Edwards both inherits and modifies the Augustinian tradition. Like Augustine, Edwards sees history as governed by the intelligent design of the sovereign God and thereby possessing an ultimate significance. Again like Augustine, Edwards saw the ultimate end of history as transcending history as such, since the finite and created existence receives an absolute meaningfulness only from an absolute and sovereign Creator and Governor who is more than the cosmos.[3] Edwards' conception of God as internally complete, all sufficient, and sovereign enables him to reaffirm the Augustinian distinction between temporal existence and its creator.

But in an important way Edwards moves beyond Augustine. God, for Edwards, is a sovereign disposition, a self-enlarging God, whose being is radically immersed in time and space, bringing about an "external existence" of the divine glory. So God is not only *in* history, accomplishing the work of redemption. For Edwards, God seeks to redeem and sanctify history itself by God's own self-extension through history. Here Edwards is a true heir of the Calvinist imperative to transform the entire creation—an imperative, motivated by the absolute sovereign will of the redeeming grace of God.[4] What Edwards has done for the transformative power of the Augustinian and Calvinist tradition is to provide it with an appropriately dynamic metaphysical grounding—a dispositional reconception of God according to which God is fully actual and complete but is also really involved in temporal process.

The unmistakable sense of history in Edwards' thought, al-

[3] For an exposition of St. Augustine's view of history, see Langdon Gilkey, *Reaping the Whirlwind: A Christian Interpretation of History* (New York: Seabury Press, 1976), pp. 159–175.

[4] For a discussion of Edwards' view of history, see "Editor's Introduction," in *Apocalyptic Writings*, ed. Stephen J. Stein, vol. 5 of *The Works of Jonathan Edwards* (New Haven: Yale University Press, 1977), pp. 24–48; John F. Wilson, "Jonathan Edwards as Historian," *Church History* 46 (1977): 5–18.

ready noted by Perry Miller, has been much discussed in connection with Edwards' postmillennialism. Alan Heimert, C. C. Goen, and others have demonstrated that Edwards, by putting the millennium on this side of the personal return of Christ, saw the ordinary course of history as the realm in which the Kingdom of God could be progressively realized though not absolutely consummated.[5] Not that Edwards believed humanity capable of saving itself and thus capable of bringing about the blessed age of peace and harmony lasting a thousand years. No one was more realistic about the limitations of human nature than Edwards. But, as Robert Westbrook puts it, Edwards believed that God "can and will do both. Moreover, He will do so within history."[6]

Edwards' postmillennialism and the accompanying positive view of history, I believe, are grounded in, and are properly understood only within, the framework of his dynamic reconception of the divine being. Edwards wrestled creatively with a theological question that today, two hundred years later, is still a lively issue: How can the absolutely perfect and actual

[5] The most important work on this issue is Alan Heimert, *Religion and the American Mind from the Great Awakening and the Revolution* (Cambridge: Harvard University Press, 1966), esp. pp. 59–158. For discussion of the specific issue of Edwards' postmillennialism, see C. C. Goen, "Jonathan Edwards: A New Departure in Eschatology," *Church History* 28 (1959): 25–40. See also Perry Miller, *Errand into the Wilderness* (Cambridge: Harvard University Press, 1956), pp. 217–239; John F. Wilson, "History, Redemption, and the Millennium," paper presented at the Conference on Jonathan Edwards and the American Experience, Wheaton, Ill., 24–26 October 1984; Bercovitch, *The American Jeremiad*, pp. 93–131; Ernest Lee Tuveson, *Redeemer Nation: The Idea of America's Millennial Role* (Chicago: University of Chicago Press, 1968), pp. 27–30, 55–57; Stein, "Editor's Introduction," in *Apocalyptic Writings*, pp. 24–48. The literature on the idea of millennialism in America is vast. See James W. Davidson, *The Logic of Millennial Thought: Eighteenth-Century New England* (New Haven: Yale University Press, 1977); James H. Moorhead, "Between Progress and Apocalypse: A Reassessment of Millennialism in American Religious Thought, 1800-1880," *Journal of American History* 71 (1984): 524–542.

[6] Robert B. Westbrook, "Social Criticism and the Heavenly City of Jonathan Edwards," *Soundings* 59 (1976): 404. See also Paul Nagy, "The Beloved Community of Jonathan Edwards," *Transactions of the Charles S. Peirce Society* 7 (1971): 93–104.

God be truly involved in the movement of history?[7] God, for Edwards, is truly actual and absolutely sovereign but not timeless or immutable in the sense of the absence of movement and teleology. The creation is the exercise of God's own dispositional essence and constitutes an extension of the very life of the divine being. Time is unqualifiedly real because God's own life is moving toward a telos within history. God's "external existence" is caught up in the becoming of the world. History, then, is the arena within which God's will can be and indeed must be accomplished.

So the thousand years of "peace and prosperity," promised in Revelation 20, are depicted by Edwards as the true realization on earth of God's end in creation although this realization is also a never-ending process. God carries out the goal of repeating his internal glory in time and space with a grand design involving the original creation of the cosmos, the Fall of humanity, the redemptive work of Christ, and the upbuilding of the Church. The external exercise of God's dispositional essence or the activity of divine providence takes the specific form of the work of redemption. This work reaches its consummation on this earth in the millennium. "Christ and his church shall . . . obtain a complete and entire victory over their enemies" at the beginning of this period. It will be a time of "great holiness," "great peace and love," and "perfection of beauty." "All nations, in all parts of the world, on every side of the globe, shall then be knit together in sweet harmony." This will be "most properly the time of the kingdom of heaven upon earth," "the principal time" of that kingdom.[8]

The temporality of this "heaven upon earth" is clearly expressed by Edwards:

Millennium. 'Tis probable that the world shall be more like Heaven in the millennium in this respect: that contemplation and spiritual employments, and those things that more directly concern the mind and religion, will be more the saint's ordinary business than now. There will be so many

[7] See Chap. 1, n. 3, above.
[8] "A History of the Work of Redemption," WC, 1: 302, 491–495.

contrivances and inventions to facilitate and expedite their necessary secular business that they will have more time for more noble exercise, and that they will have better contrivances for assisting one another through the whole earth by more expedite, easy, and safe communication between distant regions than now. The invention of the mariner's compass is a thing discovered by God to the world to that end.

Such a spiritual state as we have just described, has a natural tendency to temporal prosperity: it has a tendency to health and long life; and that this will actually be the case, is evident by Zech. viii. 4. . . . It has also a natural tendency to procure ease, quietness, pleasantness, and cheerfulness of mind.[9]

As C. C. Goen has put it, "Edwards foresaw a golden age for the church on earth, within history, and achieved through the ordinary processes of propagating the gospel in the power of the Holy Spirit."[10]

How new this "new departure in eschatology" is may indeed be an open question.[11] What clearly is new, however, is the doctrine of God that underlies Edwards' historical millennium. God, for Edwards, is essentially dynamic, and the world is the exertion of God's own dispositional essence and thus the temporal extension of God's internal glory. The conception of created temporality as the realm of God's exercise of his own disposition, combined with the doctrine of the absolute sovereignty of that disposition, would require that *this* world embody a true, though not final, repetition ad extra of God's glory. As I have demonstrated, there is a peculiar but real sense in which God has a "real and proper delight, pleasure and happiness" in seeing his internal glory repeated in time. God would be "less happy, if it were possible for him to be

[9] "Miscellanies," No. 262, HGT, pp. 207–208; "A History of the Work of Redemption," WC, 1: 494.

[10] Goen, "New Departure in Eschatology," p. 26.

[11] See Wilson, "History, Redemption, and the Millennium," p. 5. Wilson shows how a historical millennium was a conviction that had a more general currency among Edwards' precursors than Goen acknowledges.

hindered in the exercise of his goodness, and his other perfections in their proper effects."[12] Time is important to the very life of God, and what the sovereign God aims to accomplish in time cannot be hindered. The possibility and indeed the inevitability of the historical millennium is grounded in Edwards' doctrine of God's creative activity, and thus his self-enlargement, within the very fabric of time and space.

I must immediately add, however, that Edwards understands God to be transcendent and prior to the historical process as well as immanent within that process. If Edwards' doctrine of God points up the importance of temporality to God's own life (and thus the necessity of the historical millennium), that same doctrine also emphasizes God's priority over temporality, including the temporality of the historical repetition of God's life in and through the millennium. God is already God without the creation of the world. In creating the world, God did not aim at his self-realization but only his self-repetition.

This prior actuality of God ad intra means that God in God's internal glory is infinitely more than any particular repetition of that glory within the temporal passage. What has to be repeated in time is an infinite actuality of God ad intra, and such a repetition will necessarily take an infinite amount of time. Writing about the immortality of the soul, Edwards makes this relevant observation:

> Some part of the world, viz., that which is the highest, the head and the end of the rest, must be of eternal duration— even the intelligent, reasonable creatures. . . . If the world be of a temporal duration and then drops into nothing, 'tis in vain, i.e., no end is obtained worthy of God . . . and the reason is that the end could have been so small; by reason of the small continuance of the good obtained by it, it is infinitely little. And so it is still infinitely little if it stands a million of ages and then drops into nothing. That is as a moment in the sight of God. If the good obtained by the creation of the world be of so long continuance, 'tis equally

[12] "End in Creation," WC, 2: 212–213.

small, when we compare it with God, as one moment. 'Tis in comparison of Him absolutely equivalent of nothing, and therefore an end not worthy of Him. *No end is worthy of an infinite God but an infinite end.* Therefore, the good that is obtained must be of infinite duration. (Emphasis added)[13]

History, then, does repeat God's internal actuality, but this process will be completed only when it reaches an "infinite height" that alone is "worthy of an infinite God." Yet, such an "infinite height" can only be accomplished in an "infinite duration" involving an "infinite increase."[14] In short, such a moment in time will never come. However great a particular true realization of God's goal of self-repetition in time may be, it would fall short of God's infinite actuality and its infinite increase ad intra. God's internal fullness is inexhaustible.

God's internal glory, therefore, will always remain as a transcendent principle to and over any realization of the divine self-enlargement in time, including the historical millennium. As Edwards writes in the "History of the Work of Redemption," the thousand years of bliss will be followed by a period of great apostasy, and then will be "superceded" by further increases of God's glory in the "new heaven and the new earth" to be inaugurated by the personal return to earth of Jesus Christ. "All the glory of the glorious times of the church on earth is but a faint shadow of this her consummate glory in heaven." God's self-repetition in time through the history of redemption is a true repetition of God's glory, but it is a type or image of what is yet to be realized in the unending "ages" of eternity.[15]

The prior actuality of God means the actuality of God's character or quality as well as of God's infinity. The inexhaustible God is already actually God of a particular quality, and this God now repeats himself in time and space. As the above quotation says, the good obtained in time has to be worthy of the infinite God. And the good spoken of here, of course, is

---

[13] "Miscellanies," No. 1006, HGT, p. 196.
[14] "End in Creation," WC, 2: 256.
[15] "A History of the Work of Redemption," WC, 1: 495, 505–506.

the temporal repetition of the divine beauty of the triune God ad intra, which was supremely manifested in Jesus Christ, the incarnate Second Person of the Trinity. So the historical millennium is the establishment on earth of the Kingdom of the Eternal Son of God, "the Kingdom of Christ." This is another way of stating the reason that the historical millennium will truly repeat God's own life in time but will not exhaust it. The millennium is an "image of heaven" and not the final or absolute accomplishment of God's chief end in creation.[16] Since the divine beauty is already actual in God ad intra, there already *is* a divine beauty to be repeated in time; the repetition of this divine and thus infinitely perfect beauty within the temporal frame would take more than a millennium.

The God whose prior actuality is being repeated in time and space is an absolutely sovereign, all-sufficient deity who is the source of all being and creativity. The entire realm of creation is absolutely dependent upon God ad intra for its existence and meaning. God is not only the God of the future millennium but also the God of the present and the past, of history and nature. God creates and governs the entire cosmos and its entire historical span with God's own grand design. The historical millennium, then, can properly be understood only within the context of God's eternal providential rule over creation. In fact, the historical millennium has its ultimate foundation, guarantee, and significance in the fact that the entire creation is the external exercise of the sovereign disposition of God ad intra. Stephen J. Stein has observed that in Edwards' earliest apocalyptic writings the theme of providence plays a central role. Edwards' confidence in divine providence is the basis of his belief that in spite of setbacks and difficulties God will accomplish his own goal in history. In Stein's words, "Providence expands the scope of eschatology, bringing past, present, and future into focus within the divine economy and balancing both earthly and heavenly dimensions."[17] I shall

[16] Ibid., pp. 490, 494.
[17] Stephen J. Stein, "Providence and the Apocalypse in the Early Writings of Jonathan Edwards," *Early American Literature* 13 (1978–1979): 263.

discuss in the following section the future heavenly realm into which the providential activity of God's self-enlargement ad extra will be stretched.

My point here is simply that the millennium, for Edwards, has a theocentric context—the context in which the absolutely sovereign God plays out his grand design that transcends the historical millennium. Inasmuch as God's own dispositional essence is exercised in time, the temporal realization of the millennium for Edwards is necessary and possible. A true and perfect embodiment of God's beauty in time is logically founded on Edwards' doctrine of God as at once actual and also self-enlarging. However, God's prior actuality ad intra takes one beyond the millennium to the wider regions of the providential work of the sovereign God.

In light of this discussion, one can properly assess the criticism that has been directed against the focus on Edwards' historical millennium. The interpretation of Edwards' postmillennialism as the inspiration for the nationalistic ideology of the American Republic as God's New Israel has been especially controversial.[18] M. Darrol Bryant, for example, commenting particularly about the influential work of Alan Heimert, has strongly challenged any attempt to see Edwards' expectation for the dawning millennium as the impetus for the American Revolution.[19] While acknowledging that "the millennial expectation of a dawning new age served as the ground for a revolutionary critique of the old order and as the dynamic for social innovation," Bryant rejects "the assumption that the millennial impulse gains fulfillment in the American

[18] See Heimert, *Religion and the American Mind*. Some of the many other important works in this connection are Bercovitch, *The American Jeremiad*; Nathan O. Hatch, *The Sacred Cause of Liberty: Republican Thought and the Millennium in Revolutionary New England* (New Haven: Yale University Press, 1977), pp. 21–54; Sidney E. Mead, *The Nation with the Soul of a Church* (New York: Harper and Row, 1975); Bernard Bailyn, "Central Themes of the Revolution," in *Essays on the American Revolution*, ed. Stephen G. Kurtz and James H. Hutson (New York: Norton, 1973), pp. 15–18.

[19] M. Darrol Bryant, "America as God's Kingdom," in *Religion and Political Society*, ed. Jürgen Moltmann et al. (New York: Harper and Row, 1974), pp. 54–94.

Republic . . . at least in relation to Jonathan Edwards." As
Bryant sees it, Edwards' "vision is clearly fixed on a transcendent goal, not an earthly kingdom" since "the end of all creation is transhistorical and spiritual: the glory of God." The
few speculative remarks in the earlier writings of Edwards that
locate the coming of the millennium in America are overcome
and corrected, according to Bryant, in Edwards' later works.
Toward the end of his life, Edwards "has altogether forsaken
an eschatology which would see the historical process termi-
nating in any this-worldly kingdom of God." Bryant then concludes, "Thus Edwards grew to be a theologian of the glory of
God," and not "an ideologist in pious dress."[20]

This reading of Edwards' postmillennialism in the context
of his doctrine of God and the creation would indicate that
there is truth on both sides of the argument. Bryant is correct
in pointing out that God's end in creation is God's own glory
and thus not exhaustible by any particular earthly manifestation of that glory—not even by the historical millennium and
certainly not by the establishment of the American Republic.
In light of this, Heimert's oft-quoted remark that "in substance, the God of Jonathan Edwards was a supremely excellent Christian commonwealth" may be an overstatement.[21]
But there is an important element of truth in Heimert's interpretation that Bryant does not notice. In stressing the absolute
priority, sovereignty, and transcendence of Edwards' God,
Bryant tends to understate God's genuine involvement in history. Bryant's contention that Edwards' "vision is clearly fixed
on a transcendent goal, and not an earthly kingdom" is only
a half-truth. The absolutely final end of God's intention for
history is indeed beyond any earthly kingdom. But that very
final end is to have genuine though proleptic realizations
within this history and within this world. The being of this
world is the very exercise of God's own dispositional essence.
God's own life ad extra is constituted by what God does

[20] Ibid., pp. 59, 77–78, 82, 85–86.
[21] Heimert, *Religion and the American Mind*, p. 104. Although this may be
an overstatement, it does correctly stress God's ontological involvement in
temporality in Edwards' conception of the divine being.

through the Church *in this very world* as well as by what God will continue to do in future ages throughout eternity. Edwards' doctrine of the radical temporality of God ad extra undergirds his keen sense of history, which Heimert and others have emphasized.

THE RHYTHM OF THE BECOMING OF THE WORLD

One of the important issues in delineating the meaning of history has to do with the relationship between order and the temporal passage. If God as the source of all being and meaning is already actual, then there must be a divinely determined order in history and nature. If the world is conceived of as being constituted by the direct exertion of the divine disposition itself, any one single created entity or temporal event would have to be seen as a state of completed meaning and order. Every event would be a return to, and an embodiment of, the Origin. However, if time is taken seriously, as is the case in Edwards' thought, the passage of time would have to amount to something; there would have to be an advance or a telic movement in temporality. History must be conceived of not only as an eternal return to the Origin, but also as an advance to a goal.

Edwards deals with this issue of order and movement in terms of what one might call a dynamic rhythm of reality—that is, a movement of actuality to its increase. This formula of actualization and increase enables Edwards to see reality as at once completed order and also dynamic movement. History is a return to the Origin in the sense of a repetition of the Origin. There is order in history as determined by the Origin, but there also is a movement since the Origin really repeats itself within the historical process. And this principle, for Edwards, is grounded in his conception of the ultimate reality as at once truly actual as the source of all being and creativity, and also inherently self-enlarging. God's self-enlargement ad extra is to be achieved in time, and thus, temporality is real and significant even to God. But since the self-enlarging God is already actual as God, there is order and meaning in every temporal event and also in the duration of events. Genuine movement is introduced into the ordered realm of time by conceiving of the movement as a process of the repetition or increase of the event that actualizes the order.

Speaking about the significance of time, Edwards writes:

> God don't fully obtain His design in any one particular state that the world is in, in different ages, connected in a scheme. *'Tis evident that He don't fully obtain His end, His design, in any one particular state the world has ever been in; for, if so, we should have no change.* But God is continually causing revolutions. Providence makes *a continual progress*, and continually is bringing forth things new in the state of the world, and very different from what ever were before. He removes one that He may establish another. And perfection will not be obtained till the last revolution, when God's design will be fully reached. (Emphasis added)[22]

The infinite fullness of the divine being ad extra has to be repeated in the realm of time and thus requires duration. "Providence makes a continual progress," as Edwards writes, and the change or the passage of time is significant.

But Edwards also speaks of the divine providence as achieving periodic consummations. The image that Edwards uses to point to the actualizations of God's design in history as well as to the constant repetitions of those actualizations is the turning of a wheel.

> So it is in the course of things in God's providence over the intelligent and moral world, all is the motion of wheels. They go round and come to the same [place] again, and the whole series of divine providence from the beginning to the end is nothing else but the revolution of certain wheels, greater and lesser, the lesser being contained within the greater. What comes to pass in the natural world is in this respect typical of what comes to pass in the moral and intelligent world. . . .
> *Things in their series and course in providence do, as it*

---

[22] "Miscellanies," No. 547, HGT, p. 135.

were, return to the same point or place whence they began, as in the turning of a wheel, but yet not so but that a further end is obtained than was at first, or the same end is obtained in a much further degree. So that in the general there is a progress toward a certain fixed issue of things, and every revolution brings nearer to that issue, as it is in the motion of a wheel upon the earth or in the motion of the wheels of a chariot, and not like the motion of a wheel on its axis, for if so, its motion would be in vain. (Emphasis added)[23]

Edwards' point could not be clearer. History is both cyclical and linear. Created existence embodies or repeats the eternal order of the divine being but at the same time moves toward a goal to be achieved *in time*—toward the temporal increase of that eternal order. The providential wheel returns to "the same point or place whence they began." And yet there is a genuine telic movement. By returning to the "same point or place," providence attains "a further end" in the sense that "the same end is obtained in a much further degree." The movement in history, then, consists of the actualization of an end *and* of the increase of the same actualization "in a much further degree." The actualization in an event of the eternal order *and* the further increase of that actualization through further events, then, is the rhythm of created existence.

The Foundation of the World's Being and Becoming: The Father and the Son, the Son and the World

The turning of the providential wheels in the rhythm of actualization and increase (the attainment of an end and the incremental repetition of the same end) has its ultimate foundation in the dynamic life of the inner Trinity. The primordial actuality of God "in the Prime, unoriginated & most absolute manner" is the first actuality or subsistence of the deity—namely, the Father.[24] But this primordial actuality of God is also essentially a disposition. And the divine disposition continues to exert itself, bringing about an increase or repetition

[23] "Notes on the Scriptures," No. 394, in *Images or Shadows*, pp. 107–108.
[24] "*An Essay on the Trinity*," FAJ, p. 379.

of the primordial actuality in the form of the reflexive Idea of the Father—namely, the Son. And "the Father's begetting of the Son is a complete communication of all his happiness, and so an eternal, adequate, and infinite exercise of perfect goodness that is completely equal to such an inclination in perfection."[25] God's exercise of the divine disposition in taking delight in the repetition of God's self in the Son results in the Third Person of the Trinity, the Holy Spirit. God's internal life, therefore, is an eternal act of moving from actuality to its increase. In this eternal act lies the ultimate ground, pattern, and significance of the dynamic movement in time and space.

As I demonstrated above, Edwards articulates God's creation of the world in terms of the actuality-and-increase principle. God's exercise of the divine disposition ad extra is for the purpose of communicating God's internal actuality—that is, to bring about "an increase, repetition or multiplication of it."[26] It is especially to the Son, God's perfect repetition of himself ad intra, that God's self-repetition ad extra (i.e., the creation of the world) is attributed. "The Son is the adequate communication of the Father's goodness, and is an express and complete image of him." Edwards then adds, "But yet the Son has also an inclination to communicate himself in an image of his person, that may partake of his happiness." So "the Son is the fullness of God, and the Church [which the world is intended to be] is the fullness of the Son of God."[27] The world, then, is created to become a perfect image of the perfect image of God.

Strictly speaking, however, the creation of the world is the exertion of the original disposition of God's essence and thus an act of self-repetition by the entire deity. So Edwards attributes the creation to the Father and the Holy Spirit as well as to the Son. "The Father also created the world, as well as the Son, as we know; and did it for his Son," writes Edwards.[28] And it is the work of the Holy Spirit "to bring the world to its

[25] "Miscellanies," No. 104, THA, app. 1, p. 37.
[26] "End in Creation," WC, 2: 206.
[27] "Miscellanies," No. 104, THA, app. 1, pp. 37, 38.
[28] "Miscellanies," No. 148, Yale MSS.

beauty and perfection out of the chaos . . . to communicate beauty and harmony to the world."[29] So, in terms of the three Persons of the Trinity, the Father created the world "for the Son" through the Holy Spirit; and this means that the world is God's external repetition of his inner-Trinitarian repetition in the Son and in the Holy Spirit.[30]

Jesus Christ and the Church. The rhythm of actuality and increase is the principle of the dynamic life of God's internal life and also the principle that governs God's creation of the world. Since the being and meaning of the world are directly and continually constituted by God's external exertion of the divine disposition, the rhythm of the world's becoming can only follow the same rhythm of actuality and increase.

God accomplishes his self-repetition in time by creating intelligent beings who can know and love the divine beauty, thereby repeating God's own inner-Trinitarian knowledge and love of that beauty. This means, according to Edwards, that God needs to become visible in time so that the regenerate men and women may come to know and love God as their ultimate good. The Son of God, in other words, needs to become incarnate in time, and Jesus Christ is the needed presence of God in time. And it is the "sight of the divine beauty of Christ that bows the wills and draws the hearts of men."[31]

To put it differently, in Edwards' view, Jesus Christ, the incarnate Son of God, is the one event or life in which God's exertion of the divine disposition ad extra is accomplished "without measure"—that is, to a full degree.[32] In Jesus Christ, the self-enlargement of God's inner fullness achieves a perfect actuality. Thus, Edwards strongly affirms the orthodox Christological teaching that Jesus Christ was fully divine and fully human. "The man Christ Jesus" was, writes Edwards, "not an

[29] "Miscellanies," No. 293, HGT, p. 260.

[30] "Miscellanies," No. 148, Yale MSS; "Covenant of Redemption: Excellency of Christ," FAJ, p. 373; "An Essay on the Trinity," PH, p. 111.

[31] "True Grace Distinguished from the Experience of Devils," WL, 4: 469–470.

[32] "Miscellanies," No. 487, Yale MSS.

under God, as the Arians suppose, but, to all intents and purposes, Supreme God."[33] And this full presence of God in time is accomplished through the presence of the divine disposition in the form of the Holy Spirit—a presence that is "without measure."

A question, however, now arises. If Jesus Christ is the full exertion of the divine disposition in time and thus a perfect actuality of God's self-repetition ad extra, what is the significance of the created existence *before* and *after* Jesus Christ? What is the significance of the world outside of Jesus Christ? Here again the principle of actuality and increase functions. In a nutshell, in Edwards' view, the world before Jesus Christ and the world after him are the increases and repetitions of *his* actuality. The passage of time before him consists essentially of the types or "foreshadowings" of the actuality of divine beauty in Jesus Christ.[34] And the world after him is intended to be the everlasting repetitions of what is already accomplished in him. After God's disposition is truly exerted ad extra in Jesus Christ, God continues to exert that same disposition. God does so now to increase and multiply what was already accomplished in the incarnate Son. It is in light of this logic of the actuality of Jesus Christ and its increase that one can understand what Edwards has to say about the Church.

> Therefore the Church is said to be *the completeness of Christ*, Eph. i. 23, *As if Christ were not complete without the Church*, as having a natural inclination thereto. We are incomplete without that which we have a natural inclination to. . . . First we are told where the Father's delight was, and also the mutual delight of the Son, and then where the Son's delight is in the object of his communication of his goodness. "Then I was by him as one brought up with him, etc." The Son is the fullness of God, and the Church is the fullness of the Son of God. (Emphasis added)[35]

[33] "The Excellency of Christ," WL, 4: 184.
[34] "A History of the Work of Redemption," WC, 1: 306–311.
[35] "Miscellanies," No. 104, THA, app. 1, pp. 37–38. For a discussion of

Jesus Christ without the Church (i.e., the rest of the world as
intended by God) is, in other words, a true and complete actuality of God's self-communication ad extra. But the Church
adds to the completeness of Christ as the further increase of
that completeness.

To say that Jesus Christ is a true and complete actuality of
God in time is not, within Edwards' scheme, to see Jesus
Christ's life and work as a static reality. In fact, a kind of becoming is involved in the life of Jesus Christ himself, and his
becoming epitomizes and prefigures the becoming of the
world. The becoming involved here is again in the pattern of
actuality and increase. The presence of God in Jesus, as I already noted, is "without measure," and, thus, the actuality of
Jesus Christ as the incarnate Son of God is complete. But this
complete actuality increases even in the life of Jesus Christ
himself. Edwards articulates this dynamic being of Jesus
Christ in terms of the further increases of the manifestation in
his human nature of his divine excellencies. Christ's "human
excellencies . . . are additional manifestations of his glory and
excellency to us, and additional recommendations of him to
our esteem and love," writes Edwards. These "additional
manifestations" of the divine glory are "communications and
reflections of [Christ's] divine nature."[36] And these human excellencies of Jesus Christ involved a dynamic process of increase. Christ's "last sufferings," for example, have the effect
of increasing "the holiness of his nature"; they "strengthen
and increase the root"[37]—that is, the degree of the enfleshment of the Holy Spirit in Christ's human nature. In short, the
various and progressive manifestations (repetitions) of the divine nature in Jesus "added to the finite holiness of the human
nature of Christ."[38]

Edwards' ecclesiology, see Thomas A. Schafer, "Jonathan Edwards' Conception of the Church," *Church History* 24 (1955): 51–66.

[36] "The Excellency of Christ," WL, 4: 198.

[37] "Miscellanies," No. 1005, Yale MSS.

[38] Ibid. A thorough study of the Christological implications of these statements needs to be done. James Carse offers an instructive discussion of Edwards' Christology in the context of Edwards' emphasis on "the visibility of

The Church, or the people of God united with Christ through the Holy Spirit, continues to enlarge the actuality of God's self-repetition in time and the increase of that self-repetition already perfectly present in Jesus Christ. God, who is directly involved in this whole affair, never ceases to exercise the divine disposition. Thus, the increase of the being of Jesus Christ through the progressive upbuilding of the Church will continue, as shall be seen, into the everlasting ages of the new heaven and the new earth. In this way, Edwards is enabled to see the reality of the Church as an accomplished reality as well as a reality continually involved in becoming more and more full and perfect.

An implication for Christology that should be noted in passing has to do with its theocentric scope. Jesus Christ is God's real presence in time for us—that is, for the redemption of fallen humanity. But this redemptive work of Jesus Christ has a prior, theocentric context. Christ's redemption of humanity is a means toward God's own end in creating the world—namely, the repetition of God's internal glory ad extra. Thus, the ultimate scope of Christ's work is cosmic and its duration everlasting. Not only the realm of history but the physical universe also is, in limited degrees, the enfleshment of the beauty of the eternal Son of God. "The beauties of nature," writes Edwards, "are really emanations or shadows of the excellencies of the Son of God."[39] And the eternal Son was engaged in this work of self-communication already before the Incarnation, although the Incarnation puts this self-communicating work of God on a radically new level of realization. "As soon as even man fell, Christ the eternal Son of God clothed himself with the mediatorial character."[40] The visible manifestations

---

God." See James Carse, *Jonathan Edwards and the Visibility of God* (New York: Charles Scribner's Sons, 1967), pp. 95–113.

[39] "Covenant of Redemption: Excellency of Christ," FAJ, p. 373.

[40] "A History of the Work of Redemption," WC, 1: 306. Christ's work of redemption, however, according to Edwards, is grounded upon the eternal covenant of redemption among the three Persons of the Trinity, a covenant that in turn is based upon the order of subsistence among the three Persons. For Edwards, God's work of redeeming humankind is not ultimately contin-

of God's mercy before Christ's Incarnation were "types and shadows [of Jesus Christ], whereby his coming and redemption were prefigured."[41] And, then, when the incarnate Son of God "ascends into heaven," there he, now as the glorified "man Christ Jesus," continues to be the medium of God's self-communication. "The beatific vision of God in heaven," writes Edwards, "consists mostly in beholding the glory of God in the face of Jesus Christ, either in his work, or in his person as appearing in the glorified human nature."[42] The point here is that the redemptive work of the eternal Son in Jesus Christ has its true scope and thus its ultimate significance in the eternal Son's work of the glorification of God's own beauty. The salvation of human beings is important, in the final analysis, only because it fulfills the telos that is important to God's own being.

The Conversion of the Saints and Its Increase through Practice. The dynamic rhythm of actuality and increase in the becoming of the world on its cosmic level can also be traced in the life of an individual regenerate self. The progression of God's redemptive work on the individual level is an image of the same work on its cosmic level. For Edwards, a person becomes a human being in the proper sense (as God intended him or her to be) when the conversion occurs. That is, a person is enabled to know and love God and all things in relation to God only when that person's human disposition functions in a manner harmonious to the whole—to the being of God. And such a transformation of the human disposition occurs through the indwelling of the Holy Spirit. God "in his proper nature" is united with the saint's disposition and faculties and "acts very much after the manner of a natural principle or habit."[43] God's Spirit is united with the human disposition in

gent upon the sinful acts of the human beings but rather upon the inherent nature of God himself. See "Observations concerning the Scripture Oeconomy of the Trinity, and Covenant of Redemption," PE, pp. 77–98.
41 "A History of the Work of Redemption," WC, 1: 310.
42 "Miscellanies," Nos. 952, 1126, 1137, WS, 8: 579, 589, 599.
43 "Treatise on Grace," PH, pp. 72, 75.

such a way that God's actions through human beings are also the actions of human beings themselves. And all this while God retains a full sovereignty over the presence and continuance of the Holy Spirit in them. Saints do not become "Godded," but God's own disposition now acts in, under, and behind their human actions.[44]

Now the very first exercise of the divinely transformed disposition of the saint would constitute the first and a true actuality of that saint as a human being. And "the first act of the Spirit of God, or the first that 'tis divine temper exerts itself in, is in spiritual understanding or in the sense of the mind, its perception of glory and excellency"[45]—that is, in the saint's perception of the beauty of Jesus Christ and the history of redemption. The demarcation between the converted and the unconverted is sharply drawn by Edwards. Even if a person has "a faint discovery of the glory of God," writes Edwards, "yet if he has any true discovery of Him, so far as he sees this he is sensible that [God] is worthy to be loved far above all."[46]

The transformed disposition of the saint is the new direction of his or her entire self, and will be exerted in outward practice as well as through inward perceptions and affections. "The principal evidence of this power of godliness, is in those exercises of holy affections that are practical, and in their being practical." Christian practice, therefore, is the inevitable and direct outcome of the new tendency in the saint's mind and heart. "Grace is said to be perfected or finished in holy practice," Edwards asserts, "as therein it is brought to its proper effect, and to that exercise which is the end of the principle."[47] Actual Christian practice brings to actuality the real possibility to which the saint's new disposition is a disposition. In the most inclusive sense, then, the actuality of a regenerate person is realized when his or her newly transformed disposition is exercised in and through all of the inward and outward, perceptual and volitional (affectional) dimensions of the self.

[44] *Religious Affections*, p. 203.
[45] "Miscellanies," No. 397, HGT, p. 249.
[46] "Miscellanies," No. 739, HGT, p. 206.
[47] *Religious Affections*, pp. 393, 435.

So Edwards' well-known emphasis upon Christian practice is to be understood in light of his conception of disposition— both human and divine. Dispositions are active tendencies that would certainly exert themselves when the appropriate occasions arise. "Godliness in the heart has a direct relation to practice, as a fountain has to a stream."[48] And besides, the disposition of the saint is a disposition in and through which the disposition of the sovereign God is directly operating. Commenting upon Edwards' stress upon Christian practice, John E. Smith has aptly noted, "Here one can see that peculiar combination of divine necessity and human freedom, energy, and enterprise which has always accompanied the Calvinistic outlook."[49] And I have tried to indicate that behind that "divine necessity" there lies Edwards' dynamic doctrine of God as at once fully actual and also self-enlarging ad extra. Through Christian practice, the fullness of God's own being is being repeated. Thus, Edwards' insistence upon the inevitability and necessity of the practical consequences of the regenerate is rooted in the inevitability with which the sovereign God will accomplish his own aim.

The saint's transformed disposition, however, remains a disposition and will not cease to be active in the attainment of its first full exertion through the inward and outward actions of the saint's mind and heart. The regenerate person's actuality is destined to be multiplied and repeated as his or her disposition is further exercised through further acts of knowing and loving God and all things in relation to God.

> The first thing is a new heart, a new sense and inclination that is a principle of new life, a principle that, however small, is active and has vigor and power, and, as it more beats and struggles, thirsts after holiness, aims at and tends to every thing that belongs to the new creature, and has within it the foundation and source of the whole. It aims at

[48] Ibid., p. 398.
[49] John E. Smith, "Jonathan Edwards: Piety and Practice in the American Character," *Journal of Religion* 54 (1974): 176. See also Cherry, *Theology*, pp. 126–158.

perfection, and from thence are the issues of life. From thence the various things that belong to the new creature all proceed and branch forth and gradually appear, *and that more and more.* And this principle, from its first existence, never ceases to exert itself, until the new creature be compleat and comes to its proper perfection. (Emphasis added)[50]

The "more and more" of the holiness that results from the inexhaustible exertion of the saint's transformed disposition is no vacuous repetition. As the regenerate person knows and delights in the divine beauty as manifested in different contexts, the same knowledge and the same love of God is repeated in different ways and in different temporal and spatial circumstances. In Edwards' "Miscellanies," there is an entry entitled "Happiness" in which he writes:

How soon do earthly lovers come to an end of their discoveries of each other's beauty! How soon do they see all that is to be seen, are they united as near as 'tis possible and have communion as intimate as possible! How soon do they come to the most endearing expressions of love that 'tis possible to come to, so that no new ways can be invented, given, or received!

Edwards then continues:

And how happy is that love in which there is an eternal progress in all these things, wherein new beauties are continually discovered, and more and more loveliness, and in which *we shall forever increase in beauty ourselves.* When we shall be made capable of finding out, and giving, and shall receive more and more endearing expression forever, our union will become more close and communion more intimate. (Emphasis added)[51]

So as the saints know and delight in new beauties (different emanations of the divine beauty), they increase in beauty

[50] *Images or Shadows,* No. 190, pp. 127–128.
[51] "Miscellanies," No. 198, HGT, p. 195.

themselves thereby repeating their true actuality already achieved in their first acts of knowing and loving God. And "that love in which there is an eternal progress" is none other than the Holy Spirit in the saint; therefore, the saint's eternal progress in his or her increase in beauty and being is a participation in God's own self-enlargement in time. "This knowledge in the creature, is but a conformity to God. It is the image of God's own knowledge of himself. It is a participation of the same."[52] The saint's growing sanctification, then, has an eschatological dimension. Edwards writes in "The End for Which God Created the World":

> There are many reasons to think that what God has in view, in an increasing communication of himself through eternity, is an increasing knowledge of God, love to him, and joy in him. And it is to be considered that the more those divine communications increase in the creature, the more it becomes one with God; for so much the more is it united to God in love, the heart is drawn nearer and nearer to God, and union with him becomes more firm and close, and at the same time the creature becomes more and more conformed to God.[53]

The result of this unceasing dynamic of actuality and increase in the life of the saint can be summed up in this way: For one thing, it means that Christian life is already here and now a communion with God (with the divine beauty) and a participation in God's own life. A Christian's destiny is now and at every moment an actuality. But at the same time, there is a dynamic thrust toward the future in the sanctification of the saint and of history itself. The saint increases in his or her actuality, and this increase is meaningful even to God since such an increase is a participation in God's own self-enlargement. A Christian does not merely contemplate God's beauty and rest satisfied, but he or she is impelled to build God's Kingdom here in history as well as in the everlasting life to come. And

[52] "End in Creation," WC, 2: 210.
[53] Ibid., pp. 210–211.

235

the same Christian engages in this enterprise with assurance and hope since it is God who is directly involved in that same enterprise. Edwards' emphasis upon both piety and practice, therefore, is to be seen as ultimately grounded in the rhythm of actuality and increase in God's own life.

Redemption and the Eternal Life: The World, the New Heaven, and the New Earth

An important question in theology is the relationship between temporality and eternal life, between this world and the world to come. For Edwards, the essential temporality of this world is important because God's very nature demands that the divine fullness be repeated in time. And since such an aim of God, as I have already noted, will take an unending duration of time, temporality is going to be important to God in an everlasting way. Does God, then, ever complete the being of the world? Does God ever consummate the design of the redemption of fallen humanity? Here again the answer is framed in terms of the rhythm of actuality and increase. God in a sense completes the world at the eschaton; nevertheless, the world's being increases into eternity. That is to say, God's redemption of the world is attained in its actuality by the time of the return of Christ. But the fruits of this redemption forever increase in heaven.

God is the absolutely sovereign Lord of the creation and is capable of bringing about the actuality of that for which God created the world—an end that is primarily God's glorification ad extra in time and space, and, consequentially, the redemption of fallen humanity. At the end of his "History of the Work of Redemption," Edwards discusses the moment of the eschaton when God accomplishes his goal. After a period of great apostasy following the millennium, Christ comes again in person and accomplishes the final victory over Satan. The Church is now completed, and the work of redemption (and thus God's end for *this* world) is consummated. Christ appears now in his complete glory. The Church is now all gathered at one place, ready to "ascend up toward the highest heavens." "And now the whole work of redemption is finished

... the top-stone of the building is laid." Christ the bride-groom and the Church, his bride, are ready to enter heaven in their wedding robes. Is the world now no more? Is this the end of God's creation? Not exactly. "All the glory of the glorious times of the church on earth is but a faint shadow of this her consummate glory in heaven." There is more to come. "This world shall be set on fire" as the place of eternal punishment of the disobedient. So *this* world comes to an end, but the world as such does not absolutely end. The Church with its Lord will enter "on the state of their highest and eternal blessedness and glory," and will live in "a world not like that which they have left."[54]

For Edwards, eternal life is not a realm of timelessness. Eternity transcends and perfects time and space *but also includes them.* Eternity is neither timelessness nor mere unending duration (i.e., duration without a qualitative perfection of time). Eternity, for Edwards, is more than history and nature, but it certainly includes them. The new heaven and the new earth are to be lively places. Edwards chooses his words carefully when he says that the Church, when she enters heaven, will "enjoy [God's] glory *throughout the never ending ages of eternity*" (emphasis added).[55] Edwards is using the term "eternity" in the sense of "everlasting ages." This can only be so because the last end for which God created the world—God's self-enlargement in time—will take an everlasting time; thus, this process must be seen as going on in the new heaven and the new earth.

Not that redemption is incomplete. It is complete. But now the everlasting increase of the complete actuality of redemption will go on. "The work of redemption is not an eternal work, i.e., it is not a work always a doing and never accomplished," writes Edwards. Then he immediately adds: "But the fruits of this work are eternal fruits. The work has an issue. But in the issue the end will be obtained; *which end will never have an end*" (emphasis added). The rhythm of actuality and

[54] "A History of the Work of Redemption," WC, I: 504–506.
[55] Ibid., p. 505.

increase functions again here, and enables Edwards to conceive of created existence as having a distinguishable and continuing being and significance. Christ and his bride, the completely actualized Church, enter heaven to be united in marriage before the Father. And the wedding is only a beginning. So, Edwards writes, "they shall begin an everlasting wedding-day." "This wedding-day will never end . . . the joys of the wedding will be continued to all eternity."[56]

The world to come includes nature in a radically recreated form.

> As the saints after the resurrection will have an external part, or an outward man, distinct from their souls, so it necessarily follows that they shall have external perception, or sense, and, doubtless, then all their sense, and all the perception that they have will be delighted and filled with happiness—every perceptive faculty shall be an inlet of delight. Particularly then, doubtless, they will have the seeing, which is the noblest of all external senses.[57]

The new creation, then, is more than a restoration of the old. The new, however, is not totally discontinuous with the world as we know it. Edwards speaks more concretely about the recreated "bodies" in heaven in a "Miscellanies" entry entitled "New Earth":

> The beauty of the bodies of saints in the new earth, the new Jerusalem, shall not only consist in the most charming proportion of features and parts of their bodies, and their light, proportion of colors, but much in the manifestation of the excellencies of their mind; which exceeding readily will appear in their bodies, the bodies being more easily and naturally susceptive and manifestative of the affections.[58]

In another "Miscellanies" entry, entitled "Heaven," Edwards speaks further about the recreated nature:

[56] Ibid., pp. 300, 505; "Miscellanies," No. 371, WS, 8: 536.
[57] "Miscellanies," No. 721, WS, 8: 559–560.
[58] "Miscellanies," No. 139, Yale MSS.

How ravishing are the proportions of the reflections of rays of light, and the proportions of the vibrations of the air! And without doubt, God can contrive matter so that there shall be other sort of proportions, that may be quite of a different kind, and may raise another sort of pleasure in a sense, and in a manner to us inconceivable, that shall be vastly more ravishing and exquisite . . . there shall be external beauties and harmonies altogether of another kind from what we perceive here, and probably those beauties will appear chiefly on the bodies of the man Christ Jesus and of the saints.[59]

In this newly created heaven and earth, the capacities of the human mind will also be vastly enlarged. In the following entry (also called "Heaven"), Edwards speaks about the new state of the saints' capacities as well as the progressive increase of their knowledge and love:

That the glorified spirits shall grow in holiness and happiness to eternity, I argue from this foundation, that their number of ideas shall increase to eternity. How great a number of ideas soever when they are first glorified, it is but finite. And 'tis evident the time will come wherein they shall have lived in glory so long, that the parts of duration (each equal a million million ages) that they have lived, will be more in number [than] their ideas were at first. . . . Therefore, their knowledge will increase to eternity; and if their knowledge, doubtless, their holiness. For as they increase in the knowledge of God, and of the works of God, the more they will see of his excellency; and the more they see his excellency, *caeteris paribus*, the more will they love him; and the more they love God, the more delight and happiness, *caeteris paribus*, will they have in him.[60]

So, the world to come will be a radically new heaven and earth, and there will be a dynamic movement of an increase in

[59] "Miscellanies," No. 182, Yale MSS.
[60] "Miscellanies," No. 105, WS, 8: 529.

being. "HAPPINESS of HEAVEN is PROGRESSIVE and has various periods in which it has a new & glorious advancement."[61]

Thus, there will be a new heaven and a new earth in and through which God's infinite end of enlarging the divine fullness can continue. Thus, the dynamic principle of actuality and increase of God's own being is the ultimate reason and significance in which the actuality of what God intended for the world and its everlasting increase are grounded.

Edwards' vision of the eternal Kingdom of God accentuates the importance of temporality and consequently heightens the possibility of and expectation for the temporal realization of that Kingdom. After all, the Kingdom that is coming in this life is what will be repeated everlastingly in the eternal Kingdom. It is the same God who is enlarging the divine fullness ad extra both in this life and in the everlasting ages of the life to come.

H. Richard Niebuhr, in his seminal work, *The Kingdom of God in America*, traces the emergence in American Protestantism of a dynamic belief in the Kingdom of God to be realized even here in this life before it is absolutely consummated in the eternal life. How did American Protestantism, and Jonathan Edwards in particular, come to attain a disjuncted emphasis upon this worldly realization of God's eternal Kingdom? What was the key to the confidence in the coming Kingdom? Niebuhr's suggestion is that the Reformed doctrine of the absolute sovereignty of God may be the answer. The belief in God's transforming Lordship over all aspects of created existence may be the logic behind the expectation of the historical realization of the Kingdom of God. "The idea of the coming Kingdom was intimately connected, in other words, with the faith in the living initiative of God," writes Niebuhr. He then continues, "The more the idea of the end and goal of life was brought into relation to their fundamental faith in sovereignty, the more it came to be an idea of the coming kingdom rather than of the other world."[62]

[61] "Miscellanies," No. 777, Yale MSS.
[62] H. Richard Niebuhr, *The Kingdom of God in America* (New York: Harper and Row, 1959), p. 131.

My own reading of Edwards confirms Niebuhr's reading, but also proposes a supplementary point. Lying behind Edwards' linking of the sovereignty of God with the idea of the coming Kingdom is Edwards' renovative conception of the sovereign God's inherently dynamic character—that is, Edwards' reconception of the divine being as at once fully actual and sufficient and also everlastingly disposed to an everlasting process of a self-enlargement or self-repetition in time and space. In short, Edwards provided the transformative thrust of Calvinism with an appropriately dynamic doctrine of the divine being. And Edwards' achievement is that he attempted to see God's own being as really and internally involved in human history without compromising God's transcendence and prior actuality.

APPENDIX

Jonathan Edwards on Nature

THE INTERPRETATION of Jonathan Edwards' understanding of nature or the physical universe has been a particularly challenging task. Neoplatonic readings of Edwards' metaphysics have tended to leave the impression that the visible world is not really important in spite of Edwards' personal closeness to the natural environment. Edwards' idealism has made unclear the exact nature of the ontological status of the physical universe in distinction from God's consciousness as well as from the minds of human beings. An understanding of the role of nature in Edwards' thought entails a consideration of these and other prior metaphysical issues.

Clyde A. Holbrook has set forth the argument that there is a basic contradiction in Edwards between his conviction of the actuality of the natural environment that impinged upon him so vividly, especially during his youth, on the one hand, and his philosophical understanding of nature as "mental" or dependent upon human consciousness, on the other. Holbrook wonders if the physical universe has any reality distinctively its own if one takes Edwards' idealistic phenomenalism seriously.[1]

A more coherent picture of the place of nature in Edwards' thought as a whole is drawn by Paula M. Cooey and Conrad Cherry. Cooey's is a balanced study of the positive

"Jonathan Edwards on Nature" was first published in *Faithful Imagining: Essays in Honor of Richard R. Niebuhr,* © 1995 by Scholars Press, Atlanta, Georgia.
[1] Clyde A. Holbrook, *Jonathan Edwards, The Valley and Nature: An Interpretative Essay* (Lewisburg, PA: Bucknell University Press, 1987), pp. 71–2, 88–93.

role of nature in Edwards' conception of the world as the self-communication of God.[2] Cherry has highlighted the role of nature as the system of types or symbols of the divine beauty.[3] I wish to join in this attempt to discern and explicate the significant place nature holds in Edwards' philosophical theology. I have a particular interest in lifting up those aspects of Edwards' thought that turn out to be a rich resource for today's ecological concerns.

This essay will argue four main points: (1) that Edwards' dynamic reconception of God and God's relation to the world is the context in which the importance of nature for Edwards can be properly discerned; (2) that Edwards' dispositional ontology gives nature a particular kind of ontological status of its own, distinguishable from God and humanity; (3) that in Edwards' thought there is a mutuality as well as distinctiveness between nature and humanity; and (4) that Edwards' theology has a strong ecological motif with a high valuation of the physical world, as can be seen, for example, in his conceptions of the sensible knowledge of the regenerate and of the Christian's hope for the new heaven and new earth.

One word is necessary in regard to the meaning of the word "nature." Edwards' own use of it is ambiguous. We shall use it here in a "common sense" way to refer to physical and non-perceiving reality — the sense in which Edwards himself sometimes uses the term.[4] This is not to ignore the fact that the physical universe and human beings, and the corporeal universe and the spiritual realm, are overlapping realities.

---

[2] Paula M. Cooey, *Jonathan Edwards on Nature and Destiny: A Systematic Analysis* (Lewiston, NY: Edwin Mellen, 1985).

[3] Conrad Cherry, *Nature and Religious Imagination: From Edwards to Bushnell* (Philadelphia: Fortress, 1980), pp. 13–64.

[4] "Covenant of Redemption: 'Excellency of Christ,'" in *Jonathan Edwards: Representative Selections,* ed. Clarence H. Faust and Thomas H. Johnson (New York: Hill and Wang, 1962), p. 373.

THE END FOR WHICH GOD CREATED THE WORLD

Edwards makes a new beginning in Christian theology by conceiving the nature of God as at once fully actual and also dispositional. God is perfect in actuality and also inherently disposed to further actualizations — that is, to repetitions of the prior actuality.

The philosophical renovation utilized in Edwards' theological reconstruction is the replacement of the age-old notion of substance with the idea of disposition or habit.[5] The Aristotelian concepts of substance and form with which the West had for a long time done its thinking about the nature of reality had become problematic. Newtonian science suggested motion and force as the more basic categories, while the empiricistic spirit of the seventeenth and eighteenth centuries was increasingly putting in doubt the utility of the notion of unexperienceable and unknowable substance. Already in his early philosophical notes, Edwards began to think about reality no longer in terms of substance and forms but in a new language — in terms of dispositional forces.

What made this fundamental metaphysical reformulation possible for Edwards was his realist, as opposed to nominalist, idea of habits and dispositions. "In memory, in mental principles, habits, and inclinations, there is something really abiding in the mind when there are no acts or exercises of them," writes Edwards.[6] A habit or disposition, in other words, has a mode of reality apart from its manifestations in actual events and actions. A habit as an abiding principle is also "law-like" for Edwards, in that it actively and prescriptively governs the occurrence and character of actual events.

---

[5] For a fuller discussion of Edwards' dispositional ontology, see my *The Philosophical Theology of Jonathan Edwards* (Princeton: Princeton University Press, 1988), pp. 34–114.

[6] "The Mind," No. 69, *Works of Jonathan Edwards*, vol. 6, *Scientific and Philosophical Writings*, ed. Wallace E. Anderson (New Haven: Yale University Press, 1980), p. 385. Hereafter cited as "Anderson."

"All habits," wrote Edwards, "[are] a law that God has fixed, that such actions upon such occasions *should* be exerted."[7] When there is a habit or disposition, it functions like a prescriptive law that certain events will, not only may, occur whenever certain circumstances prevail. Habits or dispositions, in short, are ontologically real and causally active law-like powers.

Redefining Aristotelian metaphysics, Edwards declares in a remarkable sentence in "Subjects to Be Handled in the Treatise on the Mind": "it is the laws that constitute all permanent being in created things, both corporeal and spiritual."[8] A human being is no longer a substance or form. "[Soul's] essence consists in powers and habits."[9] Reality, in short, is a system of law-like dispositions and habits.

The being of God, for Edwards, is also essentially a disposition. God's essence, Edwards tells us, is a "disposition to communicate Himself."[10] But, unlike created reality, God's essence is not only a disposition but also a full actuality — that is, an infinitely perfect exercise of the divine dispositional essence. And the internal exercises of the divine dispositional essence constitute the inner-trinitarian life of the divine being. God's perfect actuality is God's "fullness." Because of this fullness, "God is infinitely, eternally, unchangeably, and independently glorious and perfect" and "stands in no need of, and cannot be profited by, or receive anything from the creature."[11]

Although God is internally fully actual, however, God's essence remains a disposition to communicate himself, according to Edwards. And this conception of God as at once fully actual and dispositional enables Edwards to see God as inter-

[7] "Miscellanies," No. 241, Yale MSS, quoted with the kind permission of the Beinecke Rare Book and Manuscript Library, Yale University.

[8] Anderson, p. 391.

[9] "Miscellanies," No. 241, Yale MSS.

[10] "Miscellanies," No. 107, Yale MSS.

[11] "Concerning the End for Which God Created the World," in *Works of Jonathan Edwards*, vol. 8, *Ethical Writings*, ed. Paul Ramsey (New Haven: Yale University Press, 1989), p. 420.

nally related to the world and also independent of the world in its full actuality. God's creation of the world is not for self-realization of God as God. It is rather the exercise of the disposition of God who already is God. This self-communication of God *ad extra* is an act of God's self-realization to the extent that it is a further exercise of God's dispositional essence. But it is an act of self-realization in a peculiar sense — namely, as a self-extension or repetition of what is already fully actual. So the world is meant to be "an increase, repetition or multiplication" of God's internal fullness (433).

The notion of repetition has a dual function: it protects God's prior actuality (because repetition requires something *already* there), and also relates the world internally to the divine being (because repetition is the existing again of that very thing that is already there). God's actuality that is primordially already there is now repeated in time and space. The world is intended to be God "enlarged" or "existing *ad extra*" (527). The world, however, will never completely be God enlarged but always is in a process of becoming that, since the spatio-temporal repetition of the infinite being would require an "infinite duration" (534). In this way the God-world distinction never disappears.

In short, the world does not enlarge, or add anything to, God since God as God *ad intra* is infinitely perfect. But the world does enlarge and add to God in the sense that the world is God's own life repeated *ad extra* in time and space as the exercises of God's dispositional essence *ad extra*. So "God's glory and happiness [which] are in and of himself, [and] are infinite . . . cannot be added to" (445). "And yet, in some sense it can be truly said that God has more delight and pleasure for the holiness and happiness of his creatures" (447). And God takes "more delight and pleasure" in the special sense of "a pleasure in diffusing and communicating to the creature, than in receiving from the creature" (447). The ethical implication of this discussion, of course, is that human beings ought to consider what happens in nature and history as having an ultimate significance. So God "really loves being honored by them [creatures], as all try to be well thought of by those they love. Therefore, we are to seek the glory of God as that which is a thing really pleasing to Him."[12]

A world view such as here outlined is certainly to be distinguished from that of Neoplatonism, although certain Neoplatonic elements do exist in Edwards' thought. Arthur Lovejoy analyzed the Neoplatonic system of thought in terms of "the great chain of being" with a hierarchical gradation of higher and lower beings. There are at least two basic differences between Lovejoy's great chain of being and the thought system of Edwards, and a brief look at them will lift up the world-affirming character of Edwards' metaphysical outlook.

One important difference is that in Neoplatonism the world is emanated out of the fullness of the transcendent One without there being any *telos* for the existence of the world. The One is perfect in such a way that it cannot possibly be inclined to aim at anything. The creation of the world for Edwards, however, is for the purpose of the external exercises of God's dispositional essence. Thus, the creation for Edwards is at once an emanation (an extension of God's being) and a purposive activity (the exercise of God's disposition). And, as we saw above, this purposive activity of God does not assume any imperfection of God as God because such an activity is to bring about a repetition of what already is. Thus, Edwards freely mixes emanationistic with teleological metaphors in his discussion of the creation.[13]

Underlying Edwards' emanationistic and teleological language is his dynamic reconception of the divine being. Lovejoy argued that the thought system of the great chain of being in the West contains a contradictory idea of God that juxtaposes the idea of the Good as the eternal and immutable principle behind all things, on the one hand, and the idea

---

[12] "Miscellanies," No. 208, *The Philosophy of Jonathan Edwards from His Private Notebooks*, ed. Harvey G. Townsend (Eugene, OR: University of Oregon Press, 1955), p. 129. Hereafter cited as "Townsend."

[13] See for example "Concerning the End," pp. 529–34.

of the Goodness as the creative source of all things, on the other.[14] Edwards' dispositional reconception of God represents a synthesis of these two ideas. For Edwards, God is at once the eternal and perfect actuality and also an eternal disposition to a self-enlargement. Thus, Edwards' dynamic conception of God implies a *telos* for the creation, thereby granting the creation a God-given ultimate meaning.

The other basic difference between Edwards' thought and the perspective of the great chain of being is a further elaboration of the point just made — namely, the ultimate significance of the material universe. For the Neoplatonic thought entailed in the great chain of being, the material aspects of entities are really undesirable containers of the emanations of spiritual reality, the various grades of which make up the hierarchy of being. The material universe as such, therefore, does not have any inherent ultimate meaning or reality. The salvation of the spiritual aspect of being is its deliverance from matter and not some sort of fulfillment in and through matter.

Edwards does work with a hierarchy of beings with various grades of embodiment of the spiritual within the material. Edwards also maintains that the closer to spiritual reality an entity is, the higher in the hierarchy that entity is located. To this extent Edwards is influenced by Neoplatonic thought. However, there is a fundamental difference. For Edwards, unlike Neoplatonism, spiritual realities, at whatever levels of the hierarchy of being, are embodied in the material dimension of actual entities. That is, the material dimension as such of particular beings embodies in a physical way the ultimate spiritual reality. Every entity in the world is somehow intended to be a spatio-temporal repetition of God's glory at whatever level that entity may be.[15] All levels of the hierarchy embody, and not just contain, a relation to the ultimate reality. In this sense, Edwards' hierarchy of being has

[14] Arthur Lovejoy, *The Great Chain of Being: A Study of the History of an Idea* (New York: Harper and Row, 1936), pp. 43–50.
[15] See for example "Covenant of Redemption: 'Excellency of Christ,'" p. 373.

a horizontal or egalitarian meaning. The spiritual dimension of a finite entity, therefore, cannot be separated from the material dimension, since the former does not exist except in and through the latter. In short, the material universe as such, for Edwards, has a God-given *telos* and therefore is of an ultimate and lasting significance.

THE REALITY OF NATURE: THE PROBLEM OF EDWARDS' IDEALISM

Edwards' thought system, as outlined above, requires that beings within the spatio-temporal realm, including the physical universe, have a reality of their own since the very end for which God created the world entails their being where they are and what they are. But exactly what sort of reality material beings have, and whether they have reality of their own in any way distinguishable from humanity and God, are questions that must now be raised. A consideration of these questions is necessitated by Edwards' assertion that "corporeal things exist not otherwise than mentally" — that is, "either in created or uncreated consciousness."[16]

A thorough discussion of the nature of Edwards' idealism is beyond the purview of this essay. I shall only outline a dispositional interpretation of Edwards' conception of the physical universe and indicate the implications of this interpretation for the reality and significance of nature in Edwards' thought.

As I indicated above, Edwards no longer thought about reality, including matter, in terms of substance and form. In his early writings "Of Being" and "Of Atom," Edwards critiqued the notion of material substance and reconceived matter as solidity or resisting — resisting annihilation. Edwards then quickly moved to see that this resisting which cannot be annihilated by any finite power must be the immediate activity of God himself. And it is the manner or pattern of this resisting that constitutes the quality and permanence of a

---

[16] "The Mind," No. 10, p. 342.

material entity. In "Of Being," Edwards tells us that "all body is nothing but what immediately results from the exercise of divine power in such a particular manner." A body is "the Deity acting in that particular manner in those parts of space where He thinks fit."[17] The "particular manner" of resisting or God's acting in space is "established" and "fixed" by God and is thus permanent.[18] Therefore, the "manner" or "laws of resistance" are "essential to the very being of nature." Extending this analysis to the nature of all beings, Edwards concludes: "It is laws that constitute all permanent being in created things, both corporeal and spiritual."[19]

A law of nature, as Edwards uses the term, is a dispositional force or a habit with a mode of reality apart from its exercises. Thus, when God causes resistance, God follows the law that God had fixed — that a particular sort of resisting occurs at a particular point in space at a particular time.[20] To put it differently, a body is essentially and abidingly a disposition to have a particular kind of resisting caused by God to occur at a particular space and time.

If material entities are essentially law-like habits and dispositions in Edwards' realist sense of those terms, then they have a reality of their own distinguishable both from humans and from God. Habits and dispositions have a mode of reality apart from their manifestations in actual events and actions. Here I am assuming that one can think of realness as a category broader than actuality. An entity as habit, in other words, is real in the sense of virtual though not in the sense of actual — the term "virtual" here referring to the sort of realness that falls between full actuality and a mere potentiality.[21] Therefore, in whatever manner material entities may depend upon human consciousness for their actuality, those entities have a mode of reality as habits and dispositions *be-*

[17] "Of Atoms," Anderson, p. 215.
[18] "Miscellanies," No. 1263, Townsend, pp. 184–93.
[19] "Subjects to Be Handled," p. 391.
[20] "Miscellanies," No. 1263, Townsend, pp. 184–8.
[21] For a fuller discussion of this point, see my *The Philosophical Theology of Jonathan Edwards*, pp. 42–6, 106–14.

fore human perception occurs. Perception does not exhaust the reality of material entities.

One of the problems Edwards wrestled with in connection with his idealism was the reality of unperceived objects, and Edwards' treatment of this problem illustrates the point I am arguing. How do objects in a locked room that are not seen by any human being, for example, exist? Early in his notes on "The Mind," Edwards tries the answer that objects unperceived by humans exist by being in the consciousness of God, and also the answer that they exist by being "supposed" by God in God's other actions.[22] But at the very end of "The Mind," Edwards settles for a dispositional conception. Edwards writes in No. 69:

> In memory, in mental principles, habits, and inclinations, there is something really abiding in the mind when there are no acts or exercises of them, much in the same manner as there is a chair in this room when no mortal perceives it. For when we say, there are chairs in this room when none perceives it, we mean that minds would perceive chairs here according to the laws of nature in such circumstances.[23]

To explain the reality of unperceived objects, Edwards here turns to the "laws of nature in such circumstances," laws clearly having an ontological priority to the actual events of perception. In the corporeal universe, in other words, there is something abiding that is distinguishable from human perception. It is no wonder, then, that in a philosophical note written very late in his life, Edwards observed that "there may be more in material existence than man's perception, past, present or future."[24]

Wallace E. Anderson, in his "Editor's Introduction" to the Yale volume on Edwards' scientific and philosophical writings, makes essentially the same point I am making, although he does not make much systematic application of it. Ander-

[22] "The Mind," Nos. 13 and 40, pp. 344–5, 356–9.
[23] "The Mind," No. 69, p. 385.
[24] "Notes on Knowledge and Existence," Anderson, p. 398.

son discusses Edwards' view in "The Mind," No. 27, that resistances themselves may be best thought of as mental or as "a mode of idea." For Edwards, Anderson observes, there is still something real about resistances, presumably including the resistances of material kinds, and their realness consists in the divinely established laws or "the determination of God that such and such ideas [of resistances] shall be raised in created minds upon such conditions."[25] Anderson observes:

> Edwards holds that bodies have real natures independent of the ideas and beliefs we form concerning them. But he rejects Locke's view that these real natures are unperceived and unknowable properties of substances; instead he holds that they consist in the general laws that govern the order and regularity of the series of ideas that are "raised in our minds" in the course of sense experience. These general laws, Edwards asserts, are established by God.[26]

It is not only from human minds but also from God as well, it should be noted here, that material entities are distinguishable reality. The laws and habits that make up the permanence of material beings are the manner or method of God's direct activity of causing resistances in space or of God's raising of resistances (ideas) to human minds. Whether resistances in space are mental or not, one thing remains the same: they are direct activities of God. And the laws and habits that govern them are "the proportion of God's acting."[27] These laws and habits, however, are created principles and cannot be identified with God's disposition or actuality. They are the laws of God's activity *ad extra* and have a reference to time and space.[28] They are created and thus dependent principles but do enjoy a God-given integrity as abiding

[25] "The Mind," Nos. 27 and 36, pp. 350–1, 355.
[26] "Editor's Introduction," p. 97. See also George Rupp, "The 'Idealism' of Jonathan Edwards," *Harvard Theological Review* 62 (1969): 225.
[27] "The Mind," No. 34, p. 353.
[28] This point is also made by Egbert C. Smyth in "Jonathan Edwards' Idealism," *American Journal of Theology* 1 (Oct. 1897): 959.

realities. God, according to Edwards, is "subject in His acting to the same laws with inferior beings."[29] So Edwards'
assertion that God "must comprehend in himself all being"
cannot mean that a God-world distinction is abolished; it
rather means that God is the one from whom "all are derived and from whom everything is given."[30] In his way, Edwards' dispositional ontology helps us understand the particular way in which nature, like all creation, has in Edwards'
thought an abiding, though thoroughly dependent, reality of
its own.

Nature and Humanity: Distinctiveness and Mutuality

I have thus far argued that in Edwards' theological system
the world, including the physical universe, has its own reality
that is ultimately important to the end for which God created the world. I have also indicated that there are reasons
for not thinking of Edwards' idealism as completely vitiating
the objective reality of the physical universe. Building on
these discussions, I can now enter into a consideration of
nature's relation to humanity in Edwards' theology.

Partly due to the biblical tradition that human beings are
created in the image of God, the theological tradition of the
West has accorded humanity a uniqueness that sets it apart
from the rest of the creation. Edwards follows this tradition
but also asserts a mutuality between nature and humanity —
a mutuality that is undergirded by a theocentric perspective.
The distinguishing mark of humanity, for Edwards, consists
in consciousness or perception. And Edwards sometimes
puts this matter rather sharply. "Perceiving being only is
properly being." "Spirits are much more properly beings and
more substantial than bodies." Further: "The state of the inanimate, unperceiving part of the world is nothing regarded

[29] "Miscellanies," No. 1263, Townsend, p. 193.
[30] "Miscellanies," No. 697, Townsend, p. 262.

any otherwise than in a subserviency to the perceiving or intelligent parts."[31]

Here again is a Neoplatonic influence; the spiritual is higher than the material. However, this superiority of perceiving beings has to be put in its theological context. Perceiving beings are not higher in and of themselves but rather because their special role is necessary for a theocentric reason: namely, the repetition of God's glory in time and space. God's inner beauty is repeated whenever God is known and loved in time and space, and it is perceiving beings who are capable of knowledge and love and thus capable of actively participating in God's own project.[32] Any amount of Neoplatonic bias toward the spiritual over the material is, in Edwards, undercut and qualified by Edwards' theocentric emphasis. In fact, the higher capacity of intelligent beings, according to Edwards, can turn into a greater evil if that capacity is used in an inappropriate way.[33] Even when this capacity of intelligent beings is rightly used, their superiority over the material has meaning only because it serves God's purpose and not in and of itself. So, "intelligent beings are created to be the consciousness of the universe, that they may perceive what God is and does."[34] Edwards writes further:

What could this vast universe of matter, placed in such excellent order and governed by such excellent law, be good for if there was no intelligence that could know anything of it? Wherefore, it necessarily follows that intelligent beings are the end of the creation, and that their end must be to behold and admire the doings of God and magnify Him for them, and to contemplate His glories in them.[35]

Intelligent beings are the "end of creation," but this end is qualified by a more ultimate end, "to behold and admire the

[31] "The Mind," No. 45, p. 363; "Things to be Considered," No. 44, p. 238; "Miscellanies," Townsend, No. 547, p. 136.
[32] "Miscellanies," No. 547, Townsend, p. 136.
[33] "Miscellanies," No. 62, Townsend, p. 64.
[34] "Miscellanies," No. 87, Townsend, p. 128.
[35] "Miscellanies," No. gg, Townsend, pp. 236–7.

doings of God." And this ultimate end of perceiving beings is none other than the very end of the creation itself. The uniqueness or superiority of intelligent beings, therefore, does not give them any right to dominate over other parts of the universe. Any element of anthropocentrism in Edwards is thoroughly subordinated to his theocentric outlook. In their ultimate responsibility toward God, therefore, nature and humanity are equal partners.

Perceiving beings, according to Edwards, thus have a special role in God's scheme of things. And this special role consists of "actively promoting God's glory" by virtue of their ability to repeat in time God's internal acts of knowing and loving God's beauty.[36] Now, it is upon these perceiving beings that Edwards says non-perceiving beings depend for their existence. I argued in the previous section that material things as habits and laws have a virtual reality apart from human perception. So, the dependence of material entities upon consciousness cannot be a dependence for their virtual reality. What exactly, then, is the nature of this dependence? Edwards' dispositional ontology with its undergirding theocentric perspective, the interpretative guideline of my discussion thus far, affords us at least one possible reading of the meaning of nature's ontological dependence upon human perception in Edwards' thought.

Habits and laws that make up the permanence and the virtual reality of created beings, according to Edwards, are propensities to exist in a particular manner — a manner that is fittingly related to the divine being. Thus humanity's "end is to behold and admire the doings of God." The end of nature or non-perceiving beings is no less theocentrically determined. "External things," Edwards tells us, "are intended to be images of things spiritual, moral, and divine."[37] Material entities possess what Edwards calls "secondary beauty" — the sort of harmony or regularity that does not involve the

[36] "Miscellanies," No. 547, Townsend, p. 126.
[37] *Images or Shadows of Divine Things*, No. 203, ed. Perry Miller (New Haven: Yale University Press, 1948), p. 130.

consent or love between perceiving beings, or "primary beauty." But the reason "secondary beauty" is beautiful, according to Edwards, is its resemblance to consent between spiritual beings and ultimately its analogical relation to the beauty of God.[38] Thus, material entities with their secondary beauty are essentially dispositions to be images or shadows of divine things.

At this point it is crucial to remember that for Edwards actions or relations and actual existence are identical.[39] The essence of a being is not a separate substance but the disposition to act and to be related in a certain manner. Therefore created entities, perceiving or non-perceiving, would exist as actual beings only in and through those actual actions and relations to which they are essentially disposed. Entities actually *are*, in other words, only as they are related and engaged in action.

What all this means is twofold: first, perceiving beings are fully actual — that is, moved from virtuality to actuality — only when their God-directed dispositional essence is exercised, that is, only when they know and love God; and second, non-perceiving beings would be fully actual only when their own God-directed dispositional essence is exercised, that is, when their destiny to be images or shadows of divine things is somehow played out, so to speak.

In the case of perceiving beings, knowledge and existence are explicitly correlated by Edwards throughout his writings: "The increasing knowledge of God in all elect creatures to all eternity is an existence, a reality infinitely worthy to be in itself."[40] But how can the dispositional essence of material entities with their God-directed destiny be exercised and thus made explicit and actual? How can the sun and the moon, hills and mountains, attain their end of being the images or shadows of divine things? Edwards does not explicitly state

[38] *The Nature of True Virtue*, ed. William K. Frankena (Ann Arbor: University of Michigan Press, 1960), p. 33.

[39] For a fuller discussion of this point, see my *The Philosophical Theology of Jonathan Edwards*, pp. 77–95.

[40] "Miscellanies," No. 1225, Townsend, pp. 152–3.

an answer to this question. But my thesis is that Edwards' conception of material entities as inherently disposed to exhibit a God-ward relation at least suggests an answer, namely, that non-perceiving beings could achieve their actuality as images or shadows of divine things only through a power that can see material things in their relational meaning broader than what is immediately given. This power is the imagination of the regenerate person's mind, and the true actuality of material things could then be achieved only via the regenerate person's imaginative perception of them *as* images or shadows of divine things. In perceiving beings' knowledge and love of material entities *as* images of God's beauty, their essential relation to the divine would be made *explicit mentally*, thus existing actually in a mental way.

The interpretation offered here is consistent with what Edwards actually says about the regenerate person's experience of nature. Having declared that "the beauties of nature are really emanations or shadows of the excellencies of the Son of God," Edwards continues:

> When we behold the fragrant rose and lily, we see [Christ's] love and purity. So the green trees, and fields, and singing of birds are the emanations of His infinite joy and benignity. The easiness and naturalness of trees and vines are shadows of His beauty and loveliness. The crystal rivers and murmuring streams are the footsteps of His favor, grace, and beauty. When we behold the light and brightness of the sun, the goldened edges of an evening cloud, or the beauteous bow, we behold the adumbrations of His glory and goodness.[41]

What is described here is not only an epistemic event but an ontological one. Through the regenerate person's apprehension of material things as images of God's beauty, they are not just known but actualized. As Edwards himself says of the knowledge of God's glory: "the existence of the created universe consists as much in it as in any thing: yea, this

41 "Covenant of Redemption: 'Excellency of Christ,'" p. 373.

knowledge is one of the highest, most real and substantial parts of all created existence, most remote from nonentity and defect."[42] Speaking of the world as "the expression" of God's being, Edwards writes: "The very being of the expression depends on the perception of created understandings. And so much the more as the expression is known, so much the more it is."[43]

The consistency of this interpretation with Edwards' thought can be shown also by restating the discussion above from the point of view of the purpose of the creation. As noted already, the purpose of the universe is the knowledge and love of God. And, as also noted above, Edwards correlates the creature's knowledge of God with the creature's being. How can the material universe, then, attain a knowledge of God so that it fulfills the purpose of the universe and also achieves existence? Here one reaches the same conclusion discussed earlier. Material things could attain a knowledge of God only indirectly, that is, by being known as an image of the knowledge of God. So Edwards says that "intelligent beings are the consciousness of the creation."[44]

Thus, whether one starts from the God-directed dispositional nature of material entities themselves, or from the purpose that God had in mind in creating the universe, the being of material entities appears to be dependent upon their being known by perceiving beings. Anderson notes that Edwards could have argued the ontological dependence of material things upon perceiving beings on the basis of creation's purpose. Anderson further notes that Edwards never explicitly uses this argument, but rather seems to have thought of the dependence of material things upon perception as self-evident.[45] This much is clear from my discussion, however: the dispositional and theocentric metaphysics articulated by Edwards is consistent with, or even requires, that the true

[42] "Concerning the End," p. 432.
[43] "Miscellanies," No. 662, Townsend, pp. 137–8.
[44] "Miscellanies," No. 3, Townsend, p. 193.
[45] "Editor's Introduction," pp. 78–80.

actualization of material things cannot occur apart from the perception of regenerate minds.

Thus the responsibility of perceiving beings vis-à-vis nature, according to Edwards, is weighty indeed. But fallen humanity with their narrowness of imagination cannot fulfill this responsibility toward nature. It takes nothing less than the indwelling of the Holy Spirit for human minds to apprehend the wider meanings of things. Only sanctified minds with their widened imagination are able to experience things "in their true relations and respects to other things, and to things in general."[46] To put it more accurately, it is God who works in and through the regenerate and does the creative work in time and space.

Without such a widening of the imagination, human beings do not "consent to being" but fall into a narrow or deformed perspective on reality.[47] Such a narrowness of vision is none other than sin, according to Edwards. And sin has a serious effect on nature:

This visible world has now for many ages been subjected to sin, and made as it were a servant to it, through the abusive improvement that man, who has the dominion over the creatures, puts the creatures to. Thus the sun is a sort of servant to all manner of wickedness, as its light and other beneficial influences are abused by men, and made subservient to their lusts and sinful purposes. So the rain, and the fruits of the earth, and the brute animals, and all other parts of the visible creation . . . for the creature is abused in it, perverted to far meaner purposes than those for which the author of its nature made it, and to which he adapted it. . . . 'Tis a bondage the creature is subject to, from which it was partly delivered when Christ came and

[46] "Miscellanies," No. 408, Townsend, p. 249.

[47] Edwards writes: "A natural [man] may love others, but 'tis some way or other as appendages and appurtenances to himself; but a spiritual man loves others as of God, or in God, or some way related to Him" ("Miscellanies," No. 821, Townsend, pp. 240–1). For a fuller discussion of the effect of the indwelling of the Holy Spirit upon the imagination, see my *The Philosophical Theology of Jonathan Edwards*, pp. 140–6.

the gospel was promulgated in the world; and will be more fully delivered at the commencement of the glorious day we are speaking of; and perfectly at the day of judgment.[48]

Nature or the physical universe, then, is dependent upon perceiving beings for the actualization of what it was ultimately intended to be. At the same time, there is a sense in which perceiving beings are also dependent upon material entities. As was noted earlier, this mutuality is grounded in the common God-given destiny that nature and humanity share. The essence of human beings is to know and love God and thereby repeat God's beauty in time and space, just as nature's destiny is to be images or shadows of the same divine beauty. It would follow, then, that perceiving beings are truly actual only when they know and love God. And if the physical universe is in any way helpful to the fulfillment of perceiving beings, then to that extent perceiving beings would be dependent upon, or at least benefitted by, nature.

For one thing, nature, for Edwards, is as much God's self-revelation as scripture. So there is "The Book of Nature" and the book of scripture. Scripture does have a kind of centrality:

The book of Scripture is the interpreter of the book of nature two ways, viz., by declaring to us those spiritual mysteries that are indeed signified and typified in the constitution of the natural world; and secondly, in actually making application of the signs and types in the book of nature as representations of those spiritual mysteries in many instances.[49]

So scripture is a more direct way of God's speaking, and it interprets for human beings the meaning of God's communi-

[48] "An Humble Attempt," *Works of Jonathan Edwards*, vol. 5, *Apocalyptic Writings*, ed. Stephen J. Stein (New Haven: Yale University Press, 1977), pp. 344–5.
[49] *Images or Shadows*, No. 156, p. 109.

cation in nature. However, nature in itself is also a communication of God:

> And as the system of nature and the system of revelation are both divine works, so both are in different senses a divine word, both are the voice of God to intelligent creatures, a manifestation and declaration of Himself to mankind.[50]

At the same time, the book of nature has certain advantages over the book of scripture:

> If we look on these shadows of divine things as the voice of God purposely by them teaching us these and those spiritual and divine things, to show of what excellent advantages it will be, how agreeably and clearly it will tend to convey instruction to our minds, and to impress things on the mind and to affect the mind, by that we may, as it were, have God speaking to us. Wherever we are, and whatever we are about, we may see divine things excellently represented and held forth. And it will abundantly tend to confirm the Scripture, for there is an excellent agreement between these things and the holy Scripture.[51]

So the concrete images and representations of the divine beauty in nature have a contribution to make by virtue of their being *physical*. Images in nature "agreeably and clearly will . . . tend to convey instruction to our minds" and to "impress things on the mind and affect the mind." Concrete physical images, therefore, facilitate God's communication to perceiving beings. But beyond their facilitating function, natural images as such *are* emanations, communications, or embodiments of God's beauty and God's truth. Thus, when Christ makes use of material images of spiritual truth, "these things are not merely mentioned as illustrations of meaning, but as illustrations and evidences of the truth of what he

---

[50] "Miscellanies," No. 1340, Townsend, p. 233.
[51] *Images or Shadows*, No. 70, pp. 69–70.

says."[52] So, as communications of God in their own right, natural images "abundantly tend to confirm the Scripture."

In short, just as the physical universe depends upon perceiving beings for the actualization of its God-given destiny, perceiving beings are also helped by nature in the actualization of their own being. When the regenerate person knows and loves nature as an image of God's beauty, that person's own dispositional essence is exercised. That person becomes actually what a human being is intended to be, namely, "the image of God's own knowledge of himself."[53] The dependence of humanity upon nature could not be more fundamental. And the mutual dependence of nature and humanity is ultimately grounded in their common destiny of being participants in God's own self-extension in time. To put it differently, the mutuality of nature and humanity is part of the mutuality God has with the world; and through this mutuality, God, nature, and humanity are united and thereby enlarged.

THE ECOLOGICAL PROMISE OF EDWARDS' THEOLOGY: FECUNDITY AND THE MIGRATION TO A GOOD LAND

H. Paul Santmire challenges the impression in the minds of some that Christian theological tradition in its roots is unhelpful to, or even uninterested in, ecological concerns regarding the physical environment. In his historical survey of select Christian theologies, Santmire describes those theologies that are affirming of nature with the help of two metaphors: the metaphor of fecundity (over against ascent), and the metaphor of a migration to a good land.[54]

The metaphor of fecundity represents a world-affirming perspective in which one ascends toward the higher levels of being in order to achieve fulfillment, but does so not to leave

[52] *Images or Shadows*, No. 26, p. 49.
[53] "Concerning the End," p. 441.
[54] *The Travail of Nature: The Ambiguous Ecological Promise of Christian Theology* (Philadelphia: Fortress Press, 1985), pp. 13–29.

the world behind but rather to appreciate it with a wider vision. With such a vision one sees the fullness of being and beauty in all parts of the mundane world. This metaphor of fecundity, therefore, is contrasted to the metaphor of ascent that stresses the need to leave the world behind. The metaphor of a migration to a good land has to do with the place of the earthly and the bodily in a vision for the future. This metaphor contrasts with other-worldly visions for the ultimate future, and it suggests hope for fulfillment of the earthly rather than its elimination.

Both of the metaphors are appropriate for Edwards' thought. First of all, there is ascent in Edwards' world view, but its purpose is to apprehend the fecundity of the mundane more fully, rather than to leave it behind. Here again Edwards' dynamic conception of God and God's relation to the world functions as the critical background. God's end in creating the world is that God's own life be extended and repeated *ad extra* in time and space. Thus, time and space have an ultimate significance in Edwards' perspective. And the fulfillment of the world has to be within the matrix of time and space, not outside of them.

Thus, the regenerate person's religious experience which constitutes the actualization of his or her own being and also of God's end in creation involves an ascent that has the purpose of returning. The ascent, in Edwards, is necessary because every created entity is to be a repetition or image of God's beauty, and one cannot repeat God's beauty without knowing and loving it. The knowledge and love of God, for Edwards, is the first requirement for all ontological and epistemic fulfillment.

This movement of ascent-and-back-to-the-earth is dramatically illustrated in Edwards' account of his own experience of God. Edwards writes in his "Personal Narrative":

Not long after I first began to experience these things, I gave an account to my father of something that had passed in my mind. I was pretty much affected by the discourse we had together; and when the discourse was ended, I walked abroad alone, in a solitary place in my father's pasture, for contemplation. As I was walking there, and looking up on the sky and clouds, there came into my mind so sweet a sense of the glorious *majesty* and *grace* of God, that I know not how to express. I seemed to see them both in a sweet conjunction; majesty and meekness together; it was a sweet, and gentle, and holy majesty; and also a majestic meekness; an awful sweetness; a high, and great, and holy gentleness.[55]

Edwards' ascent to his inexpressible experience of God did not in any way remove him from the earth but rather brought him right back to it — but with a difference. Immediately following the above quotation Edwards writes:

After this my sense of divine things gradually increased, and became more and more lively, and had more of that inward sweetness. The appearance of every thing was altered; there seemed to be, as it were, a calm, sweet cast, or appearance of divine glory, in almost every thing. God's excellency, his wisdom, his purity and love, seemed to appear in every thing; in the sun, moon, and stars; in the clouds, and blue sky; in the grass, flowers, trees; in the water, and all nature; which used to fix my mind. I often used to sit and view the moon for continuance; and in the day, spent much time in viewing the clouds and sky, to behold the sweet glory of God in these things; in the mean time, singing forth, with a low voice my contemplations of the Creator and Redeemer.[56]

It is true that a few times in the same "Personal Narrative" Edwards uses the kind of expression that may make the reader suspect a world-denying way of thinking. In his experience of God, Edwards felt "wrapt and swallowed up in God" and sensed "a calm, sweet abstraction of soul from all the concerns of this world."[57] Once again these are traces of

[55] "Personal Narrative," *Representative Selections,* p. 60.
[56] "Personal Narrative," pp. 60-1.
[57] "Personal Narrative," pp. 60, 59.

Neoplatonism in Edwards' thought. Yet the document is full of references to concrete natural objects, such as the sun and the moon, trees and grass, which, in being what they are, embody and manifest the divine glory. The end for which God created the world needs material objects. Time and space are not left behind in Edwards' view of the religious imagination; they rather make up the very stuff of it.

The other metaphor for nature-affirming theology is "the migration to a good land," and this also has an affinity to Edwards' thought. Nature or physical reality has a positive role in Edwards' vision of the creation's ultimate future. As noted already, the accomplishment of God's end in creation, according to Edwards, is going to take an "infinite duration" since the end befitting God is "an infinite end."[58] What has to be repeated in time is none other than the infinite glory of God, and thus this project can never come to a temporal completion. The eschaton represents the finishing of God's redemption of the fallen creation that puts it on track again, so to speak, for the accomplishing of God's end in creation. So redemption comes to a terminus. But God's end in creation does not. God's end in creation has to go on in a process of unending progress. Thus there needs to be time and space in some form for an unending duration. The spatio-temporal realm after the end of the present one is the "new heaven and new earth" in which physical reality, in a new form, will have a positive role.[59]

At the eschaton, God will put an end to the world as we know it now, "as a machine is taken down when it has answered the workman's end," and will not leave it "to a gradual decay."[60] So there is an end to this creation, but the creation does not end. As promised in Revelation 21.1, there will be "a new heaven and new earth." Noting how this new world contains a "new earth," Edwards comments:

[58] "Miscellanies," No. 1006, Townsend, p. 196.
[59] *Works of Jonathan Edwards*, vol. 9, *A History of the Work of Redemption*, ed. John F. Wilson (New Haven: Yale University Press, 1989), pp. 348–50, 508–10.
[60] "Miscellanies," No. 1263, Townsend, p. 189.

'Tis probable 'tis called by the name of the new earth, because 'tis the place of the habitation of bodies as well as souls, a place wherein their bodily senses shall be exercised. There shall be that whereon they shall tread with their feet, and an expanse over their heads.[61]

So there is a continuity between the bodily reality of this world and that of the new one. But there is also a discontinuity. Edwards does not see just a restoration of the old fallen world but a radical new construction — that is, a restoration without sin and corruptibility, and a restoration with new perfection. It will be "vastly, immensely more glorious than it was before the fall . . . a new one materially as well as in form."[62] Edwards describes the new quality of the physical universe as follows:

How ravishing are the proportions of the reflections of rays of light, and the proportions of the vibrations of the air! And without doubt, God can contrive matter so that there shall be other sort of proportions, that may be quite of a different kind, and may raise another sort of pleasure in a sense, and in a manner to us inconceivable, that shall be vastly more ravishing and exquisite. . . . [T]here shall be external beauties and harmonies altogether of another kind from what we perceive here, and probably those beauties will appear chiefly on the bodies of the man Christ Jesus and of the saints.[63]

And the saints will see "a divine person (the man Christ Jesus) with bodily eyes in the same manner as we see one another."[64]

In conclusion, nature or the physical universe has an important and positive place in Edwards' framework of thought. His dispositional ontology secures nature a reality of its own apart from perception, although nature's ultimate

[61] "Apocalypse Series," *Apocalyptic Writings*, No. 41, p. 141.
[62] "Apocalypse Series," No. 40, p. 141.
[63] "Miscellanies," No. 182, Yale MSS.
[64] "Miscellanies," No. 678, quoted from *Ethical Writings*, pp. 723–4.

destiny requires perception for its actualization. And what lies behind Edwards' high valuation of nature is his dynamic concept of God according to which God creates the world because God's inherent disposition moves him to extend his eternal reality into the realm of time and space, thereby making time and space ultimately significant. The conception of God as not only perfect but also capable of being involved in the world appears to go hand in hand with a theology in which the world, including the material universe, is important even to God himself. So the God of Edwards creates the world, to borrow Perry Miller's words, "not by sitting outside and above it, by modeling it as a child models sand, but by an extension of Himself, by taking upon Himself the forms of stones and trees and of man."[65] Jonathan Edwards belongs to the list of theologians who are helpful in the contemporary search for an ecologically responsible theology of nature.

[65] Perry Miller, *Errand in the Wilderness* (Cambridge: Harvard University Press, 1956), p. 194.

Index

Abrams, M. H., 159
abstraction, theory of: as challenged by Newtonian science and Lockean empiricism, 26–27, 120–121; as replaced by Edwards' theory of imagination, 130–131
actuality: of created existence, 85–94; as a criterion of degree of being, 109–110; of God, 178, 188–189, 198, 202, 208–209; movement from virtuality to, 106–109; and virtual actuality, 93
Addison, Joseph, 127
Ames, William, 24
Anderson, Wallace E., 15n, 31n, 33n, 47n, 51, 54, 56n, 59n, 65n, 67n, 68n, 93n, 171n
Aquinas, Saint Thomas, 15, 188, 189; on *habitus*, 20–22
Aristotle, 15, 38, 174; on habit (*hexis*), 17–19
Aspelin, Gunnar, 103
association of ideas: and the aesthetic sense, 163–164; Edwards on, 136–137; Hume on, 27–29, 121, 136; Locke on, 26–27, 120–121, 135–136
Augustine, Saint, 155, 214

Bailyn, Bernard, 221n
Barth, Karl, 204n
Bastian, Ralph J., 16n
Bate, Walter Jackson, 117n, 160n, 164
Batschelet, Margaret, 88n
beauty: as a criterion of degree of being, 110–111; dispositional es-

sence of divine being, 176–177, 179–181; divine and finite, 142; and habit, 78–79; and knowledge, 140–142; as structure of being, 82–85
Becker, William, 66n
being: as beauty, 82–85; and becoming, 96; as dynamic, 95–114; Edwards' dispositional conception of, 47–114; as involving God's continuous and immediate activity, 55; as movement from virtuality to actuality, 90, 106–114; as process of increase, 108–114; and real possibility and virtuality, 63, 79–80; as relational, 76–94. *See also* beauty; dispositional ontology; habit; substance; teleology
Bercovitch, Sacvan, 88n, 215n, 221n
Berkeley, George, 59–60
Boler, John, 16n, 36n, 39n, 42n, 44n
Bond, Donald F., 126n
Bourke, Vernon J., 19n, 20–21
Boyd, Gregory, 188n
Brumm, Ursula, 88n
Bryant, M. Darrol, 221–222
Burgersdicius, Franciscus, 22–23, 38
Burtt, E. A., 32n

Calvin, John, 190n, 214
Cambridge Platonists, 11–13, 33–34, 73, 102–104, 121–122
Carse, James, 230n
Cassirer, Ernst, 115n, 116n, 122n

269

INDEX

cause: causation by impact, 11; cause-and-effect relation and imagination, 128, 136–138; divine causality and human causality, 100–101; Edwards' aesthetic/relational conception of, 46, 105; Edwards' rejection of causation by impact, 41; Newton and causation by impact, 41. *See also* God; teleology
Chambers, Ephraim, 23–24, 38
Cherry, Conrad, 117n, 143, 144n, 243
Christ, Jesus, 73, 88, 111, 144, 160–162, 168; and beautific vision of God, 231; and Church, 227–231; dynamic being of, 229; as full external exertion of divine disposition, 228; mediatorial role, 230; second coming of, 236–239; theocentric and cosmic scope of work of, 204n, 230–231
Church, 226; as actual and becoming, 230; and Christ, 227–231; and eternal life, 237; and Trinity, 225–226, 228
Clarke, Samuel, 98
classical theism, 4. *See also* God
Colacurcio, Robert E., 117n
Coleridge, Samuel Taylor, 127, 135n, 159
Collingwood, R. G., 101–102
conversion, 143–145, 231–232. *See also* grace; Holy Spirit
Cooey-Nichols, Paula M., 89n, 166n, 243
creation: continual ex nihilo, 63; as establishment of habits and laws, 79–80; as exercise of divine disposition, 181–183; as external repetition of God's fullness, 196–210; as necessary, 201n; original ex nihilo, 69–70

Cudworth, Ralph, 11–13; influence on Edwards, 33n, 102n, 103–104, 122

Daniel, Stephen H., 3n
Davidson, James W., 215n
deism, 70–71
Delattre, Roland, 41n, 79n, 171n, 172, 176, 179, 194
Descartes, René, 31; and passions and imagination, 116
disposition. *See* habit
dispositional ontology, 63, 95; and beauty, 82–84; dating of Edwards' formulation of, 66–67; and metaphysics of substance, 50, 53–54, 77–80, 90; in seventeenth and eighteenth century, 97–106. *See also* being; habit

Eliade, Mircea, 211n
Elwood, Douglas J., 171n
emanation, 172, 198–199
empiricism: Edwards and, 122–123; and mental activity, 12–13, 26–29, 115–125; and ontology, 29–31. *See also* knowledge; sense of beauty
eschatology. *See* postmillennialism

Fall of humankind, 142
Fiering, Norman, 10n, 15n, 59n
Flavel, John, 24

Gardiner, H. N., 57n
Gassendi, Pierre, 31
Gay, Peter, 3n
Gilkey, Langdon, 214n
God: actuality of, 209–210; *ad intra/ad extra*, 204; aseity of, 50, 181–183, 186–189; beauty of, 82–83, 141–144, 176–177, 179–181, 193–196; continuous and discontinuous with humanity, 142, 177–183; and created

270